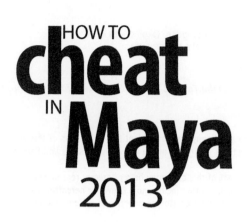

HOW TO
cheat
IN Maya
2013

Tools and Techniques
for Character Animation

Eric Luhta
Kenny Roy

Routledge
Taylor & Francis Group

LONDON AND NEW YORK

First published 2013 by Focal Press

Published 2017 by Routledge
2 Park Square, Milton Park, Abingdon, Oxon OX14 4RN
711 Third Avenue, New York, NY 10017, USA

First issued in hardback 2017

Routledge is an imprint of the Taylor & Francis Group, an informa business

Notices
Knowledge and best practice in this field are constantly changing. As new research and experience broaden our understanding, changes in research methods, professional practices, or medical treatment may become necessary.

Practitioners and researchers must always rely on their own experience and knowledge in evaluating and using any information, methods, compounds, or experiments described herein. In using such information or methods they should be mindful of their own safety and the safety of others, including parties for whom they have a professional responsibility.

Product or corporate names may be trademarks or registered trademarks, and are used only for identification and explanation without intent to infringe.

Library of Congress Cataloging in Publication Data
A catalog record for this book has been requested

ISBN 13: 978-1-138-40337-6 (hbk)
ISBN 13: 978-0-240-52590-7 (pbk)

Publisher's Note
This book has been prepared from camera-ready copy provided by the authors.

Contents

Contents

How to Cheat and Why

The truth about cheating

When we hear the word "cheating," we usually think of something negative: deception, trickery or chicanery. However in this book, cheating is a good thing. If you've watched someone who's a master of something work at it, it can seem unreal, almost like they're... cheating! But really they just have experience and in-depth knowledge of how to achieve something. They know the most efficient way to do a task and make their tools work for them.

That's the goal of this book: to give you in-depth knowledge of animating with Maya so you can skip over the trial and error, constant web searches, and poring over internet forums. Since Maya can be a technical minefield of complex menus and settings, you need someone to help you navigate this sophisticated program and get right down to the most important thing: performance. When it comes down to dodging discouragement, avoiding adversity, and side-stepping setbacks, you want all the cheats you can get! Our goal is for you to come to view this book as your on-hand reference guide as you study the art of motion.

The philosophy

Throughout our teaching experiences, one of the methods we found to be extremely effective in quickly transferring knowledge to someone else was isolation of a concept: really honing in on a single task and practicing until the knowledge is engrained. This may seem obvious but it's rare to come across an animator who didn't learn by studying performance while simultaneously wrestling all of the technical concepts. Although trial by fire can be an effective learning method, it makes for some very discouraging times. This books takes an approach that will give you a firm grasp on the technical concepts of animation, one at a time.

You will understand how to employ Maya's tools faster and concentrate on making your animation look amazing, rather than why that prop keeps popping out of the character's hand.

As luck would have it, the How to Cheat series is perfect for this style of learning. Every page spread is geared toward a specific concept, which allows you to go through the book cover to cover, or skip around to the things you want to know about. The choice is yours.

Scene files and examples

Just about all of the topics have an accompanying scene file. Most of the topics enable you to follow along, employing the given technique in a prepared animation. Once you understand the technique and have practiced using it in an animation, it will be very easy to transfer it over to whatever you're working on. For chapters that are one long project, scenes are included in a progressive order, so you can jump in anywhere and learn what you want to learn without having to start at the beginning. Having the scene files for an animation book should prove extremely useful, as you can take a look under the hood and examine the curves and see the movement for yourself. As great as books can be, you really have to see an animation in motion in the end.

Throughout the book, we use multiple character rigs that have been stress tested by students and veterans alike. We've found them to all be very fast, stable rigs, and all have just the right number of advanced features without getting too complicated.

The scene files are included for Maya 2013. If you're using an older version of Maya, just have "Ignore Version" checked in the File > Open options.

What you need to know

While this book starts at the beginning as far as animating is concerned, it does assume a basic knowledge of getting around Maya. You should be able to navigate the viewports (orbit, pan, dolly in 3D space), understand the interface, and be comfortable using the move, rotate, and scale tools. This information is covered in countless places on the web and in other materials, and we'd rather keep the book focused than rehash what's easily found elsewhere.

Going further

Visit the book's website at www.howtocheatinmaya.com. There you can find all the scene files for using the book, as well as previous material from the 2010 and 2012 editions that couldn't be included here due to space. Happy animating!

Eric Luhta
Kenny Roy

Acknowledgments

We'd like to thank the following artists for agreeing to let us use their rigs in this edition of *How To Cheat in Maya*:

"Cenk"
Özgür Aydoğdu

"Nico"
Chad Vernon

"Goon"
Sean Burgoon

"Groggy"
Zubuyer Kaolin

"Moom"
Ramtin Ahmadi

"Bloke"
Jason Baskin

And a very special thanks to Sonya Ballas for your technical support writing this book.

Note about installation: The animation files provided in this book generally have the rigs imported into each scene. A few of the scenes have the characters REFERENCED (see Chapter 10). If you open a scene and the rig produces an error, simply copy the rig from the "3D/Assets/Rigs/" directory to the chapter's directory and reopen the scene.

The "Cenk" rig requires the python script jlCollisionDeformer.py found in the Chapter 11 project directory. Open the "Readme" file for instructions on installing this script to your Maya program directory.

All of the rigs provided are for educational purposes only. Use these scene files and rigs in any non-commercial use.
Do not redistribute.

How to Use This Book

We've designed this book so that you can use it in the way that best serves your needs in learning to animate with Maya. You can start at the beginning and read it straight through if you like, as the chapters are ordered progressively. The first few talk about fundamental concepts: the principles of animation, workflow, and how animators think about the tools available in Maya. Then we start practicing some techniques in the context of animations already started for you, finally moving on to guiding you through doing projects in blocking, cycles, polishing, lip sync, and much more.

If you've been animating for a while, but need some new tips or approaches to problems you've been having, you can simply go to any topic that interests you, and pick it up right there. Even the chapter-long projects include a series of progressive files so you don't need to start from the beginning. We've also completely updated the book for Maya 2013, and cover all the exciting new animation tools and how to use them.

Throughout the book we use the abbreviation "f01" to mean frame 1, or whatever frame number we're talking about. Frame numbers are also included on every screenshot where they're relevant, to make things as clear as possible. In the upper right corner of each cheat you'll see a download icon ( ) whenever there are accompanying files, which is almost always. Underneath it the file names are listed for easy reference, and you can download all the scene files, rigs, and material from the previous edition from the book's website.

The projects are separated by chapter, and some of the projects also have QuicktTime movies of the chapter's final result. Also included is the Goon rig in several versions (regular, ninja, and demon). For additional info and updates, be sure to check out the website:

www.howtocheatinmaya.com

Squash and Stretch

STAGING Anticipation

straight ahead POSE To POSE

OVERLAPPING ACTION

follow through

Slow In / Slow Out

secondary ACTION

T-I--MI-NG

EXAGGERATION

SOLID DRAWING Appeal

1

Animation Principles

THE PRINCIPLES OF ANIMATION, identified and perfected by the original Disney animators, guide us when we make technique and performance choices in our work. They are not rules, but rather guidelines for creating appealing animation that is engaging and fun to watch.

These seemingly simple concepts combine to inform the most complex animation and performances on screen. Though some translation of these principles must occur for animators to utilize these concepts in Maya, this chapter offers a clear explanation of them and shows you how you can begin applying them in your own work.

Squash and Stretch

LAUDED AS THE MOST IMPORTANT PRINCIPLE, *squash and stretch* gives characters and objects a sense of flexibility and life. Also, this principle dictates that as characters and objects move and deform, their volume generally stays the same. Some of squash and stretch can be dictated by the object actually smooshing into something, such as a ball bouncing on the ground. With characters, squash and stretch can mean many different things. It can be combined with anticipation to make a character "wind up" for an action in a visually interesting way. One example would be as a character prepares to move, he may squash his spine, making his figure bulge out. Then as he springs into motion, his form elongates and stretches thin to retain the same volume. Whenever possible, use squash and stretch on your characters to give a sense of strain (a character reaching for something high overhead), or to give a sense of fear (a character squashes into a little ball in a corner to avoid being seen by a predator). Start looking for squash and stretch in professional animation and in life, and you'll see quickly how much this simple principle adds to the illusion of life we give objects and characters.

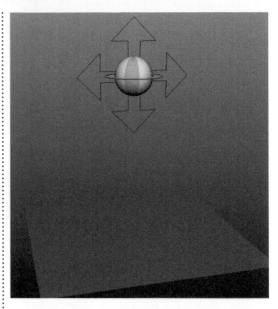

1 Open squash_Stretch_start.ma. We have an animated bouncing ball with the squash control keyed at 0 on f01 and f16. Hit play on the timeline and see how the ball seems neither alive, nor like it's made from rubber. This lifeless plastic ball is in need of some squash and stretch!

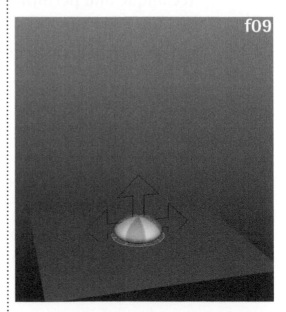

f09

4 At f09, the momentum continues downward through the ball, making it squash even more into the ground. Set the squash to -0.4 and key the control.

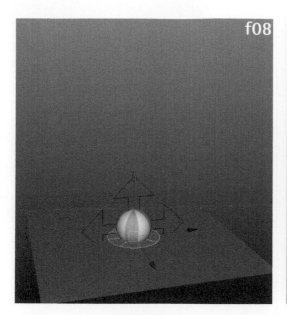

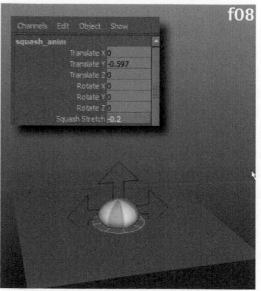

squash_Stretch_start.
ma
squash_Stretch_finish.
ma

2   Go to f08, and check out this dead ball! When it hits the ground, we expect a ball made from rubber to react! It needs to squash, so select the middle squash_anim control and translate it down in Y to the base. The location of this control determines where the ball squashes from.

3   Adjust the Squash Stretch amount in the channel box and key the entire control. The ball contacts for 2 frames, so this frame will be the start of it squashing, about -0.2 or so. Also notice that as the ball squashes down in Y, it bulges out in X and Z, retaining its volume.

HOT TIP

Squash and stretch isn't only about physically squashing and stretching in a cartoony manner. Also think about squash and stretch in the broader sense of being the contrast between compressed/contained and outstretched/extended.

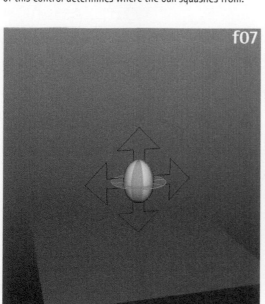

5   Go back to f07. As the ball falls, it would stretch out from the air resistance and the anticipation of hitting the ground. Translate the control back to the middle of the ball (Y is 0) so it stretches from its center, adjust the stretch control, and set a key.

6   At f11, center the squash control in Y, stretch the ball slightly and key it. Since the first and last frames are set to 0, the ball returns to its shape at the top of the bounce. Play back the animation with the controls turned off and watch this principle shine.

Anticipation

ANTICIPATION IS THE PRACTICE of moving a character in a certain way to prepare the character and the audience for the action. Most often, anticipation means moving the character a small amount in the opposite direction of the main action. Since a lot of animation is very physical, many times anticipation is a necessary part of getting the correct physical performance out of the character. For instance, a character jumping must bend his knees first. A pitcher must bring his arm back before he throws the ball. This natural motion that occurs in everyday life is what makes anticipation as an animation principle so effective. We are very accustomed as humans to tracking fast-moving objects by taking a cue from its anticipation, and then looking ahead of the object in the opposite direction. So as animators we must take advantage of this hard-wired trait of humans and use it to our advantage. We can make it so that the audience is always looking at the part of the screen that we want them to, by activating the visual cue of anticipation.

Anticipation also serves a purpose in fine tuning your performance choices. Disney animator and animation legend Eric Goldberg is known for relating anticipation directly with thought itself. This makes perfect sense; if we see a character really "wind up" for an action, it is clear to us that the character has planned the action well in advance, and is thinking about how to move. On the other hand, if a character moves instantaneously and without warning the motion comes across as unplanned. Think of the difference between the apparent thought process of Popeye swinging his arm back to punch an unsuspecting Brutus, and Brutus's head when the fist hits him on the back of the head. Popeye was planning to wallop the big bully, but Brutus was not thinking at all of the fist about to hit him! So as you are working, pay close attention to how much anticipation you are using in your animation. It may just mean the difference between a thinking, planning, and intelligent character, and a character simply reacting to the world around him.

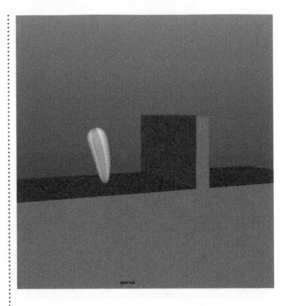

1 Open anticipation.ma. In this scene, a bouncing ball looks at a wall, and then deftly hops over. Play it a few times and see if you can spot the anticipation before the jump.

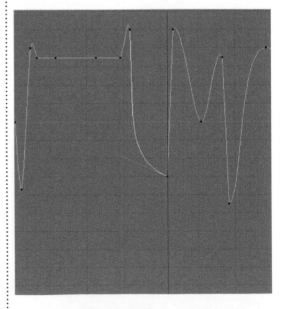

4 Now play with the handle itself! Drag it way out towards the left and play back the animation. See what a different impression you get as to the thought behind the jump? Subtle changes in anticipation can have incredible results.

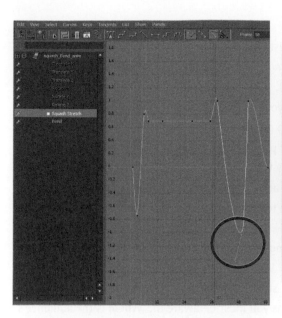

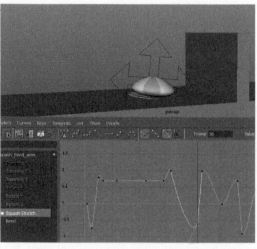

anticipation.ma

2 If you select the squash_Bend_anim control on the ball, you will see there is a keyframe on the Squash Stretch control at f50 with an unlocked tangent. This is the frame of anticipation. We are going to play with this anticipation and see what looks best.

3 Select the squash_Bend_anim control, and open the Graph Editor. See that key frame with the unlocked tangent handles? Try moving that key up and down and finding a good size of squash for this anticipation. Watch the animation over and over again to see what looks best. Remember, it's up to you!

HOT TIP

Play your animation at speed! We know that timing is vitally important in animation. You get so much more information playing your animation at speed than you do if you just scroll through the timeline.

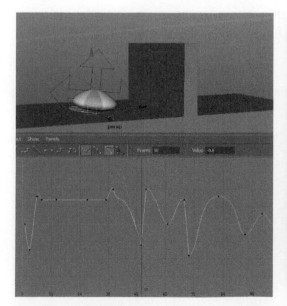

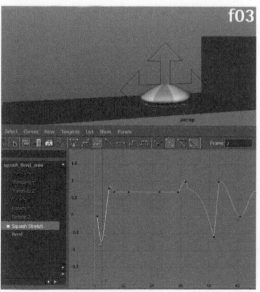

f03

5 Or does this look better? Remember, if you keep the number of keyframes you use to a minimum, you can spend more time making adjustments and less time wrestling with technical trouble. What new impression does this anticipation give you? What is the ball **thinking**?

6 At f03 is another little anticipation that I sneaked in. Play with the size and timing of this one as well, and start training your eye to hone in on the most powerful and engaging performance.

Staging

STAGING IS A FUNDAMENTAL that encompasses a mass of artistic sensibilities. Staging involves framing the camera in a way to best capture the action. It involves making sure your animation has been planned to best communicate the motion, the character arc, the story. Simply put, staging is how you create the scene.

Ideally staging starts with your planning phase. Thumbnailing your poses is the best way to make strong pose choices at the start of a shot. If you are not a strong drawer, then perhaps you rely more on photo or video references to give you cues to begin your work. At this very early phase, staging means you are thinking about how your posing and the layout of the scene are going to clearly show the motion.

As you begin your scene, staging becomes more complex. How are you going to maintain the high level of communication throughout the life of the shot? Will you be able to hit all of the poses that you'd like, or are the poses going to have to be changed to work when the character is in motion? Staging means that you are thinking about the entire action at this point. Adjusting the camera, making tweaks to the layout, and finding just the right balance in the composition all improve your staging of the scene. When you are finished blocking, generally the major staging decisions have been made. This does not mean that staging is over!

As you finish the animation, there are still staging considerations you must be aware of. Where is the audience's eye going to be looking at every moment of the shot? If you've animated the scene correctly, you have a very good idea of what the audience should be paying attention to at every second. As your shot is finished and moves through the rest of the pipeline, other decisions that hone in the audience's focus are going to come into play: lighting, effects, and editing.

As animators, our staging choices have far-reaching impact on the success of a shot in communicating an idea. We'll practice these staging concepts by repositioning a bouncing ball animation, the camera, and some lights to find the greatest impact.

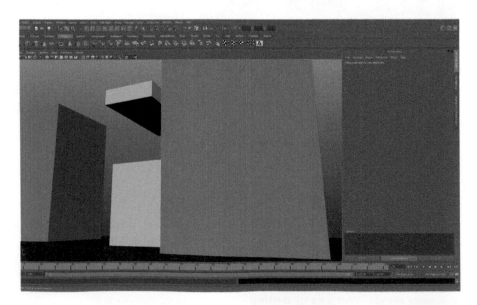

1 Open staging_start.ma, and set one of your panels to look through "renderCam". Yikes. This scene has a lot of staging problems. The camera is in a position where it cannot see any of the action, the ball has been positioned very oddly, and the light is casting a shadow on the entire main action. Let's make some adjustments.

2 Rotate, pan and zoom the camera around until you've found an angle that shows off the animation nicely when you scrub through the timeline. This is a nice angle for me.

staging_start.ma
staging_finish.ma

HOT TIP

It's easy to forget that staging is more than just the camera angle. If you're working on a production, you may not have any control over the camera angle chosen for a shot. If this is the case, you must design your staging within the camera you've been given. This might entail "cheating" poses so they look their best in a particular camera.

3 Let's adjust the position of the animated ball to make the action read clearer, shall we? Grab the "all" group in the Outliner, and scrub through the animation. See how the ball is pushed far towards the edge of the set, and hits the wall on f65? Let's reposition it to be a little more centered, and to not hit the set on its path.

Staging (cont'd)

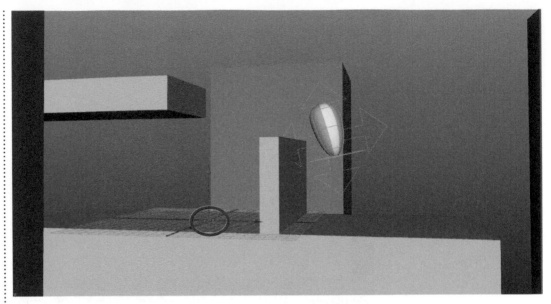

4 Much better. I moved the group back to the world origin, and the animation is working much better to camera.

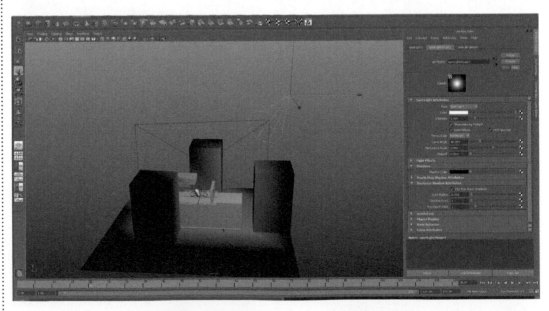

6 In a perspective panel, press the **7** key to enable the lighting, and make sure Show > Lights is enabled in the viewport menu. Select the light and transform and rotate it until it gives a nice ¾ lighting angle. The action should be lit so that we get a fully lit view of the scene, but also so that the shadows are angled to show the detail and depth of the set.

5 Hit the render button to see how the lights are positioned. Uh oh, the main action is happening in deep shadow!

7 Now click render when you have repositioned your light. Beautiful!

HOT TIP

If you select a spotlight, and then go to the Panels menu in any panel and choose Look Through Selected, it will create a temporary camera view that matches the view as seen from that spotlight. Many Maya users find using Maya's in-panel camera moving tools to position lights is a fast and easy way to stage the scene. Maya even gives you an in-panel preview of the light's cone angle!

Straight Ahead/Pose to Pose

THIS FUNDAMENTAL DESCRIBES the two basic approaches to block in a piece of animation. "Straight ahead" means that an animator creates the base animation by posing the animation in a frame, then moving forward one or more frames and posing again. This approach is akin to stop-motion animation, in which you have to pose every one or two frames because the camera needs to capture that frame on film before moving forward. "Pose to pose" means that you create the key poses, and then essentially time the rest of the animation by inserting blank or "hold-poses" in between your key poses. This is akin to a non-linear approach in which you can test different timings of a shot by simply sliding poses around on the time slider. Both approaches have their advantages and disadvantages.

Straight ahead animating should be used when the action is very mechanical or physical. This is because the ability to perceive the motion as you frame through the animation in slow motion is far greater than trying to imagine what pose the highly mechanical or physical movement is going to hit. Let's take an overlapping antenna, for instance. With this kind of highly physical action it would be impossible to imagine where the antenna is going to be without framing through the animation and adjusting the pose as you go. This is what we'll do to practice this concept.

Pose-to-pose animating should be used for creating character performances. Unlike highly physical actions, the key poses a character hits are going to tell the story. So in order to be sure that you arrive at these golden moments, you should pose them out and retime them as necessary to make the motion work. We bias our work in performance animation to feature the pose because, without a strong sense of the character's body language, the emotional story gets lost. We're going to create a pose and retime it using Maya's Dope Sheet.

1 Open straightAhead_start.ma. This bouncing ball looks familiar, but now it has an antenna on top. Let's practice animating straight ahead and make the antenna flop back and forth.

f08

4 When the ball hits the ground at f08, the antenna will not react yet because the momentum needs time to travel up through the ball. Key the antenna straight up.

f01

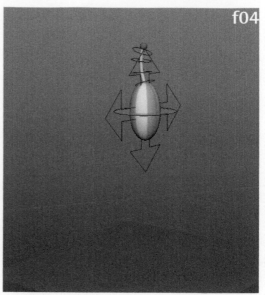

f04

2 On f01, the ball is at the top of its arc, so the antenna will be travelling upwards, trying to catch up. Select all the antenna controls, and key them upwards.

3 Go to f04. The ball has started falling and so the antenna will continue to move upwards as it catches up with where the ball was a few frames earlier. Keep an eye on the squash and stretch for a cue. Key the antenna a bit more up.

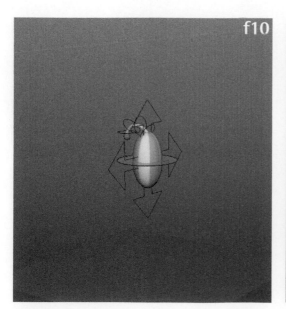

f10

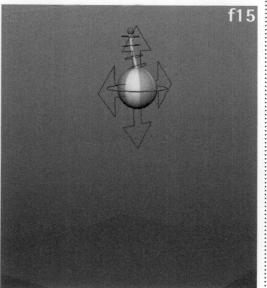

f15

5 Now at f10, the ball is traveling upwards again, but the antenna will still be moving down from the impact of the ball hitting the ground a couple frames earlier. Key the antenna bending downward.

6 Finish the scene by copying f01 to the last frame (f15) as you do with all cycles.

straightAhead_start.
ma
straightAhead_finish.
ma

HOT TIP

As we demonstrated in this example, straight ahead usually works best when there is a frame of reference to judge the movement by. In this case, we knew what the antenna should do because of where the ball was. Don't confuse animating straight ahead with animating blindly. That rarely turns out well, even for experienced animators. Always have a good plan for what you are going to animate beforehand!

Pose to Pose (cont'd)

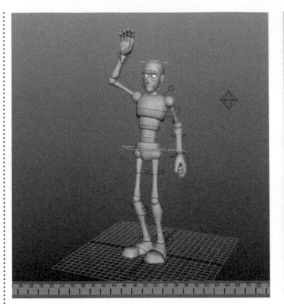

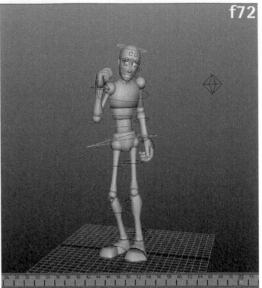

7 Open pose_to_pose_start.ma. This character is waving to someone he thinks he recognizes, but then he realizes he doesn't know them! He retracts into an embarrassed pose, and looks away.

8 Let's create his embarrassed pose on f72 and then adjust the timing using the Dope Sheet. Select all of the controls in the body and hit **S** on f72. Pose Goon with his face and body exhibiting embarrassment.

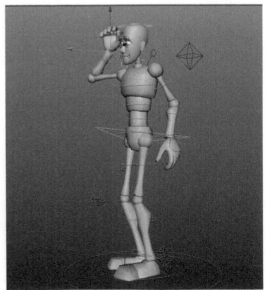

10 Frame 72 is too soon for this final pose. Select the block on f72 in the Dope Sheet and middle-mouse drag it to a later frame— whatever looks good to you! I chose 100 and I like how Goon slinks into this embarrassed pose.

11 Goon now needs a breakdown to define the arc of this movement and make it less linear. Rotate the camera to his profile. See how the arm comes very close to his face? It is common to need to add breakdowns when you retime animation created pose to pose.

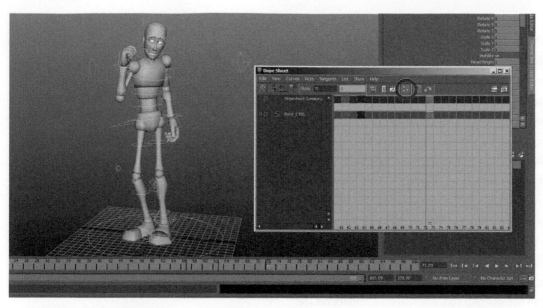

9 Open the Dope Sheet and find the Hierarchy/Below button and click it. Now if you choose Goon's root_CTRL in the panel you will notice all of the key frames load into the Dope Sheet. The Dope Sheet is a good tool for broad retiming of a scene.

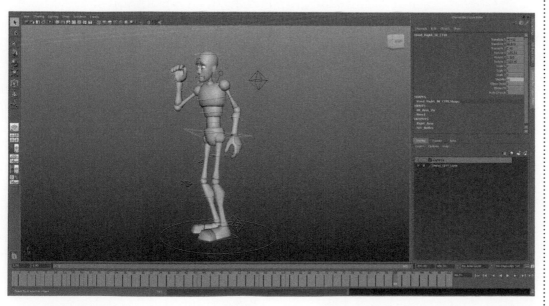

12 On f88, grab Goon's Root control and move it forward just a little. Also add a little bit of bend throughout the spine, and lastly move his hand forward so that it takes a nice arced path from the pose above his head to the pose near his face.

pose_to_pose_start.ma
pose_to_pose_finish.
ma

HOT TIP

You can get a nice settle in a pose by selecting all of your controls, then middle-mouse dragging and copying a pose from a few frames before your last key pose to a frame 6 to 8 frames later. This method needs adjustment to make it look perfect, but gives you a very quick and easy settle to start working from.

Overlapping Action/Follow-through

OVERLAP AND FOLLOW-THROUGH are the two most intuitive fundamentals in animation. Both basically deal with the principle that it takes energy to move objects and also to slow them down. "Overlap" is what we call it when an object "lags" behind the main action. "Follow-through" is what we call it when an action overshoots or goes past the end pose.

Overlap instills a fluidity in character animation. When added to your character's gestures, overlap makes the animation feel like the character has a natural limber quality. When a character swings his arm, the bending of the wrist has a nice organic quality. Natural rise and fall in the spine in a walk cycle makes it feel calm, while an extreme amount of overlap in the spine in a walk can make the character look depressed and sad. In this way we can see overlap has a very major impact on the performance of a character.

With follow-through, the main thing you can show is a sense of weight with your character. The heavier the weight, the more energy it will take to stop the character. Use follow-through to emphasize this.

We've already had some practice with overlap in the last section, but let's get some more practice with a simple animation of Goon landing from a jump.

1 Open overlap_start.ma. Playing back the animation, you can see Goon is landing on the ground from a jump. See, though, how his spine looks very stiff and unnatural. This scene needs some overlap and follow-through.

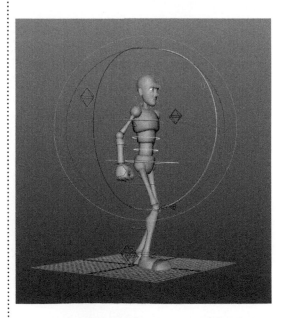

4 Don't stand him up too fast. Try a few different timings and sizes of pose at the end here as well. You'll notice that the weight of the character changes drastically with only a few frames of difference!

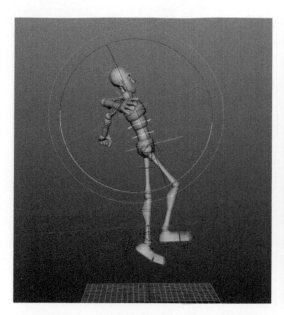

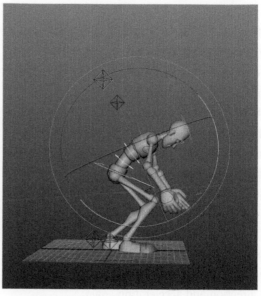

overlap_start.ma
overlap_finish.ma

2 Select the controls in Goon's spine and set a key on frame 1. Just like the antenna that you animated in the last section, we are going to have his spine "lag behind," or overlap, as he falls. As Goon falls, set a key on the spine, having him straighten up a bit. I like this pose.

3 When he hits the ground, we need the action to follow through. This means bending Goon back over as he lands. Try a few different choices of pose and a few different timings as well.

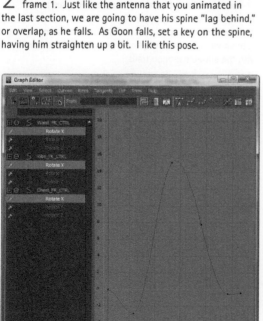

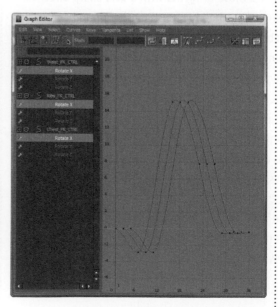

5 Let's also offset the overlap to get an even more natural follow-through in this action. Select the controls of the spine, and open the Graph Editor. Isolate just the Rotate X channels; it should look like this.

6 Offset the ribs by moving them two frames forward, and offset the chest by moving them four frames forward. Now play the animation back, and you have an even nicer, fluid overlap in the spine!

17

Slow In/Slow Out

SLOW IN AND SLOW OUT, also called ease in and ease out, refer to the spacing of the keys when an action comes to a stop or changes direction, or a character transitions from pose to pose. This principle means to animators that we typically decelerate objects as they come to a stop rather than have them come to a dead halt instantly ("slowing in" to the pose). It also means we should gradually accelerate objects as they begin to move and not have them instantly be at full speed ("slowing out" of a pose). In the Graph Editor of Maya, this principle is simply illustrated by flat tangents. It is easy to see how an object slows in to a change of direction in the Graph Editor when we look at the curves of a bouncing ball. As the ball arrives at the top of its arc, and also the flat tangent of the Y curve, it decelerates evenly before changing direction and accelerating again.

This is not a blanket rule, however! Not every action should slow in and slow out! In the bouncing ball animation, when the ball hits the ground there will be no slow in or slow out. Instead, we animate those tangents with a very sharp direction change as a result of the ball hitting the solid ground and having to change direction instantly. Consider also an animation of a character running. The feet are going to be really pounding the ground, meaning the legs are still going to be accelerating as the foot hits the ground. "Flatting" all of your tangents in the Graph Editor is a common mistake, as is having flat tangents be your default tangent type. True understanding of slow in and slow out means understanding which situations should have nice eased poses, and which ones should have stark direction changes. We are going to take advantage of Maya 2013's new editable motion trails to practice when to use slow in and slow out. Also check out the Splines (Chapter 2) for more details on slow in and slow out.

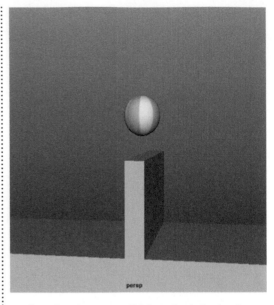

1 Open slow_in_start.ma. This bouncing ball animation has a problem. Play the animation back. See how linearly the ball changes direction at the top of the arc? We have a slow in to the pose of the ball at the top, where nothing would make it physically slow down. Let's fix that with the editable motion trails.

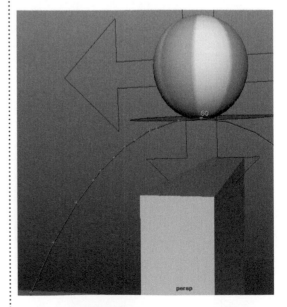

4 Select the bead furthest from the keyframe and drag it away from the keyframe. The arc smoothes out, and also the interpolation gets far less linear. Frame through the keys and see how the ball travels more distance per key than before. Undo and compare to before if you like.

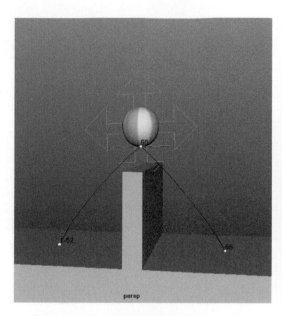

2 Select the ball_anim control and create the editable motion trail by clicking Animate > Create Editable Motion Trail. (Motion Trails are discussed in-depth in the Techniques chapter.)

3 Select the f60 keyframe on the motion trail, then right click on the motion trail and select "Timing Beads In." You can now see the frame bias, or how much Maya will slow in to the keyframe when interpolating the in-betweens. In this instance, the in-beads are squished right near the keyframe, creating way too much slow in!

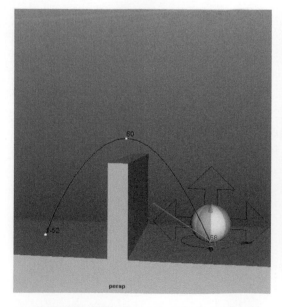

5 We also want the impact on the ground to be stronger, so let's create a "fast in" (the opposite of a slow in) on the impact. Select the key at f68 on the motion trail that is on the right side of the wall, on the ground. Right click and check "Show In Tangent."

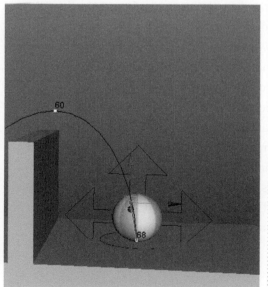

6 Select the tangent handle that is displayed, and with the move tool **W** move it to the right in the X axis until it is almost in line with the arc of the motion trail itself. Play the animation back and see the result. With character animation, VERY subtle changes make all the difference!

slow_in_start.ma
slow_in_finish.ma

19

Arcs

ARLY ANIMATORS OBSERVED the interesting fact that most natural actions follow an arced path. They then practiced applying this trait to their animation to create more appealing movement. This came to be known as the principle of "*arcs*". To avoid giving mechanical, robotic performances, check your animation constantly by tracking objects on screen and make sure they do not follow linear paths. Remember to check your arcs from all angles first, but finally and most importantly from your camera view; this is the view the audience will see!

Another very common mistake is to only track arcs on major body controls. As animators, we tend to bias our attention to the controls that give us the gross pose of a character: Root, Hand IK, Foot IK, and Head. All too often, beginning animators will then try to track the arcs of their animation, but because of all the attention and time spent using only four or five main controls, will only look to these areas for smoothing. This can lead to a visual discontinuity within the animation of the body. Instead, you have to look at the entire body, and determine the forces in the body. A fantastic resource for learning how to determine the force in a pose is the book *Force: Dynamic Life Drawing for Animators*, published by Focal Press. Investigate how the entire pose itself has rapidly changing, dynamic shapes, all of which need to move naturally and on arcs.

For our purposes, we are going to adjust the arcs on a full- body turn animation. Our character is looking towards screen left, when he suddenly turns and looks towards screen right. There is no breakdown key in the middle of the turn, meaning there is only a very drab, linear interpolation happening between the left and right poses. To fix this, we are going to add a breakdown and improve the arcs of the turn.

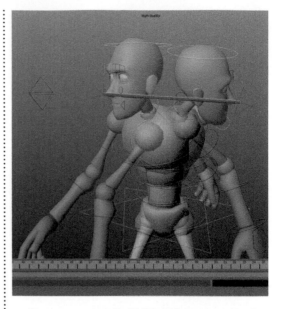

1 Open arcs_start.ma. Yuck! This body turn is unnatural and mechanical. See how linearly the body and head turns from left to right? We are going to fix this immediately by adding a breakdown in the middle of the turn.

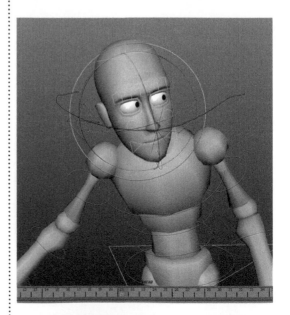

4 Don't forget the head usually leads the body in a turn! I like to have the head rotated slightly in the Z axis so that the chin is tilted on the head turn. This gives the head a little bit of natural motion.

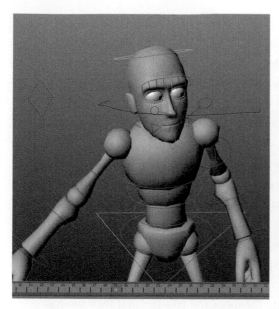

f21

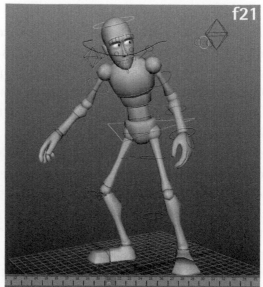

arcs_start.ma
arcs_finish.ma

2   Select the locator on the tip of Goon's nose named
    noseTrack_Loc. Then go to Animate > Create Editable
Motion Trail. We will not be editing the motion trail in this
scene, just using it for visual feedback. See how straight the
head turn is?

3   Let's add the breakdown. Select the Center_Root_FK_
    CTRL, Waist_FK_CTRL, Ribs_FK_CTRL, Chest_FK_CTRL,
Neck_FK_CTRL, and Head_FK_CTRL. On Frame 21, create a
pose in which Goon is bending a little bit over, making the
motion trail bend into an arc.

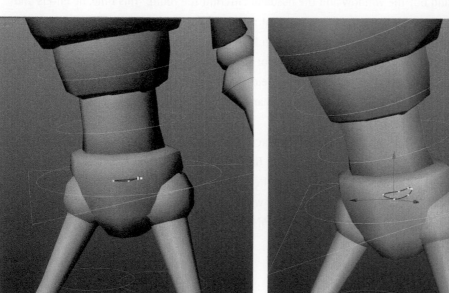

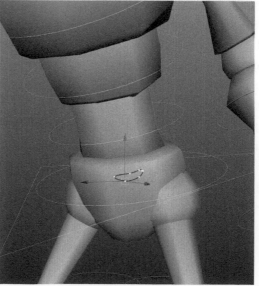

5   Now select the Root_CTRL and create another Editable
    Motion Trail. The body movement needs some arc
smoothing as well!

6   On f21 and f28, create some breakdown keys by
    translating the Root_CTRL downwards and make a nice,
arced motion. Motion trails are powerful tools included in
Maya 2013, and are directly editable in panel. Track the arcs
throughout the rest of the body to get nice smooth motion.

21

Secondary Action

THIS PRINCIPLE REALLY GIVES a scene some deep subtext. Secondary action is any action that is not the primary action in a scene. A character sharpening a pencil as he complains to his boss would be secondary action; the primary action has to do with the poses and body language involved in speaking to the boss. A character running his hand through his hair as he turns away from the mirror, giving himself a wink, would be good secondary. The main action in this example is the turn, but the hand through the hair adds a nice level of meaning to the whole scene.

The wonderful thing about secondary action is that there really is no amount that is too much. Especially with humans: we're constantly multitasking, constantly occupying ourselves with more than one thing at a time. The animation can, of course, become too busy. The fact is there is a balance, but for the most part your scenes can always use an extra level of animation and therefore subtext.

The way master animators truly utilize secondary action is by "coloring" the action to suit the subtext of a scene. This means changing the secondary action in pose, timing, spacing, etc. to distinguish it from a normal, "vanilla" performance of the same action. Let's look at an example. Let's imagine a scene where a mother is ironing clothes while looking out a window. Her husband walks into the room and tells her that their son has been killed in war. She is facing away from him, and still continues to iron. But her body language changes. Her hands start shaking. She looks like she's about to faint as her eyes well up with tears. The adjustments to the action of ironing clothes (the secondary action in this scene) is what we call coloring the action. Now imagine the same set up, with the wife looking out the window and the husband entering the room. This time, he enters and simply asks her how her day was, but this time, she found out that morning that she is pregnant. She answers him "Fine," and smiles. How would you "color" the secondary action in this scene? When she hears the husband enter the room, would she excitedly speed up her action? Maybe she got some baby clothes out of a box and that's why she's ironing. She'd then pause and look at the clothes as she describes her day to her husband. Suddenly, through secondary action, animators have access to an enormous amount of subtlety in a scene. I like to call secondary action the "window to subtext".

We are going to do a simple trick with Animation Layers to practice using secondary action to show subtlety in a scene. In our scene, Goon is sitting at the library, tapping his finger, very bored. Then someone he really likes walks by, and his eyes follow them. By animating the weight of the animation layer with the finger on it, we are going to "color" that action; basically, he forgets to tap his finger while he is captivated by this person walking by. Secondary action can be so subtle, that sometimes just STOPPING a secondary action is enough to completely color it!

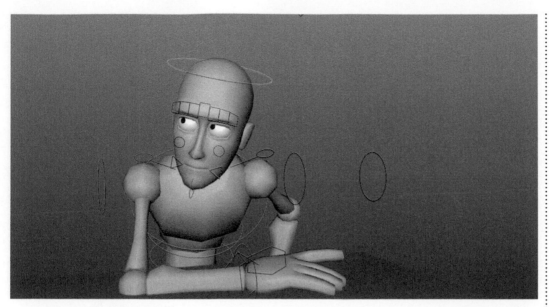

secondary_start.ma
secondary_finish.ma

1 Open secondary_start.ma. Play back the animation, and you'll see Goon is completely bored and tapping his finger at the desk. Then a person he likes walks by and he is captivated.

HOT TIP

Check out
Chapter 12 for
an in-depth look
at Animation
Layers and how
to use them.

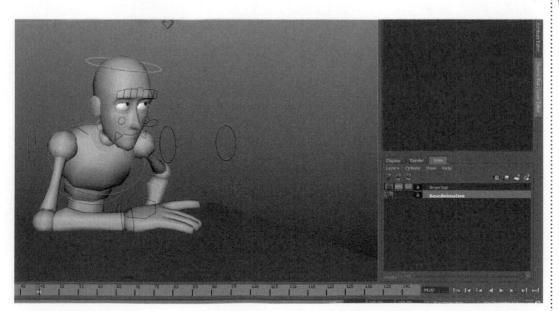

2 In the bottom half of the Channel Box your Layers tabs are all visible. When you select the layer tab labeled "Anim," you'll see that there is a "BaseAnimation" (with the entire body pose animated inside) and a "fingerTap" layer.

Secondary Action (cont'd)

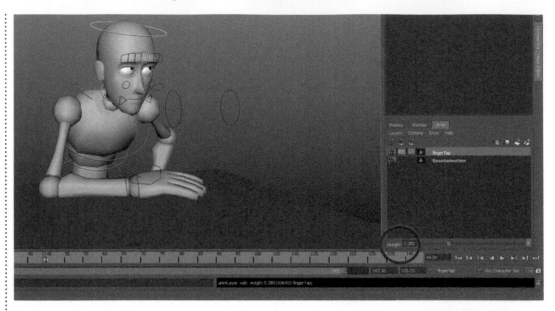

3 Maya 2013 has powerful tools for blending animation together. In fact, you can blend dozens of layers of animation together if you please; the only limit is what you can keep track of. Slide the Weight slider up and down and see how the finger tapping is affected.

5 Advance 10-20 frames in the animation and slide the weight of the fingerTap Anim layer down to 0. Goon is now so transfixed on this person that he's completely dropped his secondary action, a very powerful way of "coloring" it! To see your weight curve in the Graph Editor, right click on the Anim layer and click on "Select Layer Node."

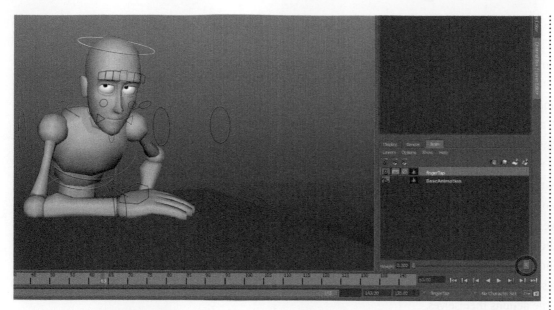

4 Not only can you blend animation, but you can key the weight! Find a good frame when you are sure that Goon has recognized the person walking by. Set a key on the weight of Anim layer "fingerTap" by hitting the **K** (set key) button next to the weight slider.

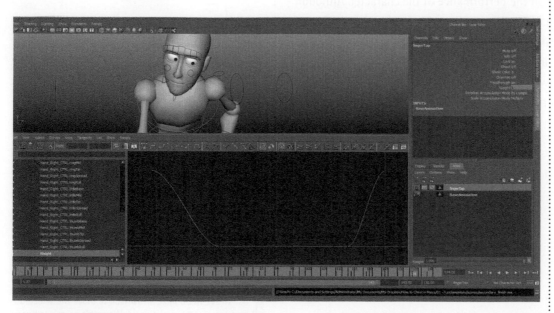

6 Experiment! Play around with the secondary action and see if you can tell different stories by animating the weight of the layer. Maybe bring it back to 1 at the end of the scene and observe the resulting change in the subtext!

HOT TIP

If you are unsure about a secondary action, sometimes it can be better to key the main action on the master animation layer, and only when it is looking solid, key the secondary action on a new Anim layer. You can always turn off the layer if the secondary doesn't work out, without fear of destroying your main action.

Timing

TIMING IS LESS A FUNDAMENTAL than it is the very foundation of the art of animation. Animation is, of course, just a series of still images that flash by fast enough to create the illusion of motion. Our task is to use timing not just to accurately portray motion in realistic scenes, but to use timing as a method to convey meaning in a scene.

In character animation the main goal is to get your audience to empathize with a character. As they succeed, the audience celebrates; when they fail, the audience feels their loss. As animators we can get so caught up in the physics and mechanics of the motions that we create that sometimes we forget the timing of a scene can be improved to tell a deeper story. The pauses in between actions can have more powerful messages than the actions themselves.

In the last section, we adjusted the secondary action of the character to show that he is so captivated in that moment that his hand just naturally stops moving. It has a subtle but powerful effect on the performance of the character. Although a full animation curriculum on timing is outside the purview of this book, we can definitely experiment with this scene to give ourselves some insight into the powerful effect subtle timing changes can have on a performance. We'll use the keyframe editing tools in the timeline and Graph Editor to make these adjustments.

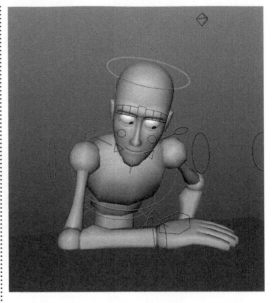

1 Open timing_start.ma. The timeline of our secondary action exercise has been extended at the end to allow us to make some adjustments here. Pay particularly close attention to the performance at the end, where Goon looks back toward the desk.

4 Use the center double arrow icon to move the selected keys forward 30 or so frames. We aren't going to choose a specific timing, because we want to observe the subtle differences that timing makes. What does this new timing tell you? To me, the longer he pauses in this in-between pose, the more it looks like he's THINKING about what he saw.

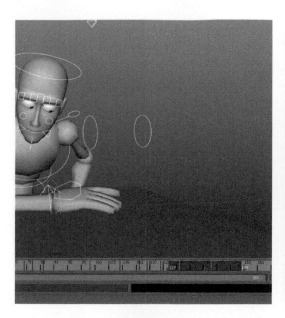

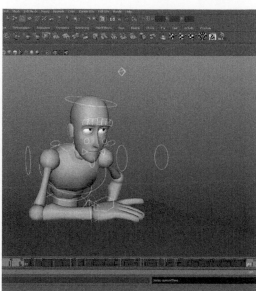

timing_start.ma
timing_finish.ma

HOT TIP

Novice animators often struggle with the difference between timing and spacing. While they are connected to each other, they're NOT the same. A movement over 10 frames can look completely different depending on how you change the spacing, even though the actual time in which it moves (10 frames) stays consistent.

2 Let's extend the time that Goon spends looking toward the desk halfway between his gaze towards screen left and the final pose back towards screen right. Select all of Goon's controls. Don't forget to select Goon's eyeTarget_CTRL too. Position the cursor over f127 on the timeline, then *Shift* LMB and drag the cursor all the way past f150.

3 This red box is your selection on the timeline. The left and right arrows scale your keys in either direction. The middle double arrow icon moves the selection through the timeline. Drag each one of the arrows around and get familiar with their use, then Undo so that you are back to the original timing.

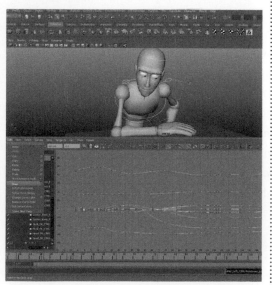

5 Let's play with the end too. Experimenting is fun! Select all of Goon's controls again and open the Graph Editor. Select the last two poses by dragging a selection box around all of the keys. Now scale the last two poses' keys by hitting *R* and then *Shift* MMB drag to the right with the cursor placed near frame 150. Release the mouse button when the last key is near frame 180.

6 Play the animation and it not only looks like he's thinking more, this slower transition to the end pose feels like he's a little melancholy. However, whenever you scale keys in the Graph Editor, your keys usually end up placed in between frames. Select all of the keys in the Graph Editor and click on Edit > Snap. Now the keys are back on integer frames.

Exaggeration

EXAGGERATION IS ONE OF THE SIMPLEST, yet most misunderstood principles of animation. Why? For decades novice animators have tried to blindly exaggerate their animation to try to recreate the amazing cartoony styles of the animators of yore. However, exaggeration doesn't necessarily mean better animation, or even more cartoony. Exaggeration must be used with a keen eye for the effect you are trying to achieve.

Find the core idea in your scene and figure out the best way to exaggerate the message. If you are animating a character getting pricked on the butt with a pin, then you are going to exaggerate the timing and spacing of him shooting into the air. If you are animating a character that gets scared by a spider, you might exaggerate the squash and stretch in his body by having his legs run away from his torso, stretching out his spine! In both of these cases we choose the main idea and exaggerate only where we need to in order to strengthen the message. Both scenes would look way over-complicated if we had exaggerated the posing, timing, spacing, composition, weight, anticipation, etc.

Your animation scenes in Maya should be as lean as possible. To illustrate how easy it can be to exaggerate a fundamental, we're going to take a finished walk cycle and adjust the overlap in the spine using the Graph Editor. Your workflow must create animation that has minimal keys, therefore making it easy to change the animation later on. For our purposes, the overlap in the spine on a walk cycle is a great fundamental to experiment with, because it has such a large impact on the performance.

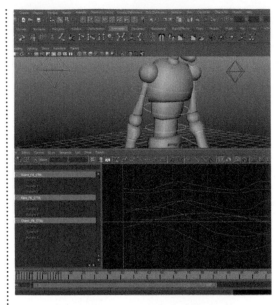

1 Open exaggeration_start.ma. Goon is walking a straight-ahead, "vanilla" walk with little performance to it. Select the controls in the spine and open the Graph Editor.

4 You can also perform the scale by using some of the math functionality in Maya. Select the controls in the spine and then in the Graph Editor value box (the right box of the two) type in "*=2". The ✱ symbol means to multiply the values and the "=2" tells Maya how much to multiply by.

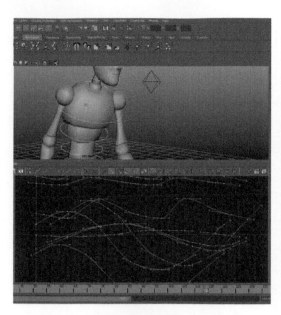

exaggeration_start.ma
exaggeration_finish.
ma

2 As you can see, as of right now these curves are not exaggerated at all. Hit **R** to use the Scale Tool in the Graph Editor. Now select the curves in the spine and MMB drag up and down to scale these keys. Notice that the point on the graph where your mouse starts the dragging motion is considered the center of the scale.

3 Scaling keys up and down in the Graph Editor scales their values, whereas scaling left and right scales timing. Without the rest of the body's controls selected, scaling the timing of the spine won't produce good results.

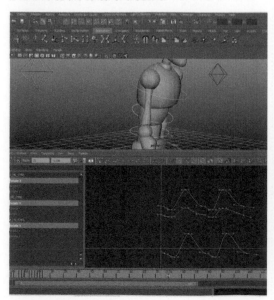

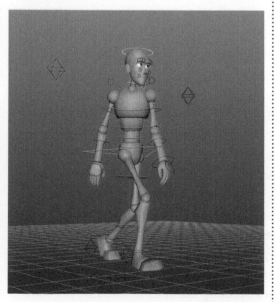

5 Playing back the animation now shows more exaggeration in his spine, but it needs some tweaking. Select just the Rotate X curves in the Graph Editor and then hit **W** to use the move tool. MM drag them upwards to get the spine to overlap more forward over his center of gravity.

6 Experiment! The best thing you can do to grow your list of cheats is to find some more on your own. Use the Graph Editor to exaggerate other aspects of the walk, like the arms, or the Translate Y in the Center_Root_FK_CTRL to get some more extreme up and down motion as Goon steps.

Solid Drawing

AT FIRST GLANCE, "solid drawing" has little to do with CG animation in Maya. What does drawing have to do with animating on the computer? On the contrary, this is an extremely important fundamental to remember when creating animation on the computer. Why? As CG animators, it is very easy to relax our artistic sensibilities and let Maya do all of the work. However, the moment you forget the art of pose, perspective, form, volume, and force, you will quickly see your animation dissolve into unappealing mush. Solid drawing is a fundamental that persists from the hand-drawn days of cel animation. What it basically imparts is a dedication to the figure-drawing principles that the master animators all adhered to. When you started your drawing, you always had to begin with the same basic construction of the character: simple shapes combined with clean, meaningful lines, taking into consideration the line of action, the force of the pose, and the weight of the character. Perhaps most of all, perspective and a sense of the character's volume had to be extremely consistent. In other words, all 24 drawings per second of animation had to look like the same character.

In CG, we have a lot of help from Maya to achieve solid drawing, but we should pay close attention to make sure we aren't being lazy. Since we are working with 3D models, for the most part Maya takes care of staying "on model." Even so, you have to be careful not to pose your character in such a way that the body or face is distorted so much that it doesn't look like the same character. Most of the time this happens when an animator hasn't thoroughly tested the rig, and is using controls to create movement that were not intended for that purpose. In CG we can indeed go off-model, and it is your job to avoid this.

We are going to fix a piece of animation that has some very bad counter-animated controls, and is also experiencing some skin-weight issues. Speaking strictly as an animator, you don't have to be as concerned with technical issues, but remember that CG animation is often a team effort, and solid drawing is the result of everyone working together.

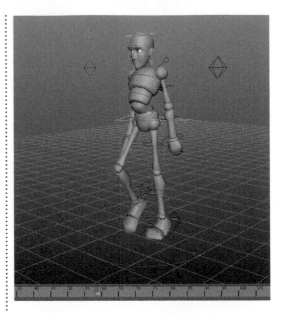

1 Open solid_drawing_start.ma. This walk cycle looks a little off. The spine controls have been animated against each other. As a general guide, body sections that work together should move in harmony with each other. Going against the natural design of how something moves, even if intentional, can create off-model-looking poses.

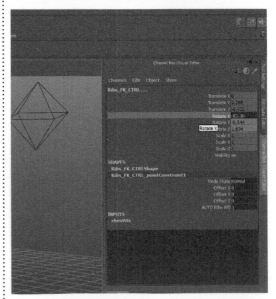

4 Delete the Rotate X curves. Notice that there are still values in Rotate X when you switch to the Channel Box. This is because Maya leaves a channel's value at the current frame whenever you delete ALL animation on a channel. Select the Rotate X channel and type in **0** and hit *Enter*.

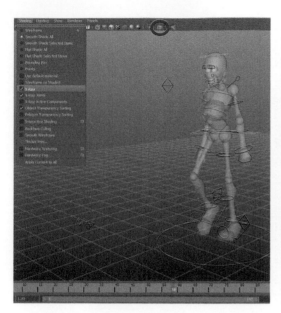

2 A good way to see your controls is to use the X-Ray rendering in panel, either in the Shading menu or with the X-Ray button. This mode makes all of the geometry semi-transparent so you can see joints, edges, and curves very easily.

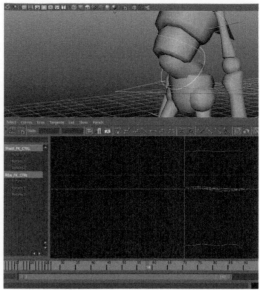

3 Select Waist_FK_CTRL and Ribs_FK_CTRL and open up the Graph Editor. As you can see, they have been posed in such a way that they are rotated against each other.

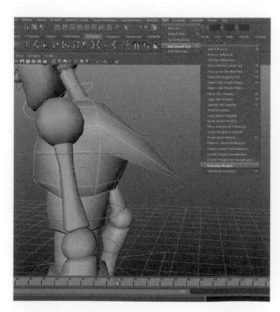

5 Now that the controls have been zeroed and the counter-animation removed, Goon is still leaving some vertices behind as he walks away. Select his chest geometry and switch to the Animation menu set. Click on Skin > Edit Smooth Skin > Normalize Weights.

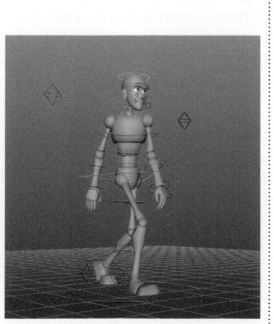

6 Now the model should be behaving! Don't worry what that did, as it's a rigging issue that most animators won't have to deal with. The point is, with CG animation, artistic choices, like posing, and some technical choices, like skin weights, can have an impact on solid drawing.

solid_drawing_start.
ma
solid_drawing_finish.
ma

HOT TIP

Instead of deleting the curves themselves in the Graph Editor, we can delete animation from a channel by right clicking on that channel in the Channel Box, and clicking Delete Selected. This will delete the animation on the channel, not the channel or the attribute itself. Remember, the channel's value will remain at the current frame value whenever you delete all animation.

31

Appeal

IT COULD BE SAID that all of the fundamentals combine to make "appeal." Beautiful, organic timing is appealing to the eye. Interesting, dynamic posing is also appealing. Character designs, contrasting shapes and rhythm, are all fine tuned, worked, and re-worked to get the most appeal. Does appeal mean "good"? Not at all: the evil villains in our most beloved animations all have appeal. From their striking silhouettes to vibrant colors, even the bad guys must be appealing. Appeal is the pinnacle of our task as animators, it is the goal. Above all else we should strive to always put images in front of our audiences that are worthy of their time.

Let's focus on posing for our discussion of appeal. As animators our work takes place far after the characters have been designed, modeled, textured, and rigged. But even with appealing characters, bad posing can ruin the entire show. For instance, an arm pointed directly at camera loses all of its good posing from foreshortening; the animation must work well with the chosen composition. Take the camera into consideration and be sure that your staging is well thought out. The silhouette of your pose should be strong, without limbs lost within the silhouette of the body. And "maxed-out" or hyperextended arms and legs never look very good.

Twinning is another major issue in posing. In nature, nothing is ever perfectly symmetrical. Without being careful to avoid twinning, it sneaks its way into our animation. It saves time, for instance, to set channels on both sides of a character at the same time. If this is a cheat you use, then you must remember to go back through the scene and un-twin your poses. Arms, legs, hands, even facial poses can fall victim to twinning.

We must be mindful of the appeal of our animation by constantly critiquing our work and showing it to others.

To practice, we are going to take a single pose and make some adjustments to increase the appeal.

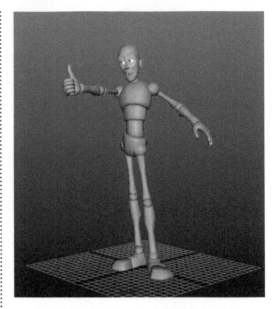

1 Open appeal_start.ma. You'll see Goon has been posed giving "thumbs up" to a character off screen.

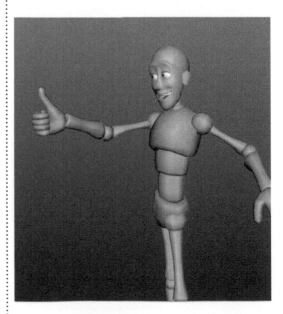

4 Let's fix the maxed-out arm as well. Bring a little bit of bend into the elbow and make the wrist look more natural.

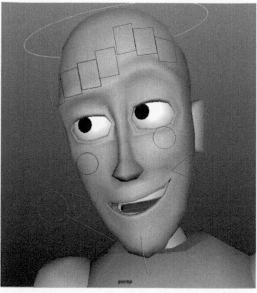

appeal_start.ma
appeal_finish.ma

2 This face pose could use a lot more appeal. Let's start with the face. It's totally twinned, and the facial controls are all at max. We can make this look better by adding some asymmetry, and dialing back some of the maxed out controls.

3 There we go! I added some asymmetry to the face in the brows, cheeks, and mouth, and Goon is already looking much better. I also made the pupils bigger and have the lids touching them so he looks more friendly and less wired.

HOT TIP

Always keep an eye on the renderCam. As animators we want our animation to work in 3D as much as possible, but when it comes down to it, the animation needs to look good through the main camera first and foremost. Working with the renderCam open somewhere is good workflow practice.

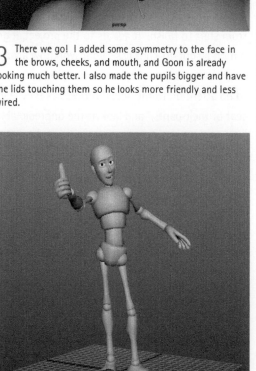

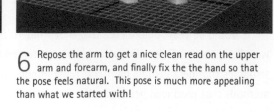

5 Surprise! Change your perspective panel to renderCam and see how we've lost the entire arm pose in foreshortening! This needs to be remedied.

6 Repose the arm to get a nice clean read on the upper arm and forearm, and finally fix the the hand so that the pose feels natural. This pose is much more appealing than what we started with!

33

What Is "Workflow"?

by Kenny Roy

IT WAS YEARS into my teaching career, with hundreds of classes and thousands of hours of animation critiques under my belt, before a student suddenly asked me, "You keep on saying the word 'workflow', but what does it mean?" I was stunned, because after all of my harping on the subject, it never occurred to me that the very concept of "workflow" itself might be unclear to beginner animators.

Simply put, a workflow is the *step-by-step* process you employ to create a shot from start to finish. It adapts to the project, it grows and changes slowly over time, but on a shot-to-shot basis your workflow always stays the same.

This may sound like a no-brainer, but the reality is most new animators pay little to no attention to the actual *process* as they learn. Instead, they animate "by the seat of their pants," and look at the unpredictable results on screen for indications of improvement. Let's take a related example in another area of art to illustrate this point.

Back in school, I had a figure-painting teacher who was very strict. His name was Yu Ji. In his class, students were subjected to a constant barrage of commands regarding how and when to do each step of a painting. First, you wipe the canvas with some highly thinned burnt umber or raw umber paint until the entire canvas is a nice, fleshy brown. Then do a quick sketch in pencil to define the form. Immediately go over that with a thin brush with umber paint, completely filling in all of the shadow areas. THEN, and ONLY THEN, do you start mixing paint to try to match the colors you see. And even when it came to finally painting with color, Yu Ji sounded like a broken record as he walked through the class to correct the color choices of his students. "Is the color warmer or cooler than the color next to it?" "Is it lighter or darker?" "What is the color tendency?" (Within warm colors, was it more red, or yellow, for example.) These same three questions were repeated at least a hundred times over the course of a three-hour class.

It would be years before I realized that what Yu Ji was doing was teaching us good workflow, above all else. Everything we were forced to do helped us avoid the major struggles that befall young painters. Most importantly, these were tried-and-true methods that produced better results. For instance, making the entire canvas brown made it so that we did not mix our colors too light just because they were competing with a blinding white canvas. Filling in shadow areas early on and foregoing minor details made the students focus on the large shapes in the form. Finally, his three questions made it so that we were mixing our colors based on the color *relationships* that we saw, barring preconceived notions from influencing our color choices. When I think back on it now, I cherish the amazing workflow that Yu Ji gifted his class, and I feel bad for thinking he was so strict!

Back to animation.

In animation, students typically start with a workflow that roughly resembles the order in which they learned the fundamentals. Pose the character with some rough timing and spacing, add some squash and stretch here, some anticipation and follow-through there. This is a messy way to work, and until you learn how to really let the fundamentals work in concert, your animation will lack the fluidity and beauty that the legends are capable of. There are just as many pitfalls awaiting novice animators as figure painters. In Yu Ji's class, we were forced to make our canvas brown so as not to wrongly exaggerate the colors; perhaps the first step in your workflow should be to not thumbnail some REALLY pushed poses and try to hit them with the model. You would be doing this because you know that as you move forward with the shot and get into polish, many of the pose choices will become watered down to accommodate timing, spacing, and compositional constraints. Yu Ji made us fill in all of the shadow areas with brown before adding any details. Sounds a bit like getting body movement looking really good before adding facial animation, doesn't it? And finally, those three questions we asked ourselves reminded us to constantly critique our choices within the painting, and with the live model. Before you move into your polishing phase, it would be a good idea to establish a workflow step in which you look at the animation one more time and ask yourself some questions. "Are my poses as dynamic as I originally planned?" "Is there still contrast in the animation in pose, timing, and composition?" "Does this resemble the reference and observation I've gathered?"

Your questions might be different, but the main point, both in figure painting and animation workflow, is that you *do it every time*. Instead of leaping at a shot with no plan in mind, just begin at step 1 of your workflow. Stop animating feverishly for huge lengths of time only to step back and realize the shot has not progressed at all.

If at any time in the middle of animating a shot you catch yourself asking the question "OK, now what's my next step?" you know you've crossed into the world of workflow. Welcome! You are on your way to becoming a great animator.

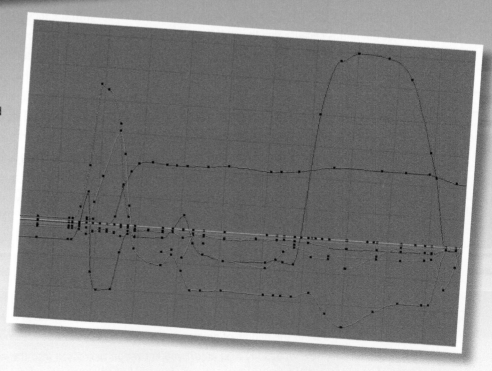

■ Splines can wrangle you, or you can wrangle them. Not into being wrangled? Keep reading! (And I just won a bet to use "wrangle" in a caption three times.)

2 *Splines*

SPLINE CURVES, or just "splines" (or even just "curves"), are the lifeblood of computer animation. They're a surprisingly efficient and comprehensive method of representing motion. Much of your time animating will be spent perusing these little red, blue, and green intertwined curves, so it makes sense to get comfortable with them. This chapter is all about facilitating your comfort.

Opening the Graph Editor to what looks like a spaghetti dinner gone bad can be intimidating, but we'll make understanding splines a quick study. We'll go through the simple concepts that make reading them easy and powerful. Then we'll try out some cheats on editing splines that will have you wrangling them under control in no time. Get ready to meet your new best friends in animation!

How Splines Work

UNDERSTANDING HOW SPLINES display their information is the key to making them work for you. Some beginner animators are intimidated when they see all those intertwined curves, but the concepts behind them are really quite straightforward. It takes a little practice to make it second nature, but only a few moments to really grasp the concepts we'll go over in this cheat. In no time, you will find that they are a surprisingly elegant way of working with your animation, and understanding them thoroughly will quickly create a noticeable improvement in your work. The main idea with splines is that they represent changes in value over time. As the curve travels to the right, frames are ticking by. As the curve rises and falls, it's an increase (travelling up) or decrease (travelling down) in the value of the attribute. If the curve changes direction, as it does at the middle key in the following diagram, the object it represents will change direction. The thing to remember, and where it's easy to get confused, is that up and down do not

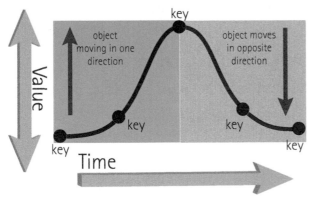

necessarily correspond to up and down for what you are seeing in the viewport. That may seem counterintuitive at first, but it has to do with how the character rig is set up and there are many possible scenarios with that. For some attributes, like translate Y, the curve will actually look like what the body part is doing, but most don't. The thing to take from this cheat is that up and down are simply changes in value, not a direct visual correlation to what you see in the viewport.

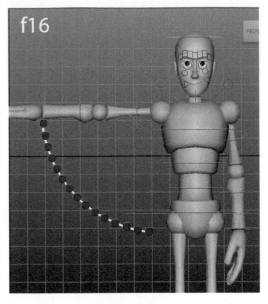

1 Open HowSplinesWork.ma. From f01–f16 the character is raising his arm. Take note of how even the movement is. Every frame, the arm moves the same amount.

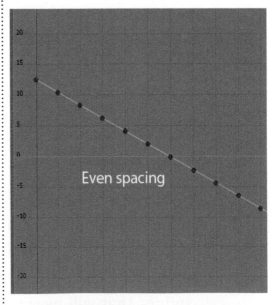

3 If I plot each frame along the curve, we see that they are all equidistant, just like the spacing tracked in the viewport. (Some curve colors in this chapter were changed in Photoshop for better clarity on the page.)

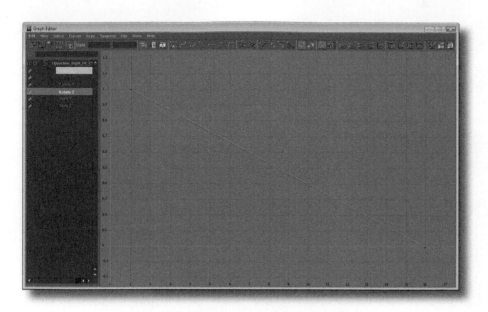

2 Open the Graph Editor and look at the upper arm's rotate Z curve. Notice that it's a perfectly straight line. This corresponds to the even spacing of the motion we see in the viewport.

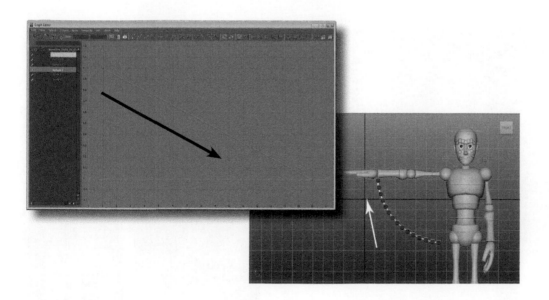

4 Also notice that the curve is travelling downward while his arm is rising. Remember that we said the up-down in curve direction is simply a change in value, not a direct representation of the viewport.

HowSplinesWork.
ma

HOT TIP

When you first start working with splines, one of the best things to do is have both a viewport and Graph Editor open. Instead of manipulating the character with the tools or channel box, move the keys in the Graph Editor and observe how it affects the character. Then do the opposite, moving the character in the viewport and observing the changes in the splines. This will help you learn how everything correlates.

39

How Splines Work (cont'd)

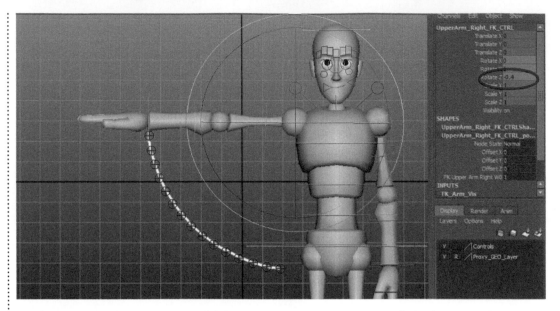

5 Select the upper arm control and rotate it in Z while watching the channel box value. Notice that rotating the arm up makes rotate Z increase in negative value. This has to do with how this particular character was rigged and is why the curve travels down, since down represents an increase in negative value in this case.

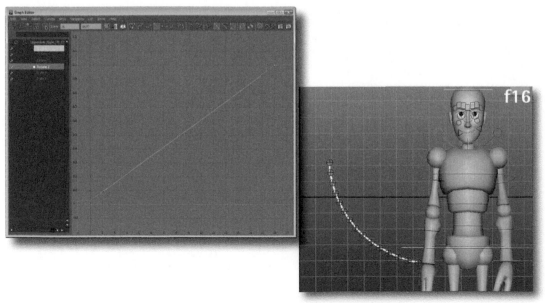

8 Continue making adjustments to the keys in the curve and watching the animation until you're comfortable with the concepts. Here I switched the positions of the keys and now he does the opposite motion.

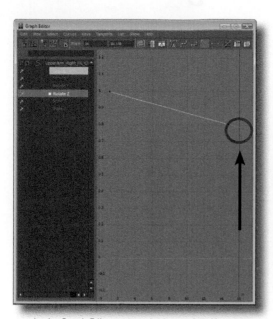

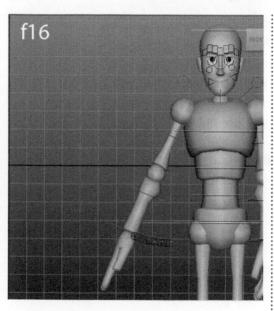

f16

6 In the Graph Editor, select the key at f16. Use the move tool **W** and *Shift* MM drag it up. Shift dragging with the move tool will constrain movement to either horizontal or vertical motion, whichever you do first.

7 Since the curve travels downward a much shorter distance, therefore increasing negative value only a little, his arm now moves up only a short distance. Tracking the motion shows us how much tighter the spacing is.

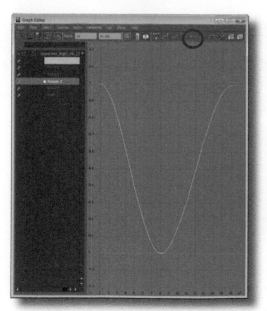

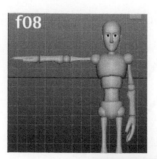

f08

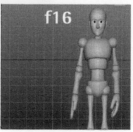

f16

9 Hold **I** and middle click the curve at f08 to insert a key. Select the entire curve and press the flat tangents button. Then use the move tool to MM drag f08's key down and f16's up to look like the graph above.

10 From f01-f08 the arm travels up. When the curve changes direction, the arm travels back down.

41

Splines and Spacing

L ET'S TAKE A MORE IN-DEPTH look at how changes in our spline curves affect the spacing of a motion. If the curve's direction over a given range of frames is mainly horizontal, the value is not changing much. Therefore the attribute will be moving very little in the viewport.

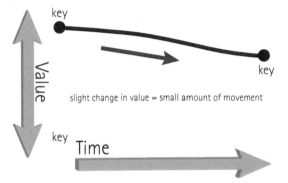

slight change in value = small amount of movement

If the direction over the frame range is predominantly vertical, a larger change in value is happening and the movement will be large.

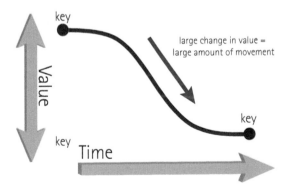

large change in value = large amount of movement

Finally, if the curve is perfectly horizontal for a frame range, that curve's attribute will hold perfectly still, as there is no change in value. We'll try some things in this cheat that will make these ideas perfectly clear.

Throughout this cheat, we'll make some pretty stark changes in the speed of the movement while never changing the number of frames it happens over (timing). Timing and spacing are intertwined, but problems in spacing tend to be less forgiving than the number of frames you're using.

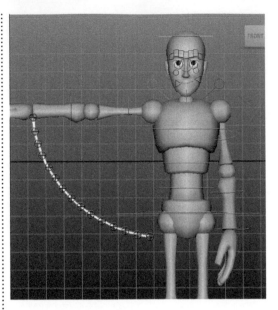

1 Open TimingSpacing.ma. We'll start with the upper arm moving up with linear, even spacing. Open the graph editor and select the R upper arm's rotate Z curve.

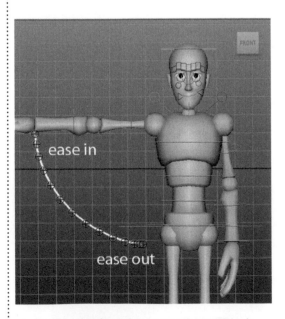

3 Play the animation and notice how the movement is much smoother. There is an ease out when the arm starts moving, and an ease in to where it stops.

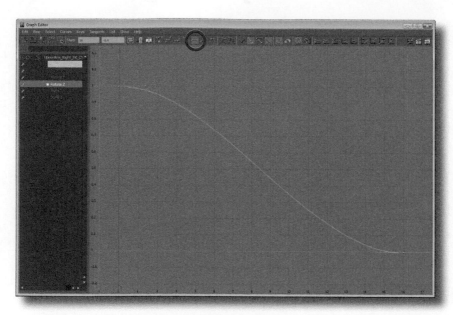

2 Select the entire curve and press the flat tangents button. The curve's shape will change from a straight line to a smooth "S" shape.

TimingSpacing.ma

HOT TIP

To track the spacing of a movement, many animators use dry erase markers right on their monitor. If your monitor is an LCD, put clear plastic over it to avoid staining the screen, and press very gently. CRT monitors should be fine as-is, since they have glass screens.

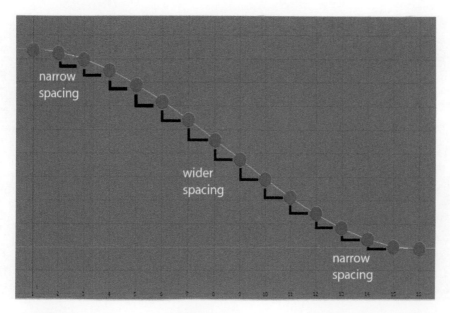

narrow spacing

wider spacing

narrow spacing

4 Plotting the spacing on the rotate Z curve shows how the curve's spacing corresponds to what we see in the viewport. The arm moves shorter distances in the beginning and end, and longer distances in the middle.

Splines and Spacing (cont'd)

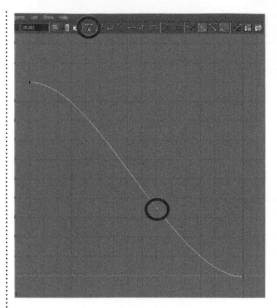

5 Go to frame 10 and set a key on the R upper arm. Select the key you just set in the Graph Editor and click the AutoTangent button if the curve is not smooth. This will keep that key's tangents smooth no matter where you move it.

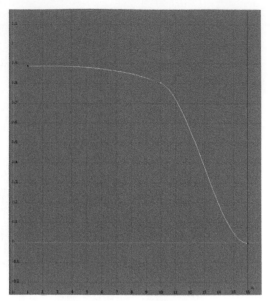

6 Use the move tool **W** and **Shift** MM drag the key up so it's a little under the value of the first key.

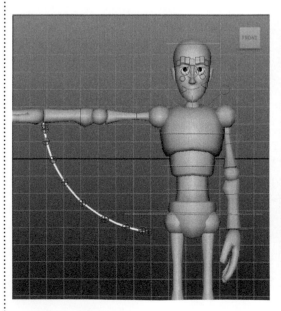

9 Now the opposite happens, with the arm moving quickly at the beginning, and easing into the end pose more gradually.

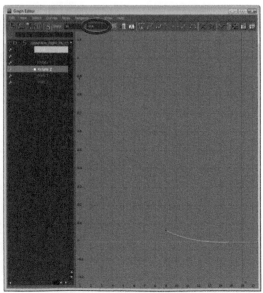

10 Select the last key at f16 and look at the value field. In my case it's -0.4.

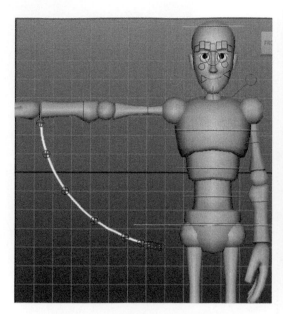

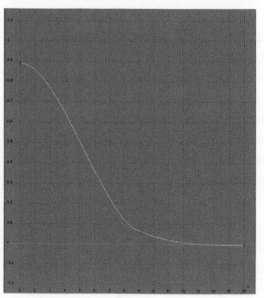

7 Play the animation and notice how much we've affected it. The arm moves very little during the first 10 frames since the spacing is so close. The value changes very little until f11, where the wide change makes it move quickly.

8 Edit the key at f10 so it's close to the value of the end key.

HOT TIP

We'll go over spline technique in later cheats, but it's good practice to avoid letting curves drift past the value of a key where it changes direction, like in step 11. Curves that do this are much more trouble to edit predictably.

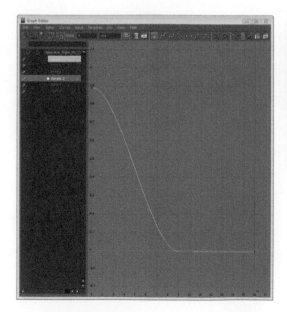

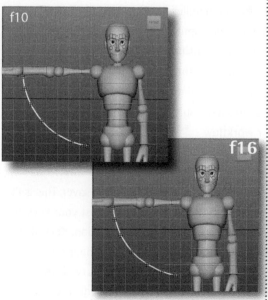

11 Select the key at f10 and enter the value of f16's key into the field to make it the same. Since we set this key to AutoTangent, it will automatically become flat. This will ensure that the curve holds at the same value through those frames.

12 Now the arm travels with an ease out and ease in from f01-f10, but holds still until f16. Since there is no change in the up or down of the curve while the frames tick by, the arm holds still.

Tangent Types

TANGENTS AND THE STYLES AVAILABLE in Maya are the other side of understanding splines. If you've used graphics programs like Illustrator, tangents will be familiar to you. They're the handles that exist around a keyframe and are used to adjust the curve's angle and direction before and after the key. As we've just seen in the previous cheats, the curve's slopes have a profound effect on the animation's spacing, so having a solid grasp on how tangents work is invaluable.

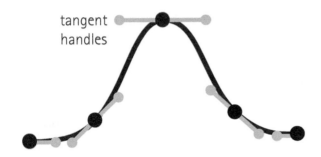

tangent handles

Maya has several different tangent types, which are really just preset angles for the handles (albeit useful ones). The handles are completely customizable, and Maya's tangent types are mostly a starting point. Using only the "out-of-the-box" tangent types tends to make the motion look very "CG" and uninteresting. However, knowing which ones will bring you most of the way to your desired result will go a long way towards speeding up your workflow.

Here we'll take a look at Maya's tangent types and what sort of situations they're best for. The icon with the "A" over it is the AutoTangent function, which is a great time saver. This isn't a tangent type per se, it's a setting that will adjust your keys' tangents automatically depending on their location. Keys at the extremes (wherever a change in curve direction happens) will be flat, while transitional keys (keys where the curve is the same direction on both sides) will be smooth. As you edit the keys, the tangents will automatically orient to whatever situation they're in. Awesome!

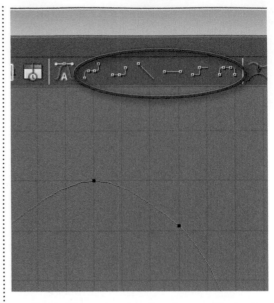

1 The tangent type icons are along the top of the Graph Editor. Simply select any or all keys and click whichever type you need. The first icon (with the "A") will enable the AutoTangent functionality for the selected keys and/or curves.

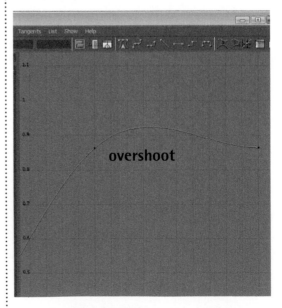

overshoot

4 Spline tangents make a smooth transition between keys and don't flatten out. They're great for keys that are transitional (going the same direction each side of the key), but with extremes (keys at which the curve changes direction) they can overshoot, which is difficult to control.

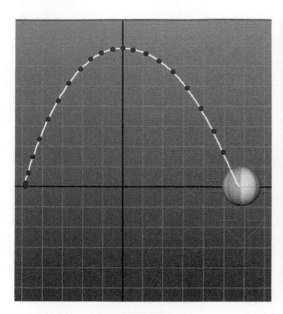

2 Open TangentTypes.ma. In the front view we have a very basic animation of a ball moving in an arc.

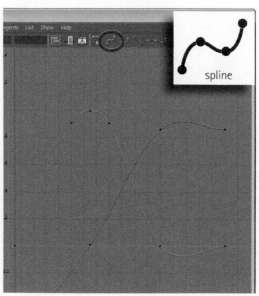

spline

3 Select the ball control (Show > Nurbs Curves in the viewport menu if you don't see it) and open the Graph Editor. Select all the curves and click the spline tangents button. Notice how the ends of the curves become straight.

TangentTypes.ma

HOT TIP

Once you're refining an animation, you usually won't use one tangent type for all keys, but rather the appropriate type for the particular key and situation you're working on.

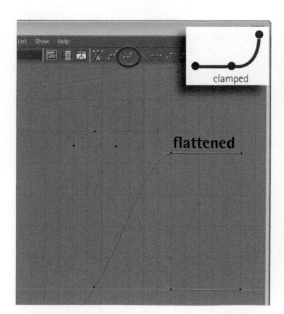

clamped

flattened

5 Select all the curves and press the clamped tangents button. Clamped are almost the same as spline tangents, except they will not overshoot on adjacent keys that are the same value or very close in value. Notice that the overshoots from before are now flat.

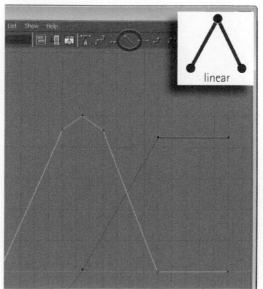

linear

6 Next press the linear tangents button. Linear tangents simply make a straight line from key to key and therefore make very sharp angles and transitions.

47

Tangent Types (cont'd)

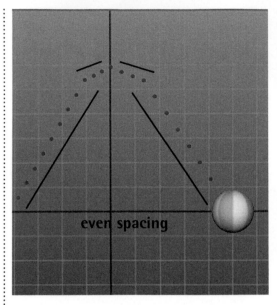

even spacing

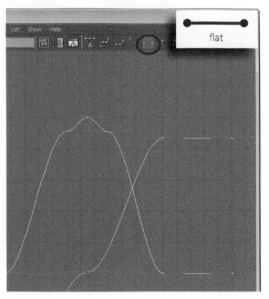

flat

7 Notice the spacing in the path of the ball is even between each key. Linear tangents are good for times when an object is traveling and then impacts another object at full momentum, such as when a ball hits the ground.

8 Next are flat tangents, which make a plateau at each key. They're common at the extreme keys, where a curve is changing direction, easing in and out of the key.
In transitional keys, they will make the object slow down in mid path.

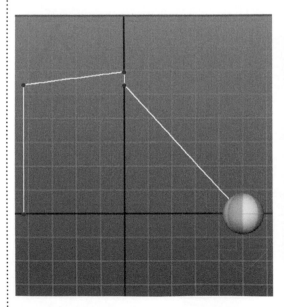

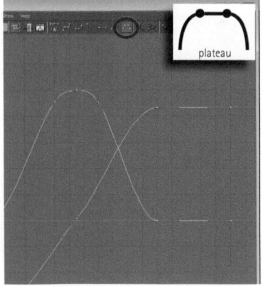

plateau

11 We see here that the ball pops to each position when it gets to that frame. Stepped keys are most commonly used for blocking in full animations, and for attributes that need to change over a single frame, like IK/FK switching or visibility.

12 Finally we have plateau tangents, which are almost identical to clamped in that they won't overshoot, and will flatten out extreme keys. The main difference is that they also flatten the start and end of the curve as well.

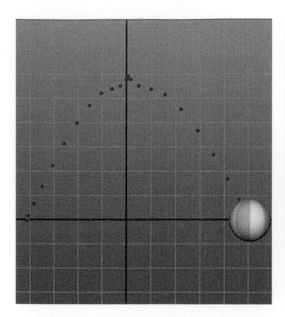

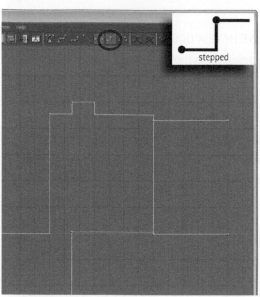

9 Notice the spacing on the ball easing out of and into each key. Flat tangents are a good starting point for keys you want ease outs and ins on. They will also hold flat through keys of the same value and never overshoot.

10 Next are stepped keys, which do not interpolate at all. They will hold still until the next key frame. Because of this they create these stair-like keys.

HOT TIP

Plateau, clamped, or auto tangents are the best all-around choice when you're moving out of stepped blocking into splined curves. They're a great starting point since you don't have to worry about cleaning up overshoots, and manually making transitional keys spline and extreme keys flat.

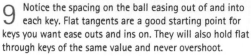

	spline	Smooth interpolation, good on transitional keys where curve is the same direction on both sides, tends to create overshoots in the curve
	clamped	Smooth interpolation, doesn't overshoot keys with close or identical values, first and last keys in curve are splined, good for moving to spline mode from stepped keys
	linear	Direct line from key to key, makes spacing between two keys perfectly even, sharp angles in curves, works well for keys where an object is meeting another at full momentum, some use for blocking to avoid any computer-created eases
	flat	Creates plateaus at keys that are perfectly flat, automatically puts an ease out and ease in on a key, never overshoots, good for keys at extremes (where the curve changes direction) and keys where a value needs to hold through frames
	stepped	No interpolation between keys, simply holds until the next key frame, commonly used for pose-to-pose blocking, and attributes that you want to switch over one frame such as constraints, IK/FK, creating camera cuts, etc.
	plateau	Same as clamped, except first and last keys in the curve are flat

13 To recap, here's a chart of some common uses for different tangent types. To reiterate, these are just starting points that may be helpful, and not rules by any means. AutoTangent isn't a tangent type, but rather an automation function. It basically sets keys to spline or flat tangents dynamically as you edit key frames, depending on the situation. Keys at extremes (where the curve changes direction) are made flat, while transitional keys (where the curve continues in the same direction) are smoothed to a spline tangent.

Tangent Handles

NOW THAT WE HAVE A GOOD UNDERSTANDING of Maya's tangent types, we can look at customizing the handles to create any type of curve we want. Maya's tangent handles offer the most flexibility of any animation/graphics program, so we should obviously take advantage of this power. Keep thinking about the spacing you want for your animation, then how a spline should look when it has that spacing, and use the handles to make it happen.

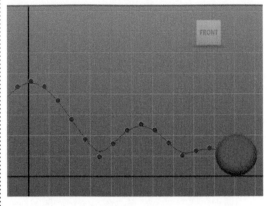

1 Open TangentHandles.ma and you'll find a simple bouncing ball animation. Select the ball control and open the Graph Editor.

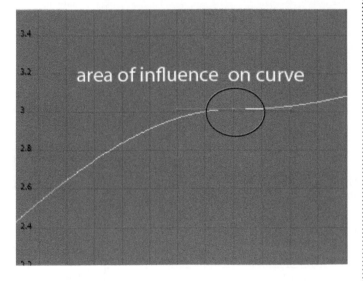

There are two types of tangent handles: weighted, and non-weighted. We'll go over them in this cheat, but they're really just styles of working and all up to preference in the end. Everything we talk about here is simply a way to get differing levels of control using the tangent handles. Note that I didn't say *more* control! Any curve shape you can get using handles you can also get by using more keyframes. At the end of the day, it's up to you and how you like working, so experiment with everything. My philosophy is it's best to get a handle (ahem) on all of the tools available, and then pick the best one for the job at hand.

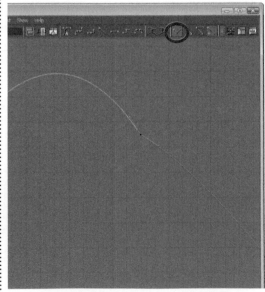

4 Select a handle and press the break tangents button. The left handle will turn blue, indicating it is now independent and you can drag select and then move the handles individually to get any curve shape you want.

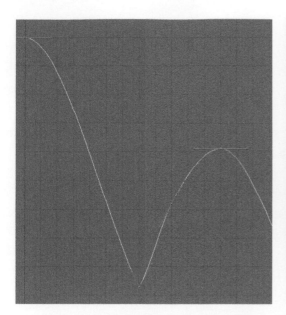

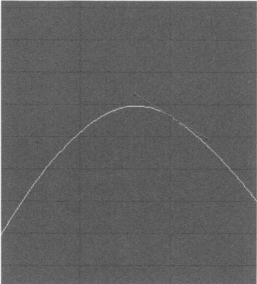

TangentHandles.ma

2 Select the translate Y curve and examine the tangent handles. They are currently non-weighted handles, which means they are all the same relative length and have the same amount of influence on a curve.

3 Select the move tool **W** and select any handle. MM drag it to rotate it. These handles are unified, which means they are attached and act as a single piece when moving either of them.

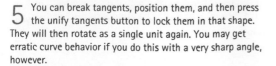

handles locked
in position

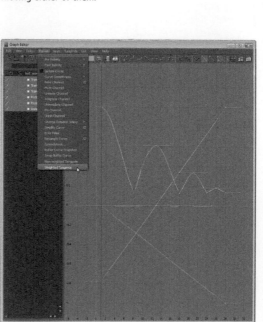

5 You can break tangents, position them, and then press the unify tangents button to lock them in that shape. They will then rotate as a single unit again. You may get erratic curve behavior if you do this with a very sharp angle, however.

6 Undo all your edits and select the entire translate Y curve. In the Graph Editor, go to Curves > Weighted Tangents and the handles will change.

51

Tangent Handles (cont'd)

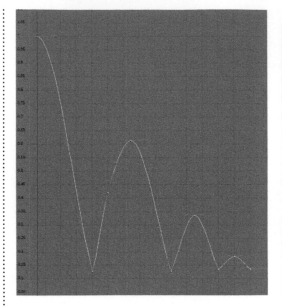

7 Weighted tangents have differing lengths which depend on the distance in terms of value between the keyframes. The longer the distance, the longer the handle, and the more influence it will have along the curve.

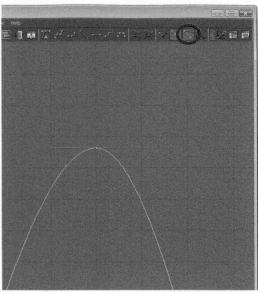

8 You can break and manipulate the handles just like you can with non-weighted tangents, but you have an additional option with weighted tangents. Select a key and click the free tangent weight button.

10 You can even break the tangent handles as we did before to create any shape of curve possible.

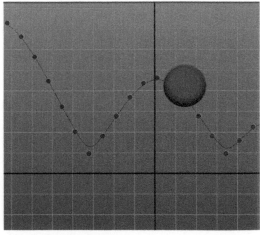

11 Continue to experiment with the tangent handles and learn how to use them to create the spacing you want.

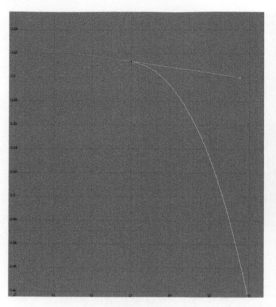 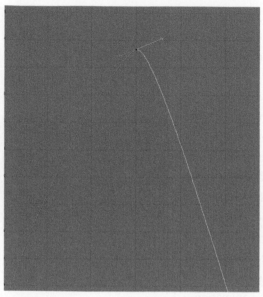

9 The ends will turn into open squares indicating free weights. You can now use the move tool and make the tangents any length you wish, increasing or decreasing the amount of influence they have on the curve.

Handles Pros
- Keeps curves less cluttered with fewer keys
- Powerful curve-shaping options
- Curves scale in time more accurately
- Good for subtle spacing adjustments without adding density
- Create sharp angles with fewer keys

Handles Cons
- Adjusting adjacent keys can affect spacing
- Some shapes not possible without keys
- Too few keys tends to feel floaty
- Can be more difficult for other animators to edit if necessary
- Less control over larger spacing areas

Keys Pros
- Exact; value isn't affected by adjacent keys
- Complete control, any shape possible
- Clearly readable in Graph Editor
- Simple to work with, not complex
- Easy to edit for other animators

Keys Cons
- Curves can get very dense and more difficult to make changes to
- Scaling time can be less accurate if you need to snap keys to frames
- More control usually translates into needing more keys

12 Remember that using handles is just another way to approach animating, not something you need to do or should never do (depending on who you talk to). Some animators never use tangents and only set keys, others use broken weighted handles all the time, but many use both methods when necessary. It's up to you in the end, but here are some factors to consider with the various methods. Ultimately, choosing the best approach for the task at hand will ensure that everything stays as simple as possible.

Spline Technique

YOU NOW HAVE a good grasp of the capabilities splines have and how you can approach using them, so let's go over some things that can tighten up your spline workflow. We're all about making things easier here, and there are a few tendencies splines have which can sabotage that. Having good spline technique means you have control, and that means you're making the animation look the way you want, not the way the computer happens to do it.

As I've said before, none of these things are really rules and there will be situations where actually doing them may be the best approach. But those are the exceptions and for general guidelines, especially if you're still becoming acclimated to splines, this cheat will go a long way towards helping you get ahead.

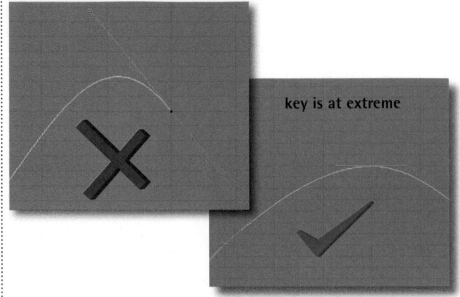

key is at extreme

1 Open SplineTechnique.ma and select the ball's move control. Look at the translate Y curve at f12. F13 is the extreme key, but the tangents are making f12 a higher value, also known as an overshoot. Use flat or linear tangents at extremes and adjust the eases to what you need.

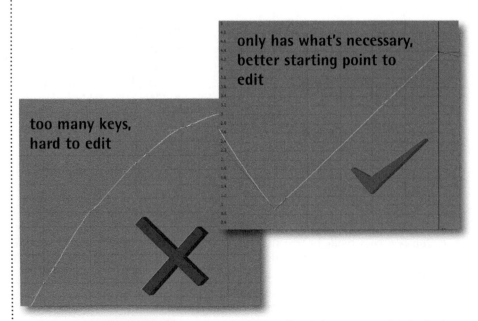

only has what's necessary, better starting point to edit

too many keys, hard to edit

3 Look at the translate X curve. Often when setting keys on all controls, we can get a lot of redundant keys. Splining can turn these curves into a wobbly mess. Only use the number of keys you need and make sure the tangents are the way you want them. Too many keys makes changes very difficult. Since this curve should be a smooth translation, we can delete almost all of these keys.

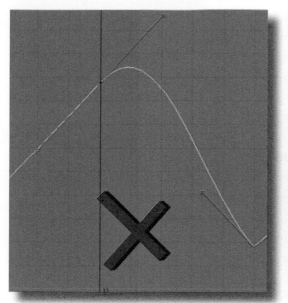

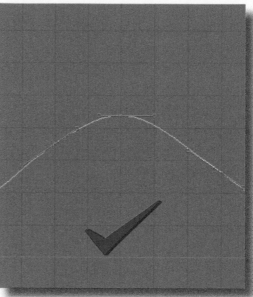

SplineTechnique.ma

HOT TIP

As awesome
as the new
AutoTangent
functionality
is, don't let it
make you lazy!
In the end it's
still spacing
and slow ins or
outs generated
by a computer
algorithm. It will
get your curves
closer to what
you want with
less work, but
you still need
to maintain
control of what
the computer
is doing. Finely
calibrated
curves are the
mark of a great
animator.

2 At f21, there's another type of overshoot, where the curve was shaped this way purposely with tangent handles. While this may look fine in the viewport, it's definitely not the best way. When the extremes have keys representing them, it makes things clear, easy to edit, and the values can't be changed without us knowing. With any kind of overshoot, moving an adjacent keyframe or handle can change where your extreme is. As much as we all love Maya, we don't want it making these kinds of decisions for us!

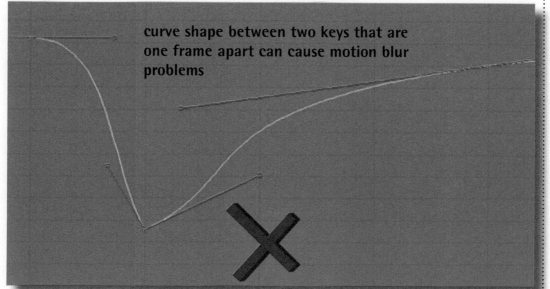

curve shape between two keys that are
one frame apart can cause motion blur
problems

4 Look at f24–f28 on the Rotate Z curve. Extreme angles are sometimes necessary, but if you need sharp angles, you're better off using keys rather than handles. Handles change when you shift keys around, but keys will always hold their value. It's good to avoid even one-frame glitches, like f27–f28, that aren't seen in the viewport. Some studios use motion blur in between the frames which will give strange results at render time with curves like this. This can actually be used to make motion blur look the way the animator wants, but unless this is intentional, don't do it!

Spline Reference

W E'VE SEEN THAT SPLINES are simple tools, yet capable of describing any movement with pinpoint accuracy. It takes some practice to make looking at them second nature, and as you keep animating, you'll get better at reading them. One thing many beginning animators don't realize at first is that reading splines is just recognizing common shapes. An ease in will always look pretty much the same as far as the general spline shape goes. The size and angle of the shape will simply determine how big (or small) of an ease in it is. You know when a circle is a circle regardless of how large or small it is. It's really the same idea.

The file for this cheat, SplineReference.ma, contains six spline shape examples that you can use as a reference for common animation spacings. Every 50 frames has a separate animation and description. Move the time range slider to start at frames 1, 50, 100, 150, 200, and 250 to see each one. The upper arm's Rotate Z curve has the animation. Memorizing these shapes will make looking at the Graph Editor an enlightening experience, rather than a puzzling one. Happy wrangling!

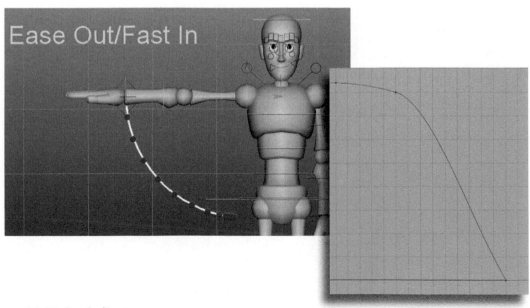

2 f50-f99: Ease Out/Fast In

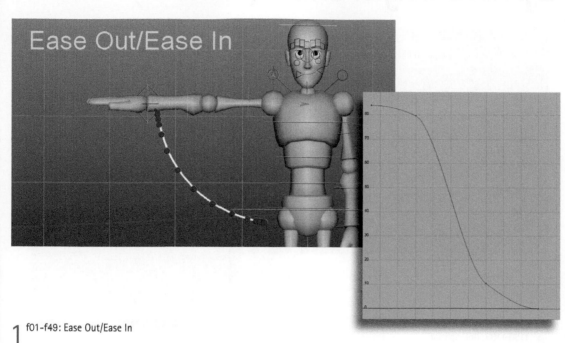

1 f01-f49: Ease Out/Ease In

SplineReference.ma

HOT TIP

Adding an extra
key to shape
your ease outs
and ease ins will
really help make
them better.
Maya's default
eases are always
the same ratio
and tend to
feel a bit flat
timing-wise.

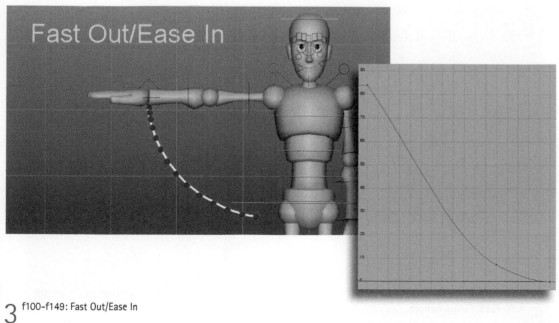

3 f100-f149: Fast Out/Ease In

Spline Reference (cont'd)

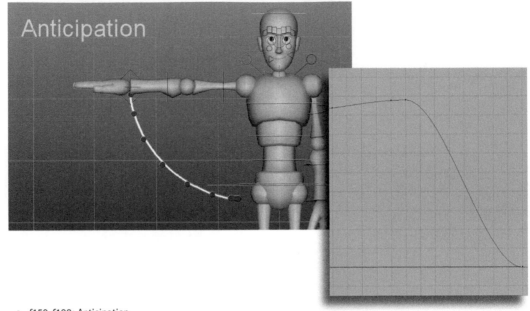

4 f150-f199: Anticipation

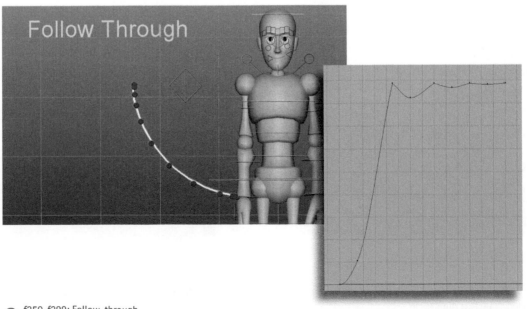

6 f250-f299: Follow-through

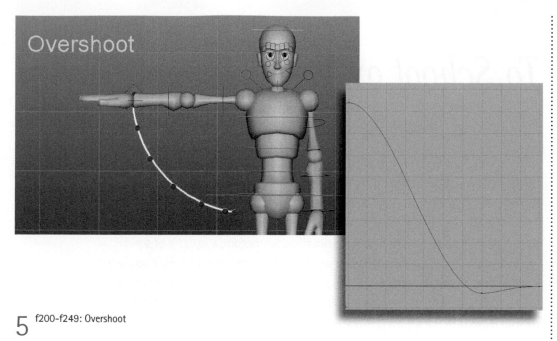

5 f200–f249: Overshoot

HOT TIP

Linear tangents are a great starting point for any key where an object is hitting another and ricocheting off of it, such as when a bouncing ball hits the ground.

To School or Not to School?

Can You Teach Yourself Animation At Home?
by Kenny Roy

THESE DAYS, THE NUMBER of animation programs out there has young artists' heads spinning. Traditional colleges have added animation curriculums by the dozens, film schools have followed in lock-step, and it seemed the minute online animation training was en vogue, as a result of trailblazers AnimationMentor.com, a handful of similar programs sprouted around the globe. Is animation a skill that you can teach yourself and still be competitive in this burgeoning industry? I think so! But there are many common pitfalls and blunders that the self-taught animator must try to avoid if they want to make it to the big leagues one day.

Let's say you want to go it alone. I am entirely self-taught, just by the way. If you think this could work for you, congratulations, but let's start off with some tips that should hopefully keep you on your feet. First off, there really is no such thing as "entirely self-taught." Okay, so I lied. You got me. What I mean is, animation is a medium that is made for consumption. If you are only animating in a vacuum, you'll never learn how to engage an audience. Viewers of your work will be left with a totally cold feeling; animation made just for oneself is a really lonely thing to behold. So if you are teaching yourself animation at the very least you need constant feedback from your peers or another audience.

Where do you go for the best feedback? Wherever there is a big audience willing to help. For me, it was posting at least five times a day on my favorite forums. Over three years, I had 5000+ posts. This kind of immersion in the craft does wonders for the speed of your learning. What happens is, the more you teach, the faster you master the concepts yourself. So giving feedback on forums is actually a very selfish thing to do! So, find a forum (for animation, the ones at www.11secondclub.com are fantastic, and for general CG, forums.cgsociety.org has an immense user base. See "Giving Feedback" on page 244 for more suggestions.) Once you have registered, put together a post with an introduction to your work. Put a couple of different pieces in there and ask for feedback on all of it. You may not actually be looking for feedback on anything you posted but you can see who comments right away on a newbie's animation. These people are going to become your best friends. Actually I've met three or four people who I knew only "digitally" when I was a member of the forums. They've all turned out to be great animators and great people. Take a second when you meet a few people on the forums to look at their old posts – maybe there's some animation that they posted for feedback, and you can oblige them. Basically, get to know your audience, and start right away looking critically at animation for the purpose of training your animation eye.

Once feedback is squared away, are you ready to really work hard to learn? Are you disciplined enough to 'chew the fat' of the early animation tests like a bouncing ball, a flour sack, a pendulum, a ball with a tail? Or are you a gung-ho animation daredevil that wants to start your education with a four-character, multi-shot dialogue sequence? SLOW DOWN! One of the biggest traps that snares beginner animators is the temptation to try to produce feature-quality animation from the get-go. This will have disastrous results. The most discouraging experience you can put yourself through is starting and stopping scene after scene, when you decide that the animation is not turning out good enough. For some reason, students of animation have a false sense of how much time and effort it takes to produce quality animation, even after they've been at it for years! To give you some perspective, it was about five years into my personal training before I was producing animation that I thought was at least worth showing to a company on a demo reel (VHS at the time!). And it was about three years after THAT I got my first feature animation job. So keep things in perspective, and don't try to create Pixar-quality work when you are just starting out. Would you be disappointed if you didn't hit a home run your first time playing baseball? Would you be disappointed if you didn't win an Oscar with your first film? Then don't base your assessment of your current skill on the ULTIMATE goal!

Create some SHORT-TERM goals that you know you can achieve. You will feel the enjoyment of creating something start to finish and a sense of accomplishment that you hit a goal. Even though you know the goal is short term and was set at an easily achievable level, you'll still feel a lot better about your progress than attempting and failing at a really difficult shot. After enough of these little shots, you may be ready to move on to something more complex. But don't go too fast! I whole-heartedly support the idea of doing many bouncing-ball and flour-sack-type character shots before even attempting a shot with a biped or other complex character. There is an extra benefit to doing these tests with simple characters; you will become very well versed in using simple shapes to convey intent and meaning. When you finally are ready for bipeds and complex characters, the amount of practice you have creating performances from simple, inanimate objects will mean your humans and animals will ALWAYS look alive and meaningful. Their body language will be stronger because you had to create a complex idea using very simple shapes; now that you have limbs to work with, everything just got easier. The motion will also be more unified and appealing; again, practicing with simple shapes means that you are looking at the overall composition and body positions of your bipeds and creating stellar staging.

You will of course need learning materials. Books like this one (ahem) are great, and there are many free and paid resources online that offer tutorials and walkthroughs; like www.kennyroy.com (double ahem). But whatever resources you use to learn the techniques of animation, you'll need a constant flow of ideas for shots to animate. That's why I highly endorse the "Mini-Challenges" that go on over at www.11secondclub.com's forums, as well as the "Animation Sessions" on forums. cgsociety.org. The advantage of participating in these is two-fold: first, the constant practice will make you improve very quickly. Second, the fact that you are taking an outside idea and animating it replicates a production environment very closely. As animators, we rarely get to work on something that is 100 percent our own creation, so these challenges will give you valuable practice as a real animator.

The great thing about animation is that many of the skills required to be a great animator are free and easy to practice. Observing humans in public places is free and easy. Watching animated films and framing through the awesome shots is about as fun as it gets. Practicing acting out shots in front of a mirror is not only a great way to spend a Saturday afternoon, but it will improve your performance choices in your shots immensely. So before you think of any excuses, know that as a dedicated student of animation, you can always be busy learning what you need to rise to the top. Now, if you are indeed looking for a school, there are a few criteria that I think you should take into account.

Many city colleges and small trade schools add "CG" or "Computer animation" to their class lists, and then hire an animator or generalist to come in and teach the course. I've seen the job postings for these positions increase more and more each year. The problem is that, in all but a few cases, this person is a professional animator or 3D artist with little or no teaching experience. In nearly all cases, there is also no set curriculum and nobody is thinking or planning on how to make sure students are learning a logical and applicable progression of skills in these courses. In effect, these schools are just trying to offer a course they know will be popular. They are taking advantage of a trend. On the other hand, these courses can be EXTREMELY good value if the instructor is talented and thoughtful. Since city colleges and small trade schools are generally cheaper, getting training in animation from a professional who does have a course path in mind can be the best bang for your buck. Just be very careful choosing a course at a school like this. Look for schools that have had the course for a long time, and see if you can see how long the instructor has been teaching the course.

Large universities have their advantages and disadvantages as well. The main advantage is you know there is a curriculum and a path to graduation that has been pored over by the faculty. The main disadvantage (for some) is that you may be required to take general education credits and be paying high tuition while doing so. It's a trade-off. Most accomplished animators are well educated and certainly well rounded. On the other hand, I've also met many animators, myself included, who only have a high school diploma. One of the other main factors for you might be financial. If animation is offered at a university and they have academic or athletic scholarships, you might actually have a better financial option in a four-year university. I was offered a full scholarship to a few schools on academic merit and this was the path I took. (I didn't graduate, I was recruited in my sophomore year).

The last category is online schools. No doubt you have heard (or perhaps are attending!) schools like AnimationMentor, AnimSchool, etc. Some of the most important criteria to consider are cost, job placements, availability for immediate help or feedback, size of classes, and the size of the student body. The teachers should all be working professionals and have good standing within the industry. Most of all, the school should offer more than a cold, online experience. Look for a school that seems like it still embodies the camaraderie and community feeling of a brick-and-mortar college.

In order to teach yourself animation, you have to be extremely self-motivated and passionate about the art. And in order to learn animation at a trade school or university, you need to be extremely self-motivated and passionate about the art! Really, it comes down to disciplining yourself to follow a steady and practical curriculum at home, or leaving the course design to a faculty. Either way, you are in for a very challenging road ahead. But it is a fulfilling road too; one that offers many rewards to the diligent and dedicated animation student.

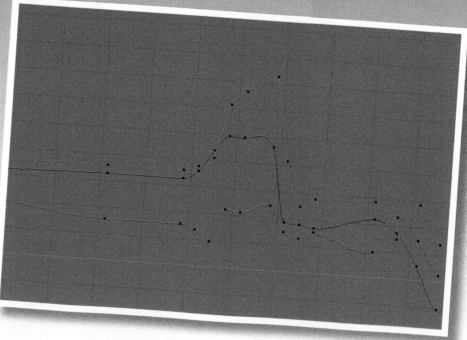

■ As your katana for cutting through a jungle of spline curves, the Graph Editor offers much in power, simplicity, and efficiency.

3

Graph Editor

MAYA'S GRAPH EDITOR is easily its most powerful
and most used tool for animating. It's likely that you
will spend much of your time working with it, so it's
a no-brainer that we learn all the ins and outs of this
fantastic editor. Maya 2013 introduces several new
features to the Graph Editor that make it even more
powerful and easy to use.

We spent the last chapter understanding splines, and now
we'll learn how to use the Graph Editor to interact with,
edit, and manipulate them.

Graph Editor Windup

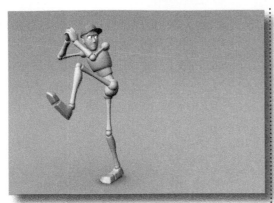

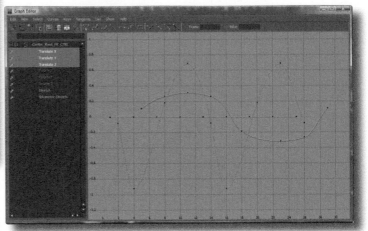

B EFORE WE LAUNCH INTO all the cool stuff
the Graph Editor has in store for you,
let's go over the basics of using it! One of the
best features about Maya 2013 is the unified
Graph Editor. This means that the curve editors
in other Autodesk products like 3DS Max and
MotionBuilder are exactly the same as what's
here in Maya. We'll be using this unified editor
throughout this chapter, as it's simpler and more
streamlined, but you can always go back to the
old editor by choosing View > Classic Toolbar.

1 Selecting a control initially displays all curves. Selecting attributes in the
left panel displays only those curves. You can drag select or **Shift** select for
sequential attributes, or **ctrl** select for multiple, non-sequential ones.

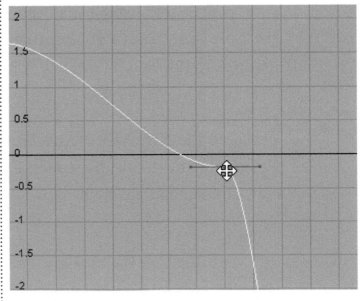

3 The move **W** and scale **R** tools work in the Graph Editor. Once selected, the
middle mouse button will drag or edit the curves or keys selected.

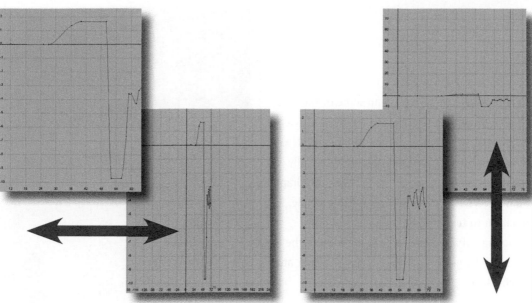

2 *Shift* *alt* and right mouse dragging horizontally expands or contracts the frame range of the graph in view, while
dragging vertically contracts or expands the value range.

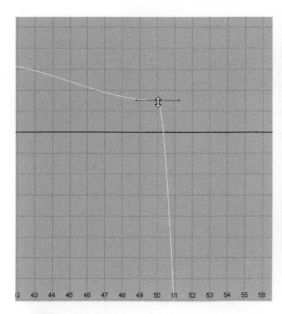

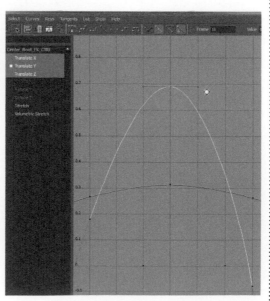

4 *Shift* middle mouse dragging will constrain the
movement horizontally or vertically, depending on which
way you initially move the mouse.

5 If you get a circle when trying to edit, it just means you
have the select tool **Q** active and need to select an edit
tool, such as the move or scale tool, to do an edit.

Visual Tools

THE GRAPH EDITOR IS FULL of goodies, and some of the most important ones let you view the curves in the most efficient way for what you're doing. Whether you need to type exact values, search for keys that may be amiss, compare drastically different curves, or want to isolate specific attributes, the Graph Editor can accommodate you. In this cheat we'll use a simple bouncing ball animation to test out the options the Graph Editor gives us for ogling curves. Make sure you are using the streamlined Graph Editor by going to View > Classic Toolbar and making sure it's unchecked.

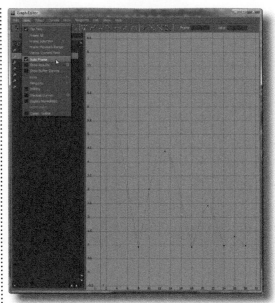

1 Open visualTools.ma, switch to the front camera, and open the Graph Editor. Select the ball's move control and its curves appear. Clicking on the attributes in the left panel isolates them, but some of the curves are difficult to see. Enabling View > Auto Frame will automatically focus on any attribute(s) you select.

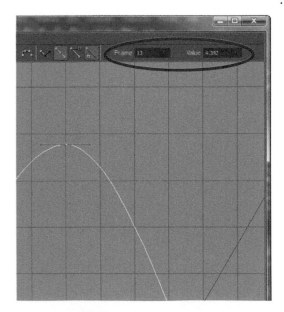

4 The stats fields show the frame and value of the selected key (or the frame length of a selected curve), which is useful for typing in precise frame numbers or values. You can also use `ctrl`+`C` to copy and `ctrl`+`V` to paste values of one key to the fields for another key or curve.

5 If you need to do precise entering of values for multiple keys, you can select curves and choose Curves > Spreadsheet. This gives you values for every key on the curve. You can use copy and paste here, and even change tangent types.

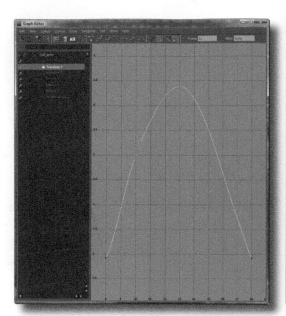

2 Select a few keys and press **F** to focus on them.

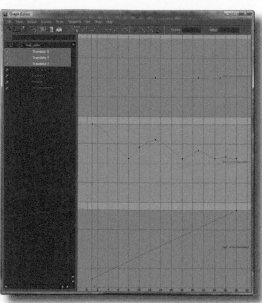

3 Maya 2013 comes with a way to visualize multiple curves. Select multiple channels and go to View > Stacked Curves. Now all of your channels are displayed in their own stacked panes.

visualTools.ma

HOT TIP

In addition to using the Graph Editor, you can also mute and unmute channels in the channel box by right clicking the attribute and selecting Mute/Unmute Channel.

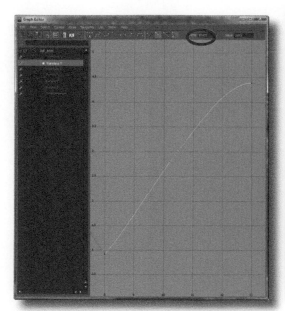

6 On the translate Y curve, select the key at f10. You'll see in the stat field that the current frame is 10.472. In the course of scaling keys or editing them, we can end up with keys that are between frames.

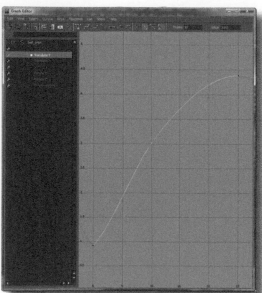

7 Select the Translate Y attribute and go to Edit > Select Unsnapped. All the keys that are not on exact frames will be selected. You can select multiple or all attributes as well. Go to Edit > Snap and the selected keys will be moved onto the nearest frame.

Visual Tools (cont'd)

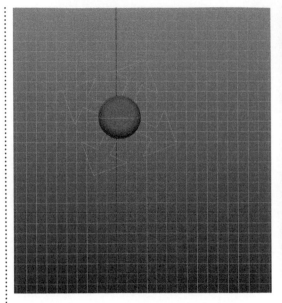

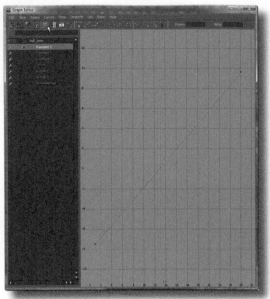

8 The ball is travelling in X as it bounces, but sometimes it's helpful to watch an animation without one of the attributes playing. Select the Translate X channel in the Graph Editor and go to Curves > Mute Channel.

9 You may have to pan the camera to see it, but now the ball no longer moves in X and simply bounces in place. In the Graph Editor, mute channels have an X next to them. Muting will use the current value as the hold point.

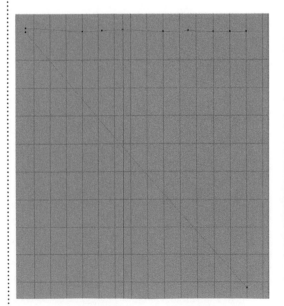

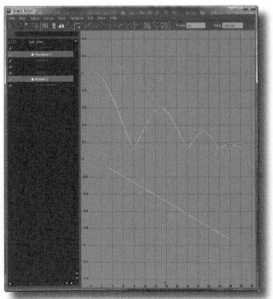

12 Select the Translate Y and Rotate Z channels. Sometimes you'll want to edit curves while comparing them to others, but it's difficult because they are in completely different value ranges. Here, we can't see any of the shapes in the Translate Y curve.

13 Select the curves and go View > Display Normalized. Now they are both displayed within a -1 to 1 range and easily comparable and editable. To go back to normal, uncheck View > Display Normalized.

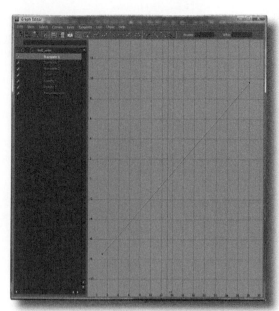

10 To unmute, select the channel, and go to Curves > Unmute Channel. Everything will go back to normal.

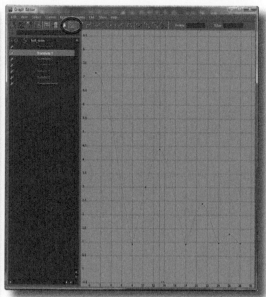

11 To quickly isolate the curves of particular attributes, select them in the Channel Box and press the Isolate Curve Display button in the Graph Editor. This is great for quickly showing certain attributes when you have multiple controls selected.

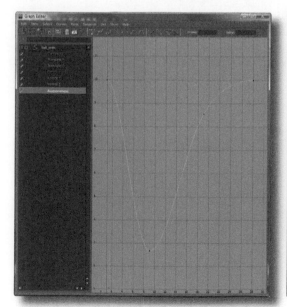

14 Extra attributes beyond the standard Rotate, Translate, etc. are colored gray, but you can change that so they stand out better. On the ball is an attribute called "awesomeness", which doesn't do anything and is just for example's sake. Select the awesomeness curve!

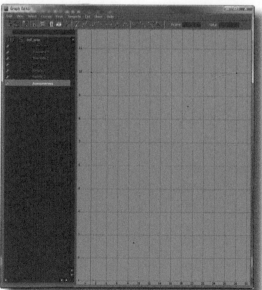

15 Edit > Change Curve Color lets you pick any color you like for the curve. Now it will stand out when looking at multiple curves simultaneously. To remove it, just select and choose Edit > Remove Curve Color.

HOT TIP

Go to the Select menu and enable Pre-Select Highlight and Maya will light up selectable objects when you hover over them. Very handy when selecting keys amongst overlapping curves!

71

Working with Keys

I N ADDITION TO its visual advantages, the Graph Editor offers some methods of working with keys that you can't get in the timeline or Dope Sheet. There are often times when we know the general shape of the curve we want to create, but setting keys and then dragging them to create that shape is time consuming. The Add Keys tool allows us to simply click keys where we need them and very quickly create a curve that can be tweaked for the results we want.

There will also be times where you want to add a key into a curve. Simply setting a key works, but the key is created with whatever Maya's default tangent is set to, which can alter the curve more than you want. Setting a key and editing the tangent is a lot of unnecessary work so Maya offers the Insert Key tool, which can be called upon instantly at any time.

Maya 2013 offers a new Retime Tool, an even simpler and more powerful way to retime animation, over the Lattice Deform Keys and Region Tools. By double clicking on a spot in the Graph Editor, you create a retime handle that can be moved back and forth in time, scaling the keys as you do so. This is an incredibly intuitive way to retime animation because the handles basically define "beats" of your scene. The Lattice Deform Keys and Region tools are still present, but the new Retime tool has far more potential to become a part of your regular workflow, so we'll show you how to use it here.

We'll be using the new streamlined Graph Editor which you can enable by going to View > Classic Toolbar and making sure it's unchecked.

1 Open workingWithKeys.ma for the start of a bouncing ball animation. Currently we have it translating in X, but no up and down. Select the Add Keys tool in the Graph Editor, then select the Translate Y attribute and select the first key.

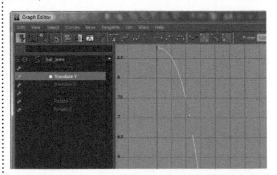

4 Without messing up our Translate Y curve, we need some extra keys at the peaks for a little extra hang time. Select the curve and hold down the **I** key. The pointer will become a crosshair indicating the Insert Keys tool is active.

7 New to Maya 2013 is the Retime Tool. This powerful tool allows you to scale the timing of keys in multiple user-defined regions. Select the Retime Tool and double click anywhere in the Graph Editor to create retime handles.

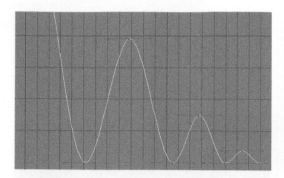

2 Middle click in the graph to add keys. In about 10 seconds I have the general shape of the curve and am ready to refine it.

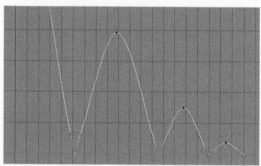

3 Converting the bottom keys to linear tangents gets us most of the way to a bouncing ball.

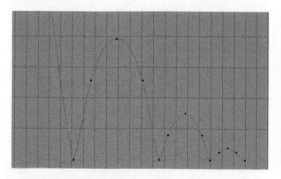

5 Middle clicking on the curve inserts a key without messing up the shape.

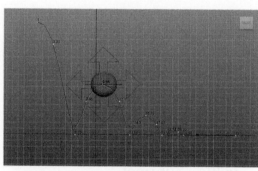

6 A few more tweaks and we have all the translation for a bouncing ball in about a minute.

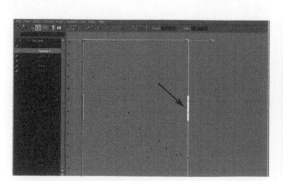

8 Now grab a retime handle and move it back and forth. Notice how the keys scale in time? You can add as many handles as you like, whenever you like!

9 To remove a handle, hit the circular "X" at the bottom. It disappears, but your retimed keys stay put. Very nice.

workingWithKeys. ma

HOT TIP

Maya has a type of keyframe called Breakdown Keys, but they're not breakdowns as animators traditionally understand them. They're simply keys that maintain an exact ratio between the previous and following key. This can put them between frames if the other keys get moved. Generally speaking, most animators just use Maya's regular keyframes for everything.

Value Operators

THERE ARE OFTEN TIMES when we need to make specific changes in value to many keys at once. For instance, we might want to see what a walk looks like if we increase the spine's Rotate X by 20 percent. Or we need to quickly scale down a curve's frame range to 33 percent of its current value. Though you wouldn't know it by looking at them, Maya's stat fields can do calculations that you can use to quickly make precise mass edits on multiple keys. By using a set of value operators, we can get results fast, without clicking on and manipulating tools. Sounds like a great addition to the cheating portfolio, eh?

The value operators are as follows:

+=value   Add

-=value   Subtract

*=value   Multiply

/=value   Divide

So if we wanted to add 5 units in value to the selected keys, in the stat Value field we would type +=5 and hit *Enter*. To increase them by 20% percent type *=1.2 and so on. This cheat will walk you through using value operators in several different situations.

We'll be using the new streamlined Graph Editor, which you can enable by going to View > Classic Toolbar and making sure it's unchecked.

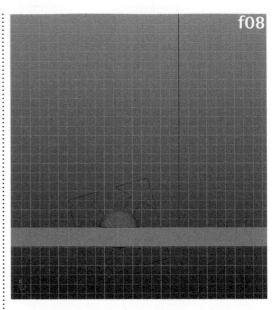

f08

1 Open valueOperators.ma for our familiar bouncing ball animation. There's a ground, but the ball is bouncing too low, about 1 unit or so, and intersecting it.

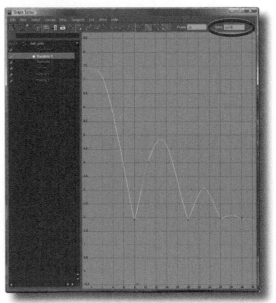

4 Let's bring the peaks of the Translate Y down 10%. Select the keys when the ball is in the air, and type *=.9 to reduce the Value by 10%.

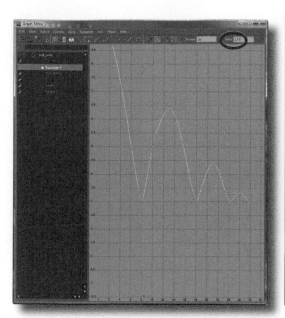

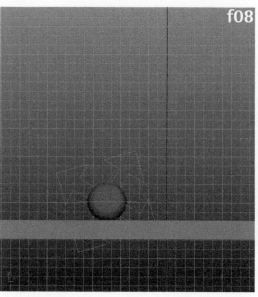

f08

valueOperatros.ma

2 Select the Translate Y curve in the Graph Editor, and in the Value field type +=1 and hit *Enter*. This adds 1 to every key selected.

3 Now every key is 1 unit higher and the ball lines up with the ground.

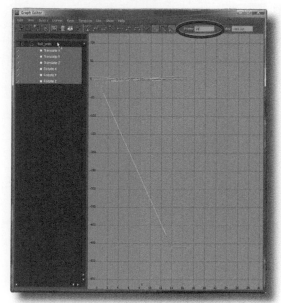

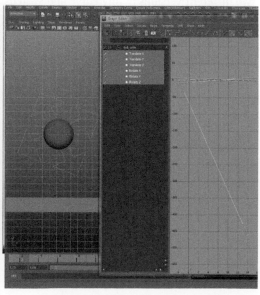

5 We can scale the time for keys as well. Select all the curves for the ball and in the Frame stat field enter /=2 to divide by 2 and cut the frame numbers the keys happen on in half. The animation plays twice as fast now.

6 You can also use -=value to subtract. Remember that all the operators work for both the Frame and Value stat fields.

75

Buffer Curves

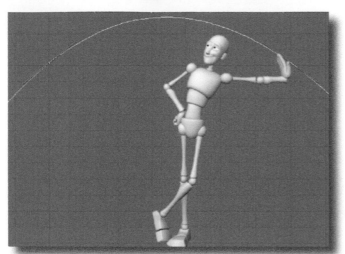

ANIMATION IS RARELY a linear process, and oftentimes we need to compare different ideas to see what works best. Looking at variations saved in different files is a hassle and inefficient, so Maya offers buffer curves in its Graph Editor functionality. We can have two different versions of any curve and switch back and forth between them instantly. For times when we're not sure if we like a certain movement over another, this allows us to experiment without having to redo or lose work.

Buffer curves are best for trying out variations on one or a few attributes. While it's possible to use them on a whole character, there's not a definitive interface for working with them. Switching between many attributes can make it easy to lose track of what you're looking at. Animation Layers are a much better approach for working with variations on a bigger scale, and they're covered in Chapter 12. But when it comes to comparing an attribute or two, buffer curves have a nice efficiency.

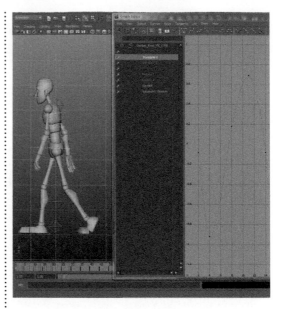

1 Open bufferCurves.ma, which has Goon doing the walk from chapter 9. Select the body control's Translate Y curve.

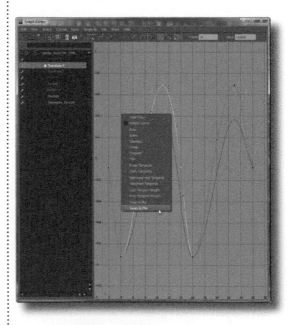

4 Hold the right mouse button and in the pop-up menu choose Swap Buffer to make the buffer curve active. The version you were working on goes into the buffer and you can edit the previous version.

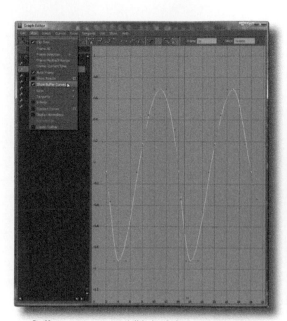

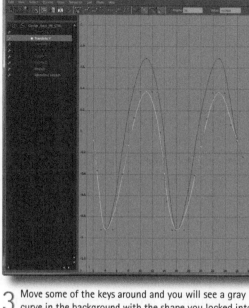

bufferCurves.ma

2 Buffer curves are not visible by default, so go to View > Show Buffer Curves. You won't see anything change yet, as both versions of the curve are currently the same.

3 Move some of the keys around and you will see a gray curve in the background with the shape you locked into the buffer. Now you can edit the curve as normal, keeping the buffer version intact and referencing it if necessary.

HOT TIP

If you want to make a curve visible but uneditable or unselectable (for instance, if you're referencing it to another curve and keep selecting it accidentally), select the channel and go to Curves > Template Channel. To unlock it, choose Untemplate Channel.

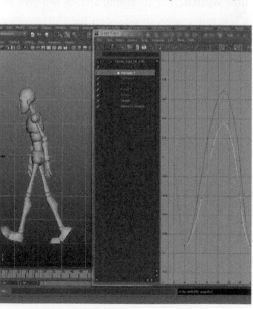

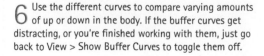

5 In the right click menu, choosing Snap Buffer will snap the buffer to the current version of the curve. This is good for quickly saving the current state of the curve, and then moving on to further experimentation.

6 Use the different curves to compare varying amounts of up or down in the body. If the buffer curves get distracting, or you're finished working with them, just go back to View > Show Buffer Curves to toggle them off.

Speed Cheats

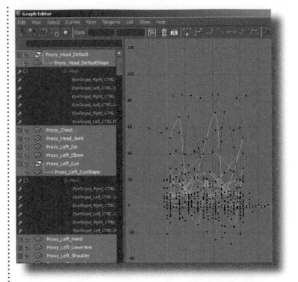

YOU WILL NOTICE as you progress in animation that you are doing a lot of the same operations in the Graph Editor. Maya 2013's Graph Editor adds some great tools that allow you to remove some of the unnecessary tasks and clutter as you work. Specifically, we're going to take a look at setting bookmarks for our commonly used curves, and isolating specific attributes (very common when doing cycles).

It will become increasingly important as you move on in your animation training to develop ways to quickly access the controller or information you need. Professionals know that time spent hunting around a scene or a UI is time wasted. The following cheats will give you a few quick ways to side-step the clutter when your scene starts getting complex.

1 Open SpeedCheats.ma. In the Persp panel, drag a selection over the entire Goon rig and open the graph editor. It should look like this – spaghetti anyone?

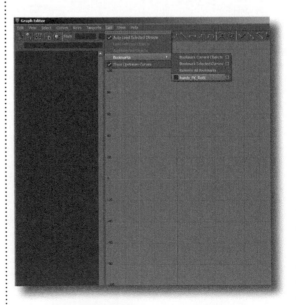

4 Now deselect everything in the panel and notice how the Graph Editor also clears out. Click on List > Bookmarks and find the "hands_FK_RotX" bookmark we just created and click on it.

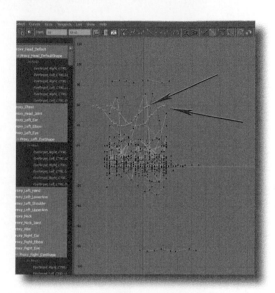

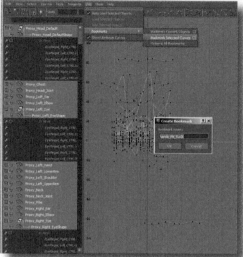

SpeedCheats.ma

2 We're going to pretend that we want to work on the hand_IK Rotate X curves over and over. Select them carefully by clicking on the first and *Shift* click the second one, as shown.

3 That's a pain! We don't want to have to do that again. Click on List > Bookmarks > Bookmark Selected Curves □. Call the bookmark "hands_FK_RotX" and hit *Enter*.

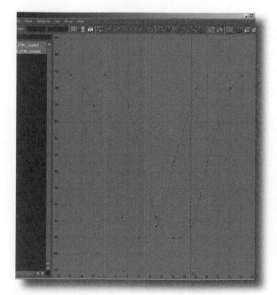

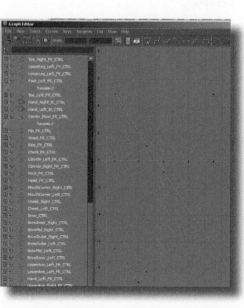

5 Now just the two curves we want to see are loaded in the Graph Editor. We can use this bookmark any time. But what if we want to just look at a certain curve type? This is very easy to do.

6 Select all of the controls in panel again, then select any Translate Z channel in the Graph Editor. Go to Show > Selected Type(s). If you select all of the channels on the left, you'll see only the Translate Z channels are in the Graph Editor!

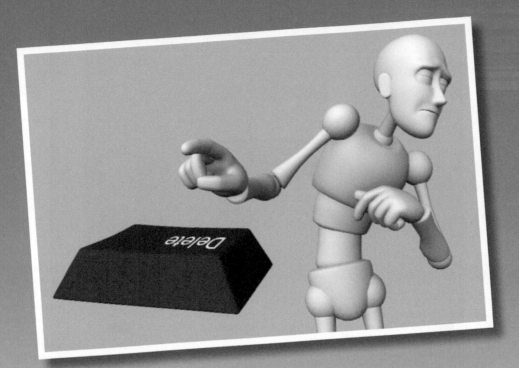

■ Making changes,
tracking arcs,
working with
multiple pivots,
using the timeline,
and much more are
discussed in depth
in this chapter.

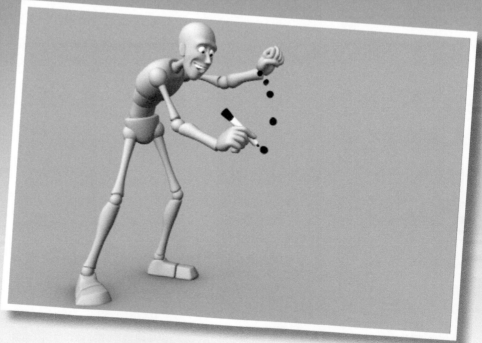

4

Techniques

FOR EVERY ANIMATOR there are a variety of techniques that are used throughout the animation process. As you develop your skills, a portfolio of mantras that you call upon regularly will also develop: your kung fu, so to speak.

This chapter contains a wide selection of very useful tools and techniques for animating. While creating a piece of animation, you may call upon some of these techniques dozens of times, others only once, but all of them will make a regular appearance in any animator's workflow. Prepare, grasshopper, for efficiency lies within...

Auto Key

HAVING TO PRESS THE **S** KEY incessantly
while animating does two things: gets
tedious, and wears out your **S** key. So in the
interest of preventing tedium and extending
your keyboard's life, let's look at the different
ways we can use Maya's Auto Key. This feature
eliminates most of your manual keying, and
while it's pretty straightforward, it works great
with the Hold Current Keys option, which is
easy to overlook.

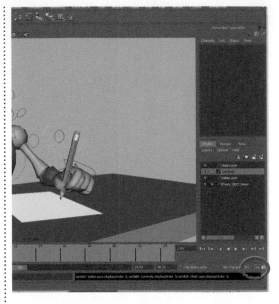

1 Open AutoKey.ma. The quickest way to turn Auto Key on
or off is the button in the bottom right corner. Make sure
it's red to indicate Auto Key is on.

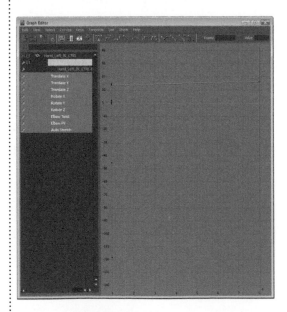

4 Looking at the Graph Editor, we see that there are keys
on all the hand attributes at f01, but only on Translate
Y at f08.

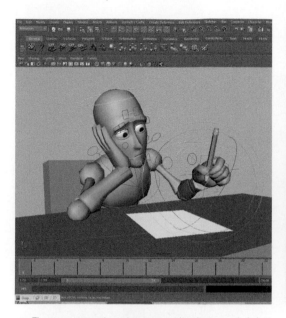

f08

AutoKey.ma

2 There are currently no keys set on the character, he's just posed. Grab the L hand and move it, and you'll notice no key is set. Auto Key only sets keys on controls when you've manually set a key on it first. Undo the move and set a key on it by pressing **S**.

3 Go to f08 and move the hand in Translate Y. Now a key will be set, but only on Translate Y. By default Auto Key only sets a key on the attributes that are changed, not the entire control.

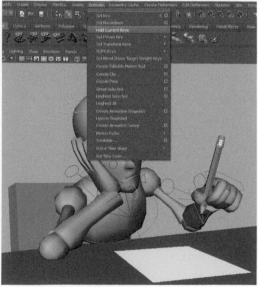

5 In the Channel Box, select the last of the attributes on the L hand control, right click and choose Delete Selected to erase all keys on this channel.

6 Move to f14 and go to Animate > Hold Current Keys. When using Auto Key, you may want to keep some attributes unkeyed, yet still set a key on all keyed attributes. Using this menu option will set a key on all keyed attributes of a control, but not on unkeyed ones.

83

Timeline Techniques

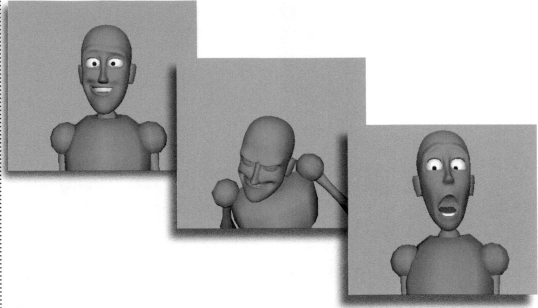

T HE TIMELINE is the interface element
you will use more than any other when
animating in Maya. It has a lot of functionality
beyond scrubbing, but its simple appearance
can hide how powerful it is. There are lots of
edits you can do without ever leaving it, from
copying and pasting keys, to reordering them
or setting tangent types. Even playblasting is
readily available. After working through this
cheat, you'll have some timeline chops that will
serve you as long as you animate.

We're going to use a simple animation of
the Goon doing a take. We have three basic
poses and right now that's all they are: poses
that interpolate to each other. Let's use some
fancy timeline editing to make it less poses and
more animation.

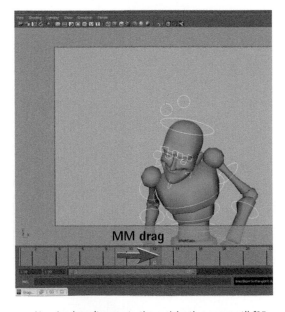

MM drag

3 Now he doesn't move to the anticipation pose until f05,
but he needs to hold there also. MM drag from f09 to
f12 and set a key to copy that pose also.

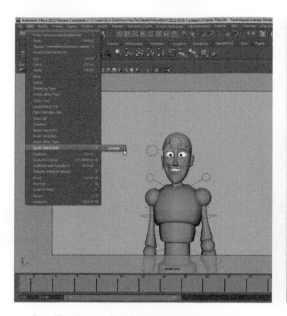

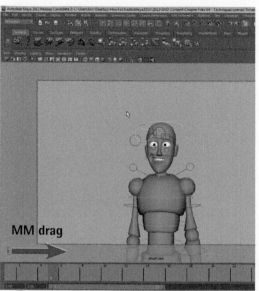

Timeline.ma
Timeline_end.ma

1 Open Timeline.ma. The first pose needs to hold a few frames longer before the anticipation pose. Go to Edit > Quick Select Sets > controls to use a predefined set to select all of the Goon's controls.

2 In the timeline MM drag from f01 to f05. The animation doesn't change like when you scrub. MM dragging holds the frame on wherever you started, so it's a quick way to copy poses. Make sure the tangents are set to Auto, and set a key at f05.

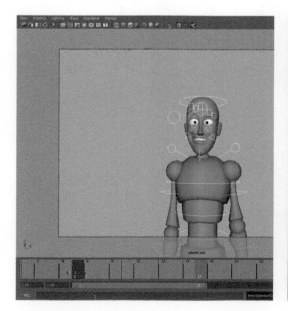

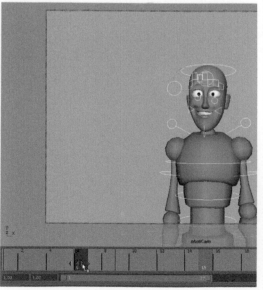

4 It's looking better, but let's make the transition into the anticipation a little snappier. *Shift* click f05 and it will turn red.

5 Click and drag on the two center arrows to move the key to f06. Now the transition is only three frames, which feels better.

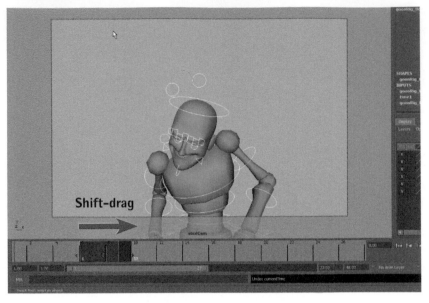

6 He hits the anticipation pose very hard, so let's cushion him hitting that pose. Shift drag from f06 through f09 to highlight them red.

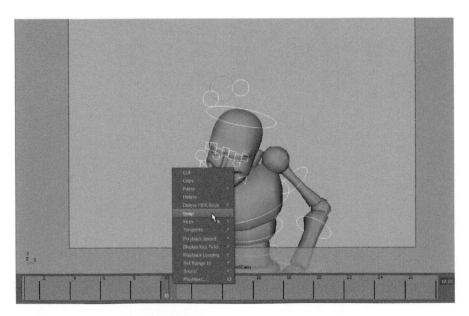

8 That feels much better, but the scaling has put the key between f11 and f12, which can make refining more unpredictable and cause motion blur problems. Right click on f11 and choose Snap to snap the key to the closest frame, which puts it back on f11.

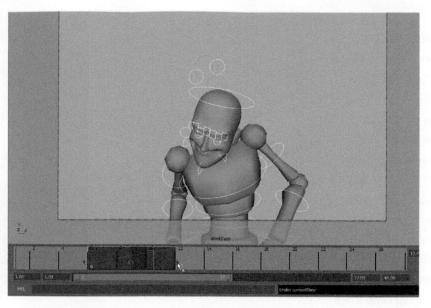

7 Grab the end arrow and drag it through f12 to scale the keys' values out and ease into the anticipation pose.

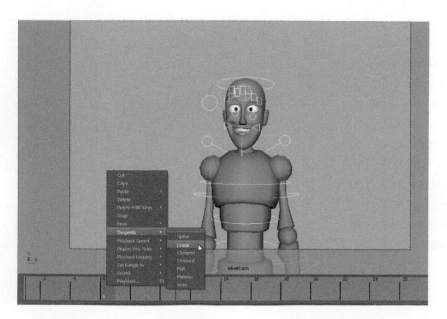

9 The timeline right click menu has many options. You can change the tangents of keys without the Graph Editor, playblast, adjust speed and display options, and more. Use these for speeding up your workflow considerably.

HOT TIP

The timeline is where you can activate sound for dialogue animations. Import the sound file through the File menu, then right-click on the timeline and select the sound to activate it during scrubbing and playback.

Cartoony Motion

CARTOONY STYLE IS A VERY DIFFICULT style to attain. Most novices make the mistake of trying to push all of the fundamentals. By exaggerating EVERYTHING, they feel like the animation will automatically become cartoony. This could not be further from the case.

To create cartoony movement, we need to create the IMPRESSION of an exaggerated movement by picking a visual simile. What does that mean? Choose a motion that is realistic, and can be observed in everyday life, and put that motion into your character.

You've seen it all before – a character's head rings LIKE A BELL after he gets punched. A character falls the ground LIKE A SHEET OF PAPER after he gets flattened. A character's arm wobbles LIKE SPAGHETTI after he gets a shot of Novocain in it. All of these examples reference REALISTIC motions that, when we put them into the body of our character, become cartoony. You will notice none of these examples mention anything about exaggerating. We're going to be creating the last example of the numb arm in this cheat, using some reference geometry. Using reference geometry we do not have to guess the motion we're trying to get out of the wobbly arm, it's right there in front of us to copy. Use this cheat whenever you need to closely reference any motion for cartoony-styled animation.

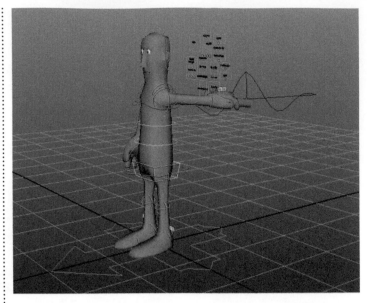

1 Open cartoony_Start.ma. We have a character just gliding through the scene. We can imagine they are running away. We want to give the impression his arm is totally numb, and flopping around like spaghetti. Let's get started.

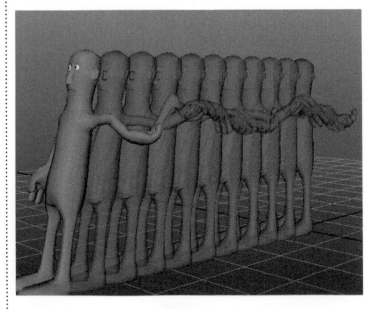

4 Continue going through the animation on 2s, and then back again on 1s, until the arm matches the movement of the cylinder in the entire shot.

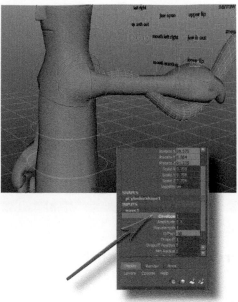

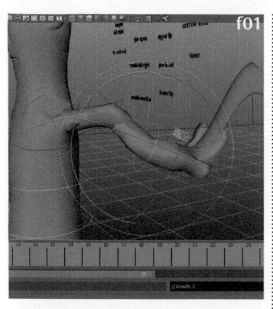

cartoony_Start.ma
cartoony_End.ma

2 There is a cylinder attached to Bloke's arm. That is the piece of geometry we are going to use to apply the wobbly motion for reference. Select the cylinder geometry, and in the Channel Box, go down to the wave1 input and turn the Envelope parameter up to 1.

3 Now that the cylinder is wobbling very Spaghetti-like, let's key our arm to follow it. Grab all of the arm controls and set a key matching the pose on f01.

5 Done! Hide the cylinder and play your animation back and watch the awesome wobbly motion come to life. Remember, we didn't just exaggerate, we used motion inspired by real life. This is how true cartoony action comes to life.

89

4 Techniques
Trax Editor

THE TRAX EDITOR, apart from being the best place to import and manipulate audio, was actually built to load animation "clips" onto character sets. This can be very fun and intuitive.

Manipulating clips is kind of like "mixing" animation. You can create a library of clips and mix and match the animation to create entire performances, or, perhaps more usually, multiple permutations of background animation. Imagine how easy it would be to animate a small crowd if you can just drag and drop animation clips onto the characters, mixing movement into cycles and blending between clips. The Trax Editor does just that.

Some things to know about using clips is that the character sets normally have to be identical, so working with a finished rig is highly recommended. Also, you want to make sure your animation is created to be mixed and matched. Meaning you should be thinking about creating actions that are modular and/or layered to be used in a non-linear fashion.

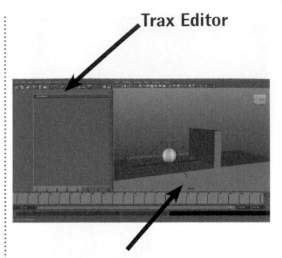

Trax Editor

Perspective Viewport

1 Open trax_Start.ma and set up your panels like these above are arranged, with the Trax Editor on the left and persp camera on the right. Just go to Panels > Panel > Trax Editor.

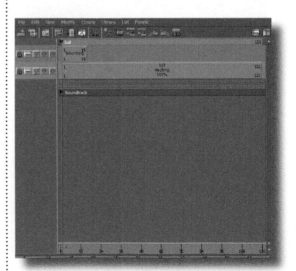

4 Import another clip by going to File > Import Animation Clip to Characters... Choose Vaulting_Clip.ma and it will load into a new track.

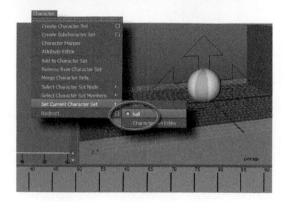

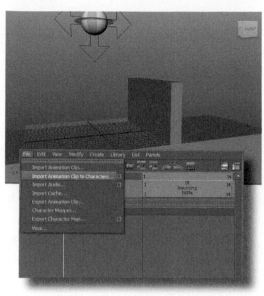

trax_Start.ma
trax_End.ma

2 Set the current character set by hitting F2 to switch to the animation menu set and then going to Character> Set Current Character Set> ball. Then create a track in the Trax Editor by clicking the button in the top left corner.

3 Import the first animation clip (the ball bouncing) by going (in the Trax Editor) to File > Import Animation Clip to Characters. Choose Bouncing_Clip.ma. It will load into the Trax Editor and you can find it using the normal camera tools or by hitting **A** to frame it.

HOT TIP

These clips were exported with the animation taking place in "relative" space. This setting means that the position of the controls will start from the end position of the last clip. So, you can have a clip where a character starting at 0 walks forward 5 units, and then in the next clip he'll automatically walk from 5 to 10.

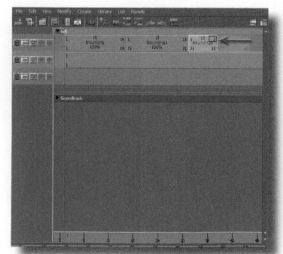

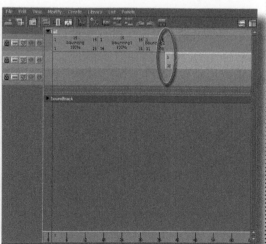

5 Now copy the bouncing clip by selecting it and hitting **ctrl**+**C**. Paste it twice by hitting **ctrl**+**V**, and arrange them one after another on the same track. Drag the clip range of the last clip to end on f08 of the clip, by grabbing the top right corner and dragging it left to "8".

6 Finally, drag the Vaulting_Clip so that frame 1 lines up with frame 8 of the third Bouncing_clip. Play back the animation, and you'll see the ball bounces twice, then lands, and vaults over the wall.

Copying Curves

COPYING DATA GOES BACK to the earliest functionality of computers, and it is alive and well in computer animation. Maya's curve-copying abilities are rather extensive, and it offers many options for shuffling animation data around to save time and effort. We're going to build on a laughter animation in which the character is yet a bit too static, by copying curves onto his head, neck, and body to make him much more, well, animated.

As we'll see in this cheat, copying isn't only for putting the same curve on another control. Any attribute's curve can be copied to any other attribute. This is great for taking a curve that is similar in shape to what we want onto another control (even if it's a rotate going to a translate, for example) and using it as a starting point. Tweaking a curve can be much faster than positioning the control and setting keys. Faster = good.

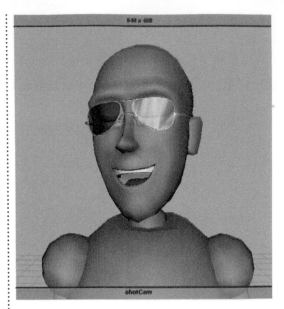

1 Open CopyingCurves_start.ma.

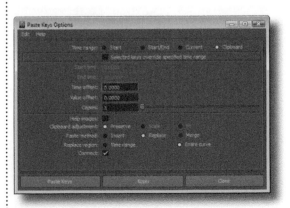

4 Select the neck control. Before we paste these curves, go to Edit > Paste > ☐. Set the Time range to Clipboard (to use the curves we just copied), Paste Method to Replace, and Replace Region to entire curve. Then press Paste Keys.

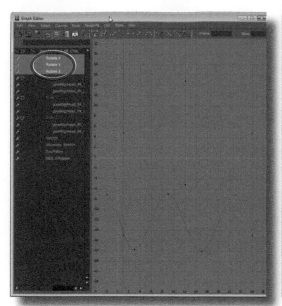

2 In the Graph Editor, select the Rotate X, Y, and Z attributes for the head control. Be sure to select the attributes in the left panel, not the curves themselves.

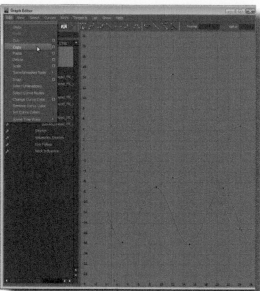

3 Go to Edit > Copy in the Graph Editor menu to copy the curves.

CopyingCurves_
start.ma
CopyingCurves_
end.ma

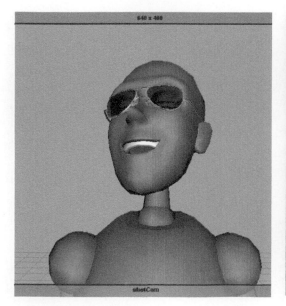

5 The curves will automatically be placed on the same attributes they were copied from if nothing is selected in the Graph Editor. They've been copied to the neck, but now his head is back a bit too far.

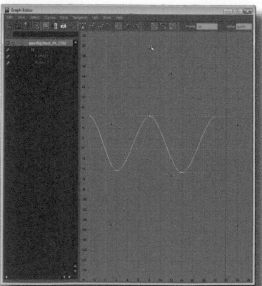

6 I moved up the entire Rotate X curve to bring his head forward, then scaled the whole curve down. Now his movement is bigger, but not too much.

Copying Curves (cont'd)

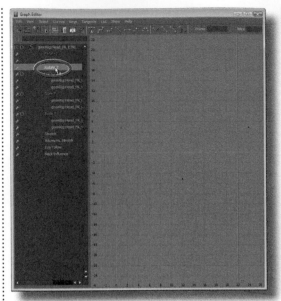

7 Let's use some of these curves to add side-to-side movement on the chest. The head's Rotate Z curve has a similar contour to what we want to start with, so select the attribute in the Graph Editor and go Edit > Copy.

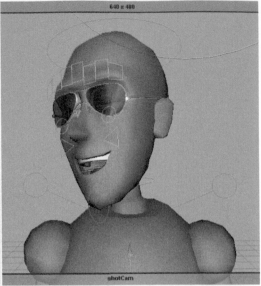

8 Select the chest control and set a key at f01. Since we'll be putting the head's Rotate Z on the chest's Rotate Z and Rotate Y, we need to be able to select those attributes in the Graph Editor. Without a key they won't appear.

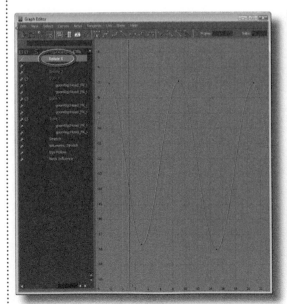

11 Finally, let's add some bounce on his body. The curve most similar to what we want is the head's Rotate X, so select that attribute on the head and copy the curve.

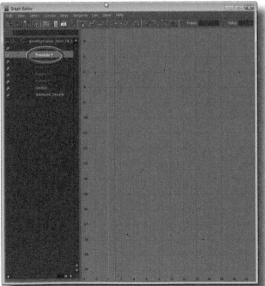

12 Select the main body control and set a key at f01. Select its Translate Y attribute and paste the curve onto it. He'll move out of frame because of the values, so let's quickly tweak this curve.

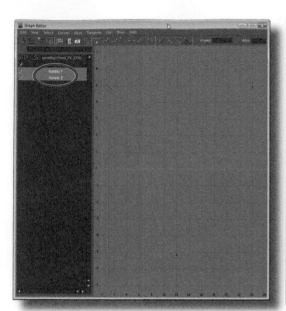

9 In the Graph Editor, select the chest's Rotate Y and Z attributes and go Edit > Paste. The curve will be put on both attributes.

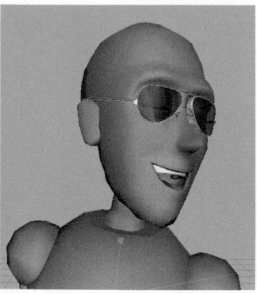

10 I shifted both curves one frame earlier for a little offset, and scaled them up. Now his movement is much more energetic.

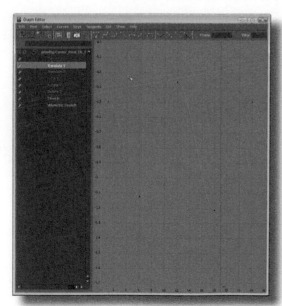

13 I edited the curve so it starts on f01 and his bounces stay in frame. There are also some differences in the values so everything doesn't feel exactly the same.

14 The animation can be refined a lot from here, including adding some bounce in the shoulders, but now you see how we can quickly get a smooth starting point simply by copying curves, without doing any character positioning.

HOT TIP

Copying curves is a great technique, but it's almost always best for quickly giving you a curve to start refining, rather than a finished result. It can also work well for starting overlapping action on things like tails and floppy ears.

95

Editable Motion Trails

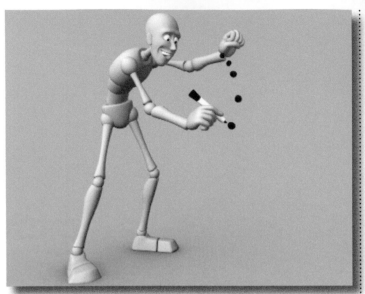

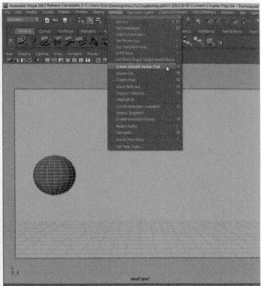

I N ORDER TO GET APPEALING, polished animation, it's a good idea for the motion to travel in pleasing arcs. After all, it is one of the twelve animation principles! There have been plenty of tools made for Maya to track arcs, but what about fixing them directly in the viewport? Wouldn't that be nice? Or even adjusting your spacing without having to go into the Graph Editor? If only there was a way...

There is. One of the best features in Maya 2013 for tracking and editing arcs (and other things) is the Editable Motion Trail. Not only does it show you the path an object is taking through 3D space, but it also allows you to edit that path directly in the viewport. Needless to say, this has been a feature animators have desired for quite some time, and Maya 2013 makes it a reality.

Editable Motion Trails give you lots of power. They work in conjunction with the other keyframe tools (the Graph Editor, and the Dope Sheet) so anything you edit on them will be reflected everywhere else. You can adjust the path of action, timing, and spacing, as well as add, delete, and move keyframes right on the path. This cheat will give you all the ins and outs of this most welcome addition to Maya's animation toolset.

1 In the project file EditableMotionTrail.ma, double check that your tangents are weighted, and that the tangent type is set to Auto (see Chapter 2 for more information on this). The motion trail's behavior is dictated by what tangent settings are present on the curves. Select the ball and go to Animate > Create Editable Motion Trail.

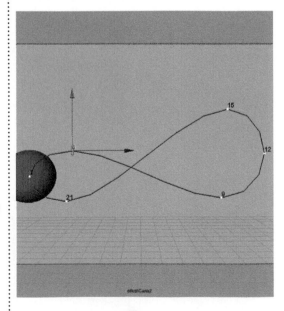

4 Select the move tool *W* and select the key at f04. Just like moving an animation control, you can move the key in 3D space and adjust the path instantly.

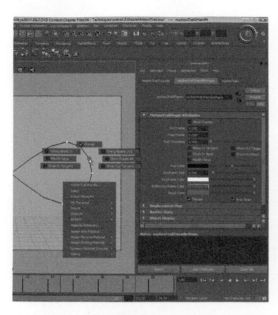

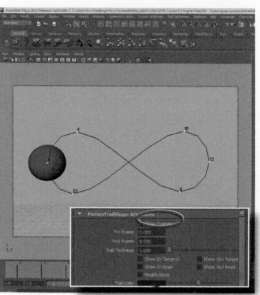

EditableMotionTrail.ma

2 Open the Attribute Editor if it isn't already and click on the motion trail to bring up its options. You can also right click directly on the trail to quickly access the settings most commonly toggled on and off.

3 The trail shows the path the object takes in 3D space. The white beads show where keyframes exist along the trail. Click the Show Frames box in the Attribute Editor to display the frame number for each key.

HOT TIP

The Trail Color slider is very handy for when you have multiple motion trails happening. Keeping the colors different makes it easier to remember what is what.

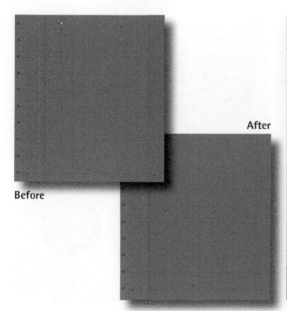

After

Before

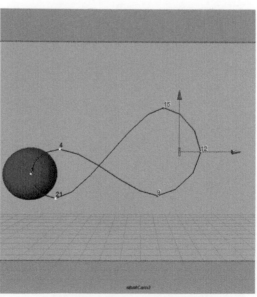

shotCam2

5 Notice the Translate Y curve before and after the change made in the previous step. Adjusting keys in the motion trail is really just another more visual and natural way of editing the curves.

6 You can select multiple keys and move them just as easily. *ctrl* dragging will move the selected keys perpendicular to the viewport (i.e., backwards or forwards), without having to change cameras to make an edit.

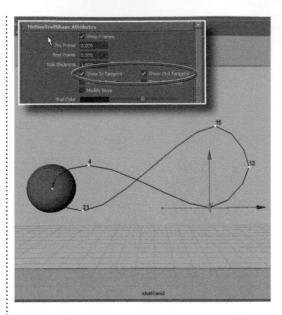

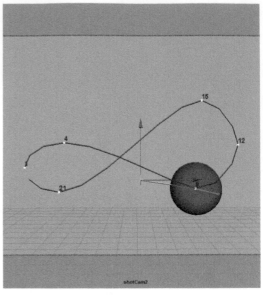

7 Select the key at f09 and in the Attribute Editor (or right click menu) turn on Show In Tangent and Show Out Tangent to show handles for the key. Remember that the way these handles will behave depends on the settings for the curves they are found on.

8 Marquee select the handle and you can use it to edit the spacing in the motion path, just like in the Graph Editor. Editing handles is easiest when you only use one axis on the manipulator at a time, rather than grabbing them in the middle and dragging all axes freely.

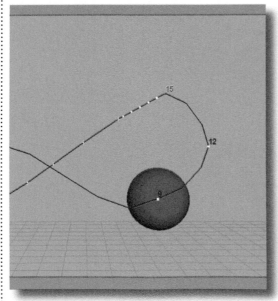

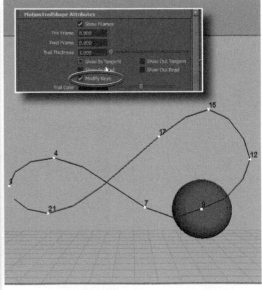

11 Simply clicking and dragging on the beads lets you adjust the spacing. Remember, if you don't see any beads, it's because your tangents on this key are not weighted.

12 Click the Modify Keys box in the Attribute Editor or right click menu. When this is turned on, simply clicking on the trail will add keys, which will use whatever default tangents are currently set.

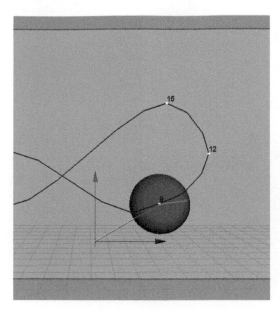

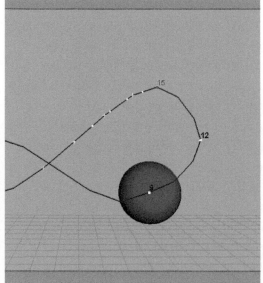

9 If you break the tangent handles (select the curves or keys in the Graph Editor and click the break tangents button), you can edit them independently in the viewport as well.

10 Select the key at f15 and click Show Out Bead In the Attribute Editor or right click menu. Beads representing the in-between keys appear on the trail. Notice that you cannot show both tangents and beads at the same time, as they're really just different representations of the same thing — spacing of the in-betweens.

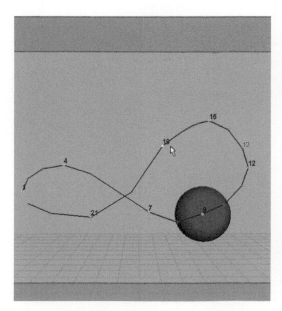

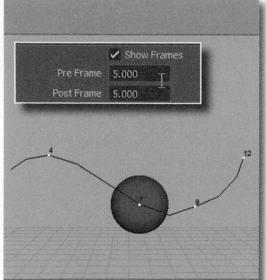

13 For making quick timing changes with Modify Keys, simply hold S and MM drag keys. You'll see the frame number adjust, as well as the marks indicating the current position of the in-between frames. Very nice!

14 In the Attributes, you can enter Pre and Post Frame values. This controls how many frames before and after the current frame to display. This helps if the path crosses over itself multiple times in a small space, which makes the trail hard to read. Setting 0 shows all frames.

IK and FK

ALMOST ANY RIG that is intended for character animation will have the arms and legs available in two modes, IK (inverse kinematics) and FK (forward kinematics). Many animators have a mode they prefer to use when either is viable, but there will often be times when you have to use a specific mode, at least for part of the animation. If your character is going to plant his hand on something to support his weight or push or pull it, you will have no choice but to use IK arms if you want acceptable results. Switching between the modes can seem tedious at first, but when you understand how switching works, it's really quite simple.

For a quick refresher, FK (forward kinematics) means that the position of the hand (or foot) is dependent upon the joints leading up to it. This is how our bodies work in the real world. To reach up and grab something with your hand, your shoulder must rotate, taking your upper arm with it, which takes your forearm with that, which takes your hand up to the object. You can't raise your hand without at least raising your elbow, and so on. With FK, if you move the character's body, it will move the arm as well. This works well for things like walks and gesturing, but not for pulling or pushing things.

IK (inverse kinematics) is the opposite. The hand is positioned on its own, and Maya figures out where the rest of the arm would be angled based on that. You can think of the hand almost as a separate object that's tethered to the body. If you move the body the hand will stay where it is, making it ideal for pushing or pulling. This way we can work on the body animation without losing the positioning of the hand.

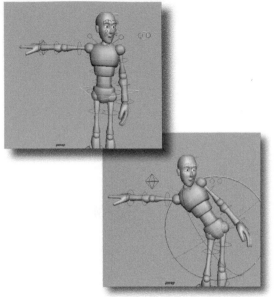

1 Open IK_FK.ma. The left arm is currently in FK. Rotating any of the body controls brings the arm along with it.

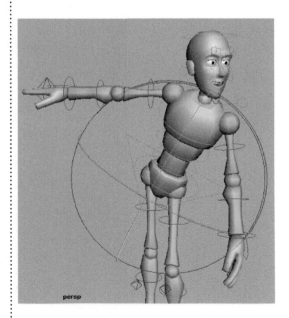

4 When Chest Influence is 0, the FK arm will follow with translation of the body, but not rotation. Some animators prefer this because you need to do much less correction on the arms if you change the body.

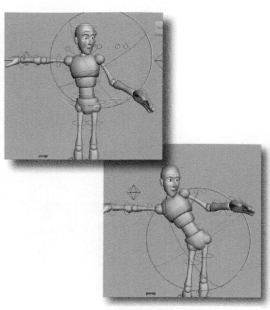

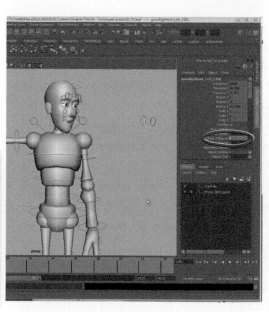

IK_FK.ma

2 Undo the body rotation and put the L arm in any pose you wish. Again, the arm will follow along with anything we move in the body and spine.

3 Undo everything and select the hand control. In the Channel Box is the Chest Influence attribute. Change it to 0. The arm may jump slightly when you do this, which is normal.

HOT TIP

Some rigs have advanced options for IK arms. These hands are in world space, but it's possible to switch that if it's built into the rig. For example, it can have a root space option, which means the IK will move if the root does, but nothing else.

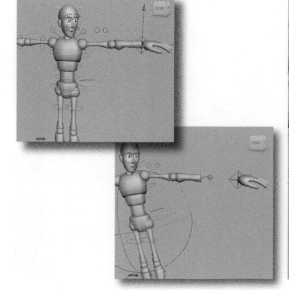

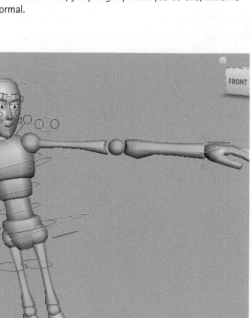

5 Undo everything. Select the hand control and set the IK weight to 1 (100%). The arm will move to the IK control and is now an IK arm. Move the body and the hand will stay in place no matter what you do.

6 On the IK control if you set Auto Stretch to 1, the geometry will stretch between the hand and body, rather than separating at the wrist.

IK/FK Switching

WHEN PLANNING AN ANIMATION, an important step is determining if it's best to use IK, FK, or both at different times. When we need to use both, switching between them in a way that's smooth and seamless is the key to quality work. While some animators may dread this element of animating, when you keep in mind how switching works under the hood, it's very straightforward.

The thing to realize is that there are actually two different arms as far as the joints underneath the geometry are concerned. One arm isn't switching between IK and FK modes, we're actually moving the geometry to another joint skeleton. So when you switch to from, say, FK to IK, keep in mind that the frame where IK takes over, the FK arm is still in its last position, following along (albeit invisibly). Remembering that there are two arms at work will make switching clearer in your mind.

While it's possible to blend into the other arm over several frames, I believe it's almost always best to do the switch over a single frame. When you blend, there are frames where the geometry is partially attached to both arms, so both controls affect the geometry to varying degrees. This makes it difficult to be precise in both posing and timing. It can work, of course, but I always prefer complete control at every frame.

Some rigs do have IK/FK snapping, which makes life much easier by automatically aligning either arm to the other. Many rigs don't, however, and you just have to pose the switching frame manually, which is how we'll do it here.

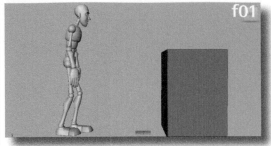

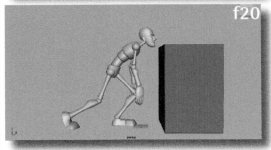

1 Open IKFKswitching_start.ma. There's a simple blocking animation of the character standing, then stepping to push the box. The arms aren't animated yet and they start in FK.

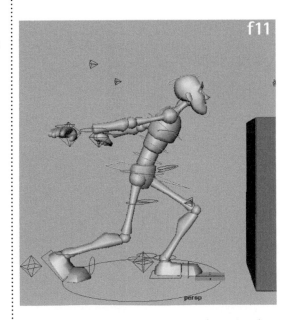

4 At f11, key the IK weight attribute at 1 (for 100% IK). The arms will snap back to where the IK arm skeletons are located.

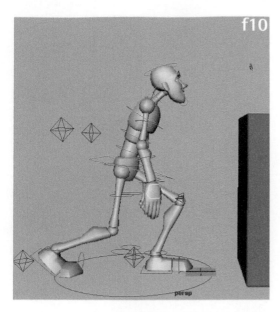

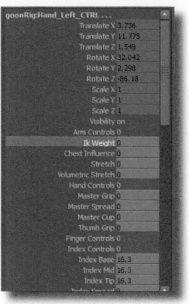

IKFKswitching_
start.ma
IKFKswitching_end.
ma

2 First we'll do the switch manually, without the snapping tool. F11 is where the switch to IK will happen, so select the hand controls and move to f10.

3 At f10, in the Channel Box right click and choose Key Selected on the IK weight attribute. This keys it again at 0 so we hold in FK up to f10.

HOT TIP

For any kind of IK/FK switching, don't sweat the small stuff until the transition is working. Focus on just the hands and hide or ignore the fingers until the foundation is set.

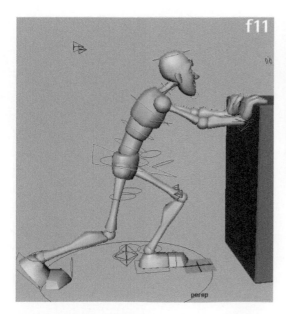

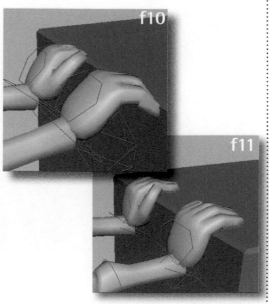

5 At f11, pose the IK hands and fingers on the box. Use the shoulders to help you get a good pose. When doing a switch, it's helpful to first establish the pose you're switching to, rather than basing it on the transition into the pose.

6 At f10, key the FK arms and pose them going into the IK pose. Try to ignore the fingers and just focus on the palm, since we'll need to edit them again anyway. It won't be perfect yet, as we'll also have to adjust the IK pose again in a moment, so just get it in the ballpark.

IK/FK Switching (cont'd)

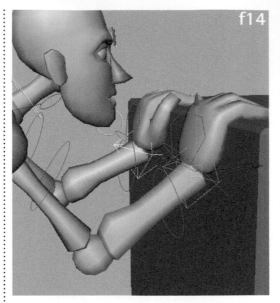

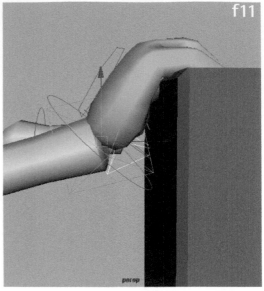

7 Now that the transition is better, we can improve the contact point. Right now his hand just kind of sticks to the box and we don't feel it compress into it. Select the IK controls and set a key at f14 to set the same pose a little later.

8 Go back to f11 and pull the IK controls away a bit and rotate them down slightly. Again, focus only on the palm and don't worry about the fingers yet. Make the palms ease in nicely to f14 to give a feeling of the palms pressing.

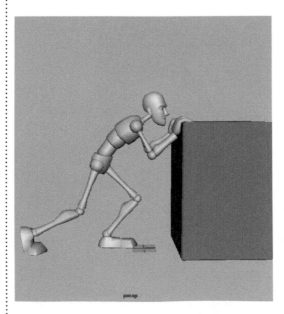

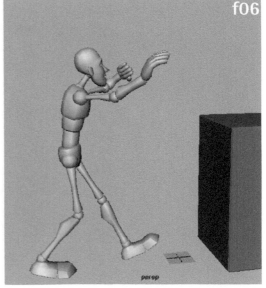

10 You probably noticed that once you get the switch frame, the rest is just normal animating except you're switching between two different types of controls.

11 You may or may not have the problem of his arms going crazy during the transition. If so, it's because of gimbal lock, which can happen from time to time.

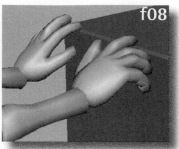

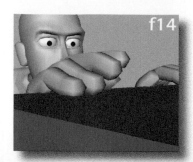

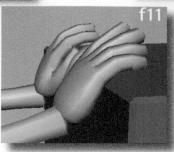

9 With the press working better, now is a good time to rough in some finger poses and have them trail the palms pressing for some overlap.

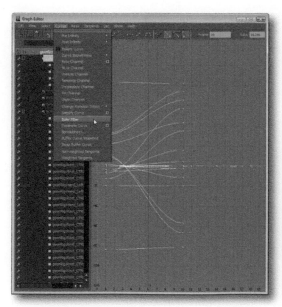

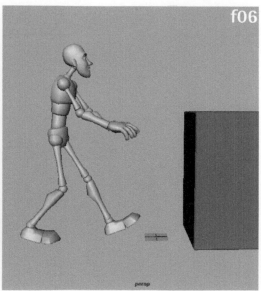

12 To fix it, select all the FK arm curves in the graph editor and use Curves > Euler Filter.

13 Now his arms interpolate to the push pose the way we'd expect and we can continue to refine the animation from there.

4 Techniques

Character Sets

DURING PART OR ALL of their animation process, some animators like to use character sets, which are basically selection sets you don't need to select to key. They're kind of a legacy feature, as they've been around since the earlier versions of Maya, but a number of animators still find them useful. Personally, I think they work best in situations where you have to do a lot of keyframing on specific channels of a control, such as the fingers, and for that they can be handy. In this cheat we'll look at how to create and edit character sets.

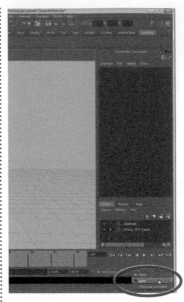

1 Open CharacterSets.ma. The Character Set selection menu is at the bottom right, next to the Auto Key button. Click the arrow next to it and select spine.

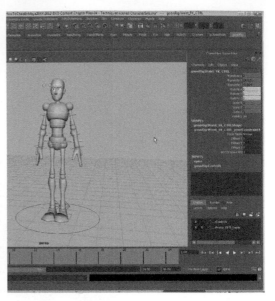

2 Without selecting anything, press **S** to set a key. This set contains all the spine controls, so they will automatically be keyed with any key. Notice their channels are yellow, indicating they are connected to a set.

5 With the arms set selected, setting a key will now key all the controls. Open the Animation Preferences and turn on Auto Key if it isn't already. On character sets, set to Key all attributes.

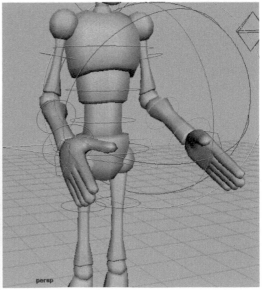

6 Now adjusting any of the arm controls will set a key on all the other arm controls automatically. This can be handy for blocking if you make a set for all controls.

106

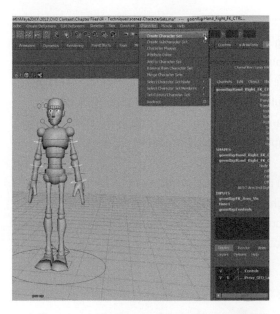

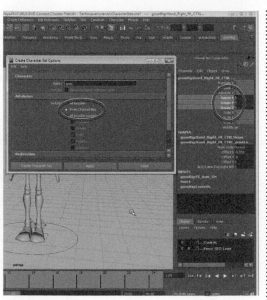

CharacterSets.ma

3 Let's create a set for the arms. Select all the arm controls and in the animation menu set (F2) go to Character > Create Character Set > Options box.

4 In the options, name the set "arms" and select From Channel Box. Highlight the Rotate XYZ channels in the Channel Box, and click Create Character Set.

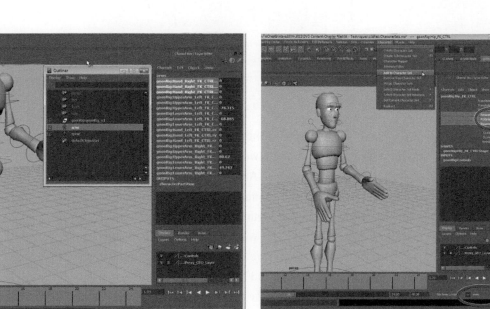

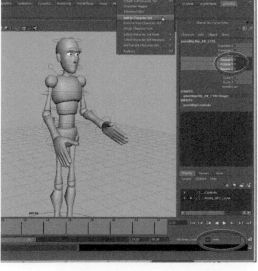

7 To remove attributes, go to Window > Outliner and select the set you want to edit. The attributes will appear in the Channel Box. Select the attributes you want to remove and go to Character > Remove from Character Set.

8 To add to a character set, have it selected in the list at the bottom, select the objects or attributes you wish to add, and go to Character > Add to Character Set.

HOT TIP

It's best to create character sets before you start animating. If you need to create a set with controls that are already animated, create a new set with nothing selected. Then add the controls or attributes to the set using Add to Character Set.

Multiple Pivot Points

ONE ISSUE THAT CAN ARISE when animating props is needing different pivot points at different frames. Being able to rotate an object from other pivot points when you need to makes animating much easier. While it is possible to key the pivot point of an object to different spots during the animation, this method is difficult to make changes to and keep track of. It also does not give a clear indicator, such as a Channel Box attribute, that the pivot point is being animated. Instead, then, we're going to use grouping to achieve the control we need and make animating multiple pivots more straightforward.

Grouping is basically parenting your object to an invisible object that can be moved, rotated, and translated just like any other object. You might think of it as a container for an object or objects. We can define the pivot point of the group wherever we like, and we can nest groups as many times as we need to get the number of pivots we require.

The important thing to remember is, once the groups are created, always animate from the top group down. In other words, the last group we create (the highest in the hierarchy, group 2 in the above diagram) is the first one we animate. Also, once you "leave" one group and move to the next one down for the next pivot point, you cannot go back to the previous one at a later frame. You must plan ahead beforehand so you don't animate yourself into a corner.

It may sound a bit precarious, but this cheat will give you all the info you need to have as many pivots as your heart desires. Always be sure to plan your animation first, determine how many pivots you need, where you need them, and the order in which they happen. For this animation, the shuriken will be flying through the air, so we will need to first animate it from its center, meaning that's the last group we will create for it. It will then stick into a wall with one of the tips. The shaking from hitting the wall will resonate from that tip, so that's where the other pivot will be, within the first group.

So in a nutshell, create the groups working backwards from the end of the animation. Animate them starting at the top group (the last one you create).

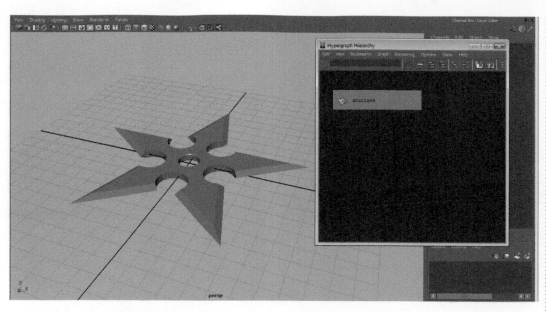

1 Open MultiplePivots_start.ma and go to Window > Hypergraph : Hierarchy to open the hypergraph. This editor displays objects' hierarchies (what they are parented to). Currently the shuriken is by itself.

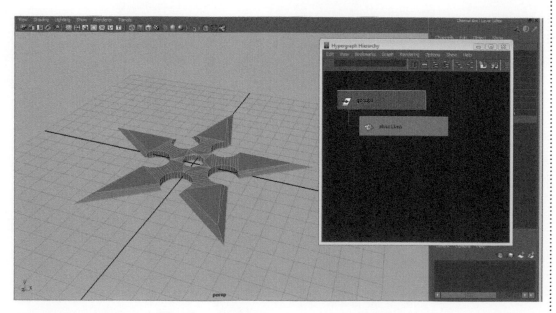

2 Select the shuriken and press *ctrl* + *G* to create a group node and put it inside. You can see in the hypergraph it now appears underneath the group object, meaning it's the child and the group is the parent.

MultiplePivots_
start.ma
MultiplePivots_end.
ma

HOT TIP

Never use grouping on a rig, as adding a parent–child relationship can break it. Only use it on props and simple objects. If you need this type of pivot control in a character, it must be built into the rig.

109

Multiple Pivot Points (cont'd)

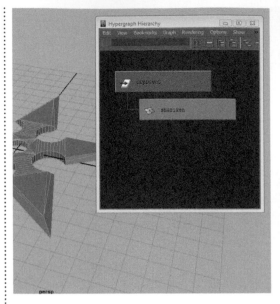

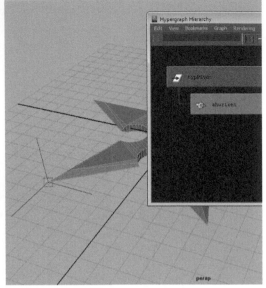

3 Rename the group to reflect what pivot you're animating by **ctrl** double clicking the name. Again, we're creating them backwards from how we'll animate them, so this is the tip pivot.

4 With the tipPivot group still selected in the hypergraph, select the Move tool and press the Insert key. The tool goes into pivot mode (the arrowheads disappear). Move the pivot to a tip and press Insert again to exit pivot mode.

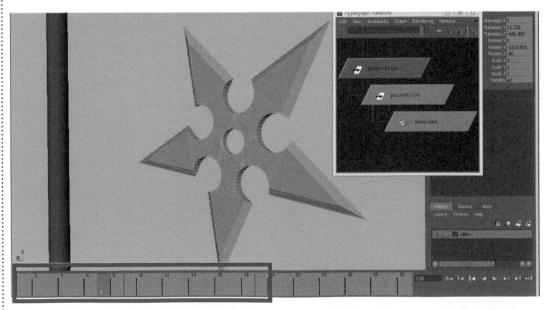

6 Open MultiplePivots_end.ma to see how the animation works. The centerPivot group is animated from f01 to f19. As stated before, the last group that's created is the first one that's animated. As the frames progress and the pivots change, you simply work your way down that list, and never go back to a pivot after the following one has been keyed.

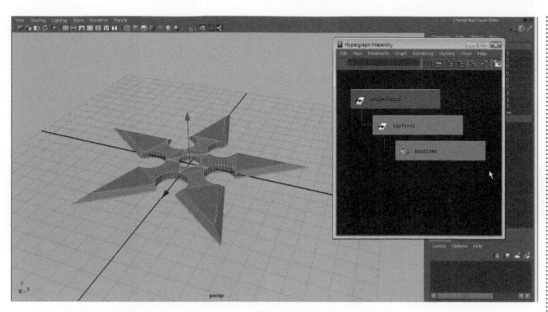

5 Making sure that the tipPivot group is selected, press **ctrl** + **G** again to create another group at the top of the hierarchy and rename it "centerPivot". This is the center of the object which we will animate first, as the shuriken is flying through the air. We won't change the pivot on this one since it's already where we need it to be.

7 From f19 to the end the tipPivot group is animated for the residual energy from hitting the wall.

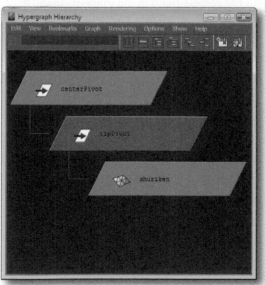

8 When animating multiple pivots, it's easiest to use the hypergraph to quickly select the group you want to animate. You can also select the object and use the up or down arrow keys to move through the hierarchy.

Reblocking

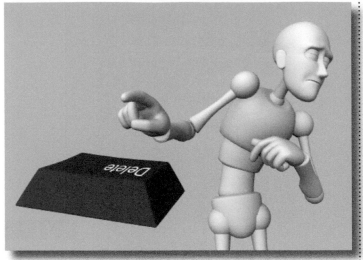

I T IS INEVITABLE, IT IS YOUR DESTINY... as an animator the time will come (and regularly at that) where you'll need to make changes to work you already started refining. It can be frustrating when it happens, but it's one of the tiny cons to the major pro of doing the coolest thing in the universe. Doing a reblock in the middle of an animation is just a fact of life for an animator. The key to making changes smoothly is knowing how to save what you can, when to shuffle around poses that can be salvaged for other spots, and not allowing the new stuff to derail what's already working.

We're going to look at a sort of test case where we take something that's already in the refining stages of animation, and insert another acting beat into it. We'll start with a simple take animation, and imagine we've been given the direction to have him see a spider first, which then makes him do the take.

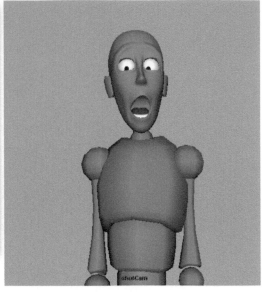

1 Open MakingChanges_start.ma. We have a simple animation of the Goon doing a take, and we need to add a spider coming down screen left, which he sees and then does the take from there.

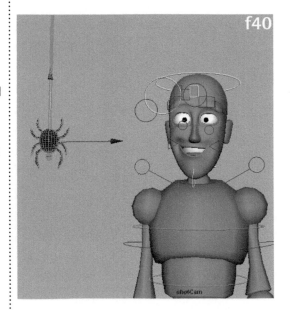

f40

4 He'll be looking at the spider when he starts the anticipation, so that's a good spot to begin. Select the spider, move it into position at f40, and set a key.

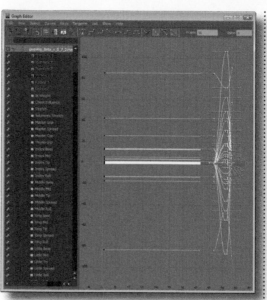

MakingChanges_
start.ma
MakingChanges_
end.ma

2 The first thing we need to do is expand the frame range. Click in the Display End field and enter 70. Typing a number greater than the whole range here automatically expands the entire range.

3 Go to Edit > Quick Select Sets > controls to use the predefined selection set to select all his controls. Select all the keys from f06 on, and move them to start on f50.

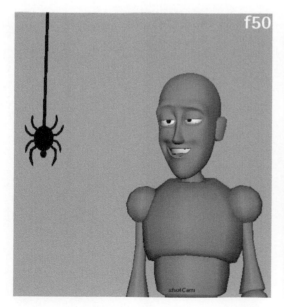

f50

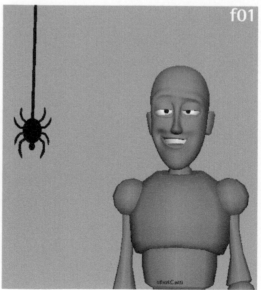

f01

5 At f50 alter his pose to make him look at the spider calmly.

6 Let's keep his eyelids low until he does the actual take, so select the two eye controls. MM drag to f01 and set a key to copy the eye pose.

Reblocking (cont'd)

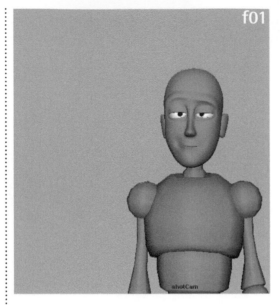

7 Alter his mouth pose to give him a smug, vacant expression. This will add some variety when he changes to the smile as he looks at the spider, and hopefully make it funnier.

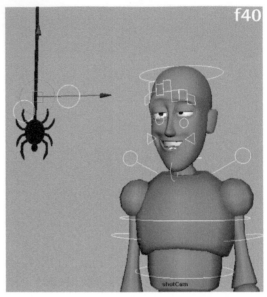

8 We'll have him hold while looking at the spider for 10 frames for a delayed reaction. Select all controls, and in the timeline MM drag from f50 to f40. Set a key to copy the pose.

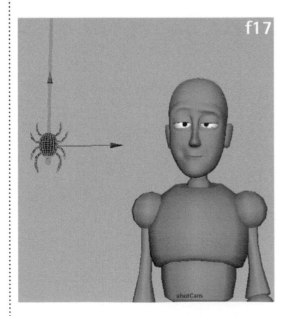

11 On the spider, MM drag from f10 to f17 so he has a 7 frame drop down.

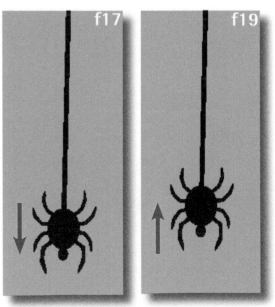

12 Rekey the spider at f19 with the same pose as f17. Then go back to f17 and lower him a bit more. This will give him a little overshoot when he hits the bottom.

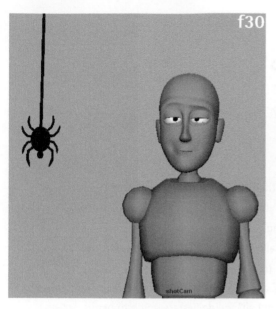

f30

9 MM drag from f01 to f30 and key all to hold the first pose for 30 frames.

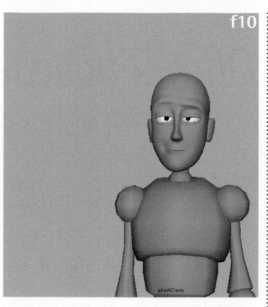

f10

10 Select the spider and, at f10, translate it up out of frame and key it.

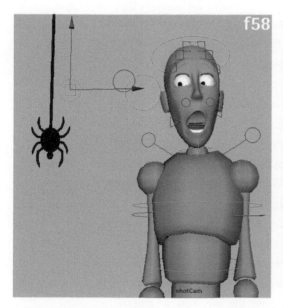

f58

13 To finish this reblocking, we just need to make him look at the spider at the end. At f58, move the eyes to a better position.

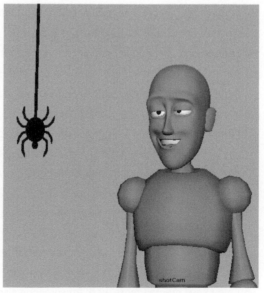

14 With a minimum amount of work, we are able to make this animation much more interesting than its previous version. It's now ready for some more detailed refining with the face and overlap.

Office Etiquette

by Kenny Roy

IF YOUR GOAL IS TO WORK in a production setting there are some things you should know about the studio environment that may help you avoid problems in the workplace. The guidelines below will ensure a copacetic working environment for all.

It is always a good idea to sit silently in a few dailies sessions to observe the culture before offering any feedback to another animator. This not only differs from studio to studio, but from project to project; different clients, different supervisors, budget and schedule constraints all have an effect on how "town hall" the dailies are going to be. See if the supervisor or director gets all his or her comments out before opening up the floor for discussion. If you are encouraged to give feedback, ALWAYS phrase your feedback positively. In fact, I'd only offer ideas when a supervisor asks for it, at least until I get to know my coworkers very well.

Always listen to your music or your dialogue tracks through headphones. Always use headphones that have good sound insulation. Heavy metal has a way of being even more annoying when you can hear the sound escaping someone else's headphones. The rule of thumb is that your ideal working conditions cannot disturb other artists.

I feel this should go without saying, but you have to bathe regularly and manage your body odors. Animators' desks are commonly placed end-to-end and you will be working in close proximity to others for at least eight hours a day. It is unfair to put others in the uncomfortable position of having to ask you to remedy rogue aromas. Animation is hard enough to create without an awkward air in the room (pun intended). I am not above sending an animator home to shower if it is necessary.

Pipeline is more than just a suggestion; it's a rule. And in relation to office politics, adhering to pipeline will keep you out of a lot of trouble. For instance, it is common that your animation will be handled by a few different departments before it finally goes on screen. However, if for some reason your work goes against the studio pipeline, you may have created more work for someone else down the line. You can quickly alienate other artists if you are constantly straying from the established pipeline.

Equipment can be a point of contention. Hopefully the studio has a bit of standardization; everyone gets dual monitors and the same speed workstation, etc.

It's not always best to be the squeaky wheel when it comes to equipment, including desks and chairs. The more senior artists may become upset if you get the brand-new chair, widescreen LED monitors and a screaming fast workstation on your first day after complaining. Until you have established yourself , Wait to bring up your equipment woes to your supervisor, or worst-case scenario you cannot get your work done with the equipment you've been given. And never steal someone else's chair!

Another thing that should go without saying, wash your hands every single time you use the restroom. Colds and the flu can travel around studios at light speed because of the close proximity. If you are sick, always cover your mouth (preferably with your sleeve and not your hands) when you cough or sneeze.

Never go over anybody's head. If you have a lead, bring your questions and concerns to him or her. If the problem is big enough, it will be elevated to the supervisor or director. The established hierarchy is set up to make it so that the amount of work that needs to be completed is done in an orderly fashion. Breaking the pecking order not only hurts your relationship with your higher-ups, it's bad pipeline.

Finally, make an effort to be courteous and generous to your coworkers. The animation industry is an exciting business, but that doesn't mean every day is a picnic. There's overtime, challenging work, computer crashes, schedule delays, and nightmare clients. You're all on the same team, so always be cheerful and helpful and the whole team will brave the difficulties together.

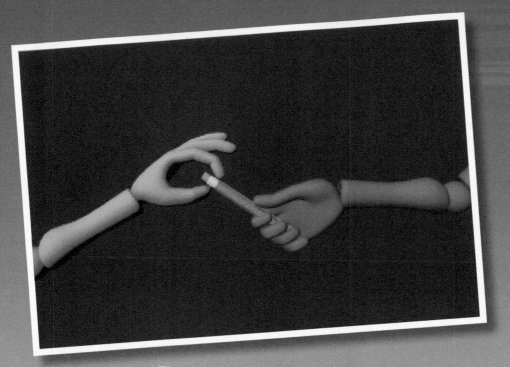

■ Constraints can get a bad rap sometimes. Once you understand the nuts and bolts and how to think about them, they become a great tool in creating more expressive animation.

5 Constraints

SOONER OR LATER every animator must have a character interact with a prop, and that means we need to work with constraints. They can seem a tad complicated at first, but once you understand how they work, you can design a constraint system that is simple and flexible. The next few cheats will tell you what you need to know about constraints as an animator. Then we'll look at some tools that will make constraining a breeze.

Parenting

NOVICE ANIMATORS SOMETIMES confuse parenting and constraining. These two processes behave somewhat similarly, but are quite different under the hood. First let's look at how parenting works.

Parenting is essentially indicating the center of an object's universe. By default, an object created in Maya exists in 3D space, and the infinite area inside the viewport is its central universe.

When we parent an object to another object (referred to as the parent), we are making the child object's central universe the parent object, instead of the 3D space. The child can still be moved independently, but its location is defined by where it is in relation to its parent, not where it is in space.

Think of it like this: you are currently parented to the earth. If you are sitting at your computer reading this book, as far as you're concerned, you're not moving. If you get up to get a soda from the fridge, you would say you've moved to a new location. Now think beyond earth and consider your position in the galaxy. When you're at your computer thinking you're not moving, you actually are moving through space (at 65,000 mph!) because the earth is moving through space and you are on it. It's your own perspective that you're not moving, but in relation to the entire universe, you are. This relationship of you to the earth to the galaxy is the same as a child parented to its object in Maya's 3D space. Let's observe this in Maya.

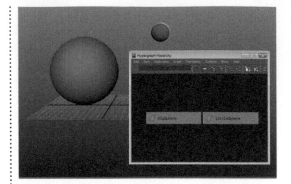

1 Open parenting.ma. Here I've created two spheres, and right now they're independent of each other. We can see in the hypergraph (Window > Hypergraph: Hierarchy) that they're side by side, indicating two separate objects.

4 This is also indicated in the Channel Box, where we see that, although nothing has changed in the viewport, the little sphere coordinates are different, to reflect the new relationship.

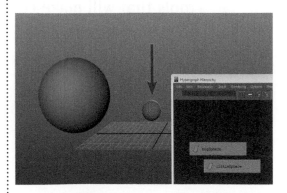

7 Use the move tool again to translate the little sphere.

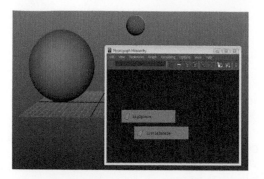

parenting.ma

2 Notice the coordinates for the little sphere in the Channel Box, indicating their position in world space. Move the little sphere and you will see these coordinates update accordingly.

3 First select the little sphere (the child), then shift select the big sphere (the parent) and press **P** to parent them. We can see in the hypergraph that they are now connected. We've created a hierarchy. The little sphere now uses the big sphere as its reference point.

HOT TIP

When parenting, the order you select the objects in determines what is parented to what. Think "child runs to the parent" to help you remember to select the child first. To unparent, use *Shift*+**P** with the child selected.

5 Move the big sphere using the move tool **W**, and the little sphere follows accordingly, maintaining its position.

6 If we look at the little sphere's coordinates in the Channel Box they're still the same. Its reference point for moving is only in relation to the big sphere, just like our intro example: our perception of moving is related to the earth, rather than the universe.

8 Now the translate channels for the little sphere change, because it's in a different position relative to the parent.

9 What's this have to do with animating? Knowing the difference between parenting and constraining will help you make a flexible system when using props with your characters. Next we'll look at how constraints work, and then how to use these methods together.

121

Parent Constraints

Parent Constraint

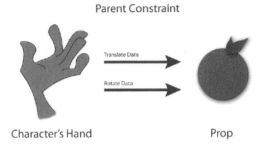

Character's Hand → Translate Data → Prop
Rotate Data

CONSTRAINED OBJECTS are fundamentally different from parented ones in that they still ultimately reference their position from the origin. They simply get their translate, rotate, and/or scale information told to them by their master object. Think of it as a direct line from the master object's attributes to whichever attributes are constrained (which can be any or all of them) in the target object. When we have constrained a prop to a character's hand, it isn't actually "stuck" there; it just receives the same location information which makes it follow along.

Because of this direct line, we can't move constrained objects, because they're "hardwired" to the master object. We can turn the constraint off (using what's called the weight), but if it's on, the constrained attributes cannot be altered independently of the master object.

We can see that there is sort of a yin-yang balance with parenting and constraints. Parenting cannot be turned off or on over the course of an animation, but you can move the child object independently. Constraints can be turned on or off yet are locked to their master object while on. In setting up effective constraint systems, we can use the strengths of each to get the results we need.

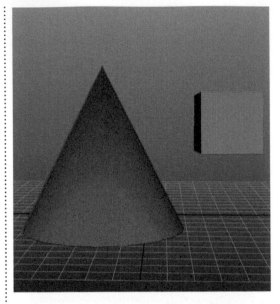

1 Open parentConstraint.ma. There are many types of constraints, but as an animator you'll probably use parent constraints most of the time. Parent constraints connect the translate and rotate attributes, and the constrained object behaves as if it were parented, except for not being able to move it independently.

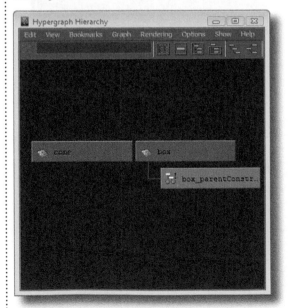

4 In the hypergraph, notice that the objects stay disconnected, and we see a constraint node appear. This is connected to the box, because it looks at the translate and rotate data of the cone, and "tells" the box to do the same.

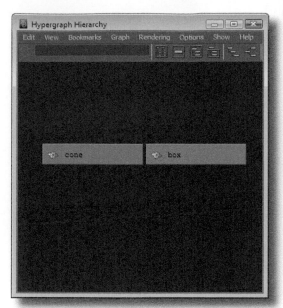

2 In this scene we have two independent objects, a cone and a box. Go to Window > Hypergraph: Hierarchy. Notice how they are not connected.

3 Constraint selection order is the opposite of parenting, with the master object being selected first. Select the cone, then shift select the box, and in the Animation menu go to Constrain > Parent. The names can make things confusing, but keep in mind this is a constraint, so you are not actually parenting these objects.

parentConstraint.ma

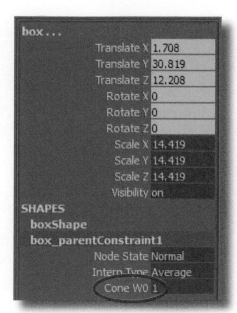

5 In the Channel Box the box's translate and rotate channels are blue, indicating they're constrained to something. If you click on the box_parentConstraint1 node, you'll see "Cone W0." This is the weight, or how much the constraint is affecting the object. 1 = 100% influence.

6 Translate and rotate the cone and the box follows. Notice how it maintains its position relative to the cone. This is why it's a parent constraint, because it assumes the pivot point of its master object, just like in a parent-child relationship.

HOT TIP

Constraint weights are used when we need to have an object constrained to different objects at different times in an animation. For instance, if we had a character throw a ball to another character who catches it, the ball would need to be constrained to their hands at separate times. We set keys on the weights to tell Maya which constraint to use at a given time. It's also possible (but not common) to have multiple weights on. Two objects at 100% influence would keep the object halfway between both of them. We'll look at weights in the cheat on pages 126-7.

123

Constraints

Constraining a Prop

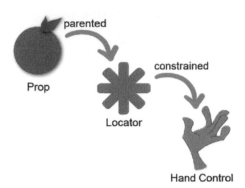

parented

Prop

Locator

constrained

Hand Control

W E'RE GOING TO USE both parenting and constraining to get the most flexibility in animating our props. Instead of just constraining the prop itself, we're going to constrain a locator that has the pencil parented to it. A locator is simply a blank object that you can translate, rotate, and scale. Not only does this create insulation between the rig and prop, but it also gives us the flexibility to reposition the prop and animate it. We're using the benefits of parenting and constraining in conjunction to make animating flexible and easier.

This approach can be very handy if you want to make some adjustments to a prop after you've already constrained and animated with it. We'll see how this can allow us to animate the writing movement of the pencil while keeping it in sync with the moving hand.

In a nutshell, the pencil is parented to the locator, which is constrained to the hand. Parenting the pencil lets it follow the locator, but still allows us to keyframe it. Since the locator is constrained to the hand, it follows how we want it to, while still giving us control to animate the pencil movement, keeping it isolated from the rig.

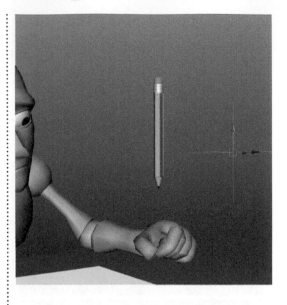

1 Open propConstraint_start.ma. Go to Create > Locator and move it in the area of the prop. If you can't see it, make sure Show > Locators is enabled in your viewport menu. Use the scale tool **R** to make it larger.

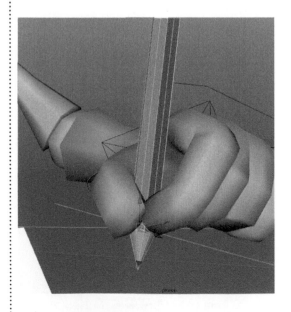

4 Select the pencil, then the locator, and press the **P** key to parent them. Moving the locator will now move the pencil. Using the locator, position the pencil in the character's hand. Keep in mind where it will pivot from between the fingers.

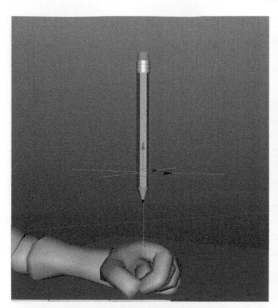

2 In the perspective view, position the locator at the pivot point where the character will hold the prop and where the fulcrum of movement will be. It doesn't have to be mathematically exact, but get it as close as you can, being sure to check the position from all angles.

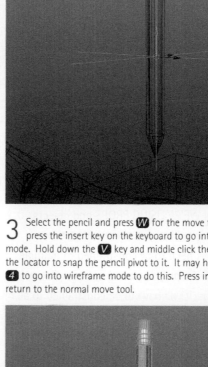

3 Select the pencil and press **W** for the move tool. Then press the insert key on the keyboard to go into pivot mode. Hold down the **V** key and middle click the center of the locator to snap the pencil pivot to it. It may help to press **4** to go into wireframe mode to do this. Press insert again to return to the normal move tool.

propConstraint_
start.ma
propConstraint_
end.ma

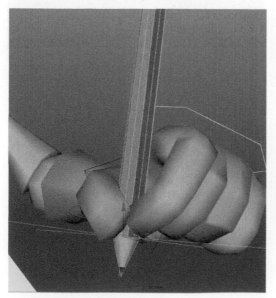

5 Select the hand control, then the locator, and go to Constrain > Parent. The channels on the locator will turn blue indicating a constraint.

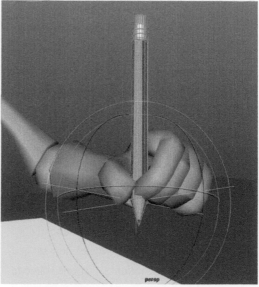

6 Now when we translate or rotate the hand, the pencil follows along. We can now easily animate the hand and arm writing. For the subtle movement of the pencil, we can simply key the pencil itself (perhaps with some animation on the fingers as well).

5

Constraints

Constraint Weights

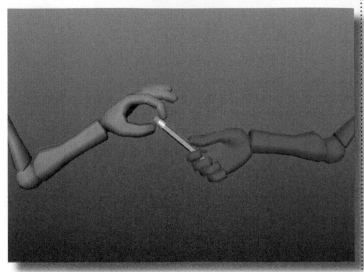

WHEN WE'RE USING PROPS and objects in our animations, there will be times when things need to be constrained to multiple characters. If a prop is passed between two or more things, it will have to be constrained to all of them at some point in the animation.

To tell Maya which constraint we want active at a specific time, we need to use the constraint's weight attribute.

It may be helpful to think of the weight as an on/off switch. Every time we constrain an object to something else, a weight attribute for that particular object is automatically created in the constraint's node in the channel box. Then we simply need to key it at 1 (on) and 0 (off) at the appropriate times.

In this simple animation of one hand giving another a pencil, we're going to see how to switch the constraint weights over one frame to get a seamless transition.

1 Open constraintWeights_start.ma. In a viewport menu, go to Panels > Perspective > shotCam to see the camera for the animation. If you like, press the viewport's Film Gate button to frame the animation more accurately.

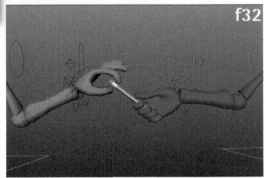

f32

4 Go to frame 32. We want to constrain the pencil to the hand on this pose, as the blue hand will take control of it from this point on. Select the blue hand IK control, then the pencil control, and go to Constrain > Parent.

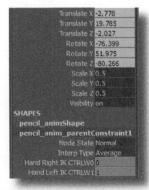

7 Go to frame 33 and switch the weights values to the opposite, turning off the pink hand's constraint and turning on the blue hand's. Select both weights, right click and choose Key Selected.

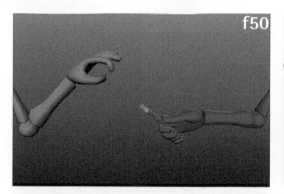

f50

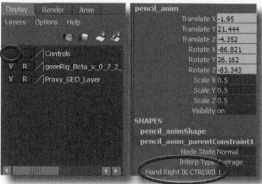

constraintWeights_
start.ma
constraintWeights_
end.ma

2 Scrubbing through the animation, we can see that the hands go through the motion of giving the pencil, but the blue hand doesn't actually take it. Right now there is only a parent constraint on the pencil for the pink hand.

3 In the layer panel, turn on the Controls layer to see the rig controls. Select the control on the pencil and click on pencil_anim_parentConstraint1 in the Channel Box. Here we can see the weight attribute for the right hand since the pencil is constrained to it.

HOT TIP

Constraint weights don't have to be switched over one frame. They can blend over however many frames you want by simply setting the weight keys further apart. Then the constraint will gradually drift into the next one. You can even edit the blend's curve in the Graph Editor. For animations like this one, that obviously wouldn't work, but for situations without obvious contact changes it can be handy.

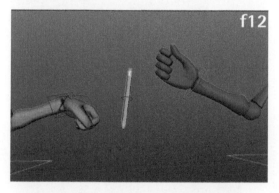

f12

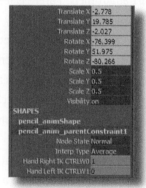

5 You'll see the new weight for the left hand (the blue hand) created in the Channel Box, but now the pencil floats between both hands. This is because both weights are on, pulling the object equally to keep it exactly between them.

6 Select the pencil control. At frame 32, set the Hand Left weight to 0 (off). Then select both weights, right click and choose Key Selected to set a key on both weights. If you scrub through now, the pencil stays with the pink hand the entire animation again.

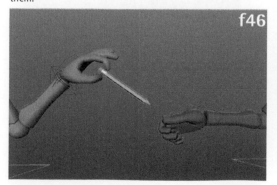

f46

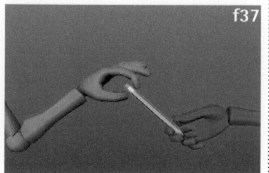

f37

8 The pencil should now get taken by the blue hand after frame 33. On your own projects, remember to design your animation so you have the right pose to pick up a prop and make the switch look natural.

9 You'll notice that the pencil goes through the pink hand's fingers after it is taken. Once we have the constraint working properly, its much easier to animate the fingers following the pencil as they let go. Open constraintWeights_end.ma to see the final result.

Animating with Constraints

THERE WILL INEVITABLY be situations where the easiest way to animate something is to keyframe it at certain places, and constrain it in others. Maya makes this simple with an attribute called "Blend Parent," which we can key on and off depending on what we need at a given moment. When Blend Parent is set to off (0), Maya will ignore any constraints on an object and follow the keyframe data. When Blend Parent is on (1), it will ignore keyframes and conform to any constraints currently active. The best part about Blend Parent is it's created automatically whenever you set a key on a constrained object, or constrain something that already has keyframes set on it. When either of these situations happens, Maya creates a pairBlend node that allows us to switch between the two modes (or even blend somewhere in between, hence the name...).

Many times, I find animations that need this approach are simplest when done in a rather straight-ahead fashion. That isn't to say the animation isn't planned out, it most certainly is, but I've always found keeping track of things easiest if the constraints are done during the blocking process. We're going to take that approach here, where we'll start by animating an object (a bouncing ball: the cornerstone of animation education), constrain it to a platform, then keyframe it again, constrain it to a claw, and finally keyframe it through the end. Sounds complicated in theory, but this exercise with a living ball as our character will show you how simple it really is.

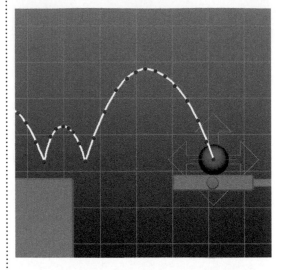

1 Open ballCourse_constraints1.ma and switch to the front view. I've done some preliminary animation of a ball hopping over to a platform, which is also animated. Scrub through and you'll see that the ball doesn't follow the platform after frame 41.

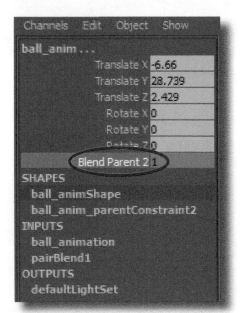

4 At frame 41, right click on the Blend Parent attribute and do Key Selected to set a key on it. This ensures that we will be at 1 (on) at the frame where we want the ball to start following the platform. The channel will turn orange once you set the key.

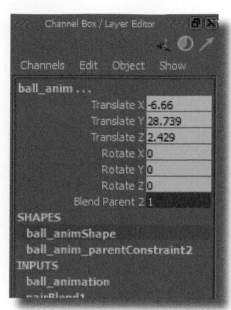

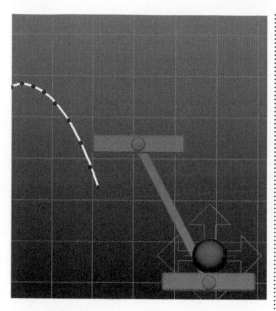

ballCourse_
constraints1.ma

2 Select the platform the ball is on, then the ball move control, and in the animation menu set go to Constrain > Parent. Notice that our channels turn green, indicating both keyframe and constraint data, and the Blend Parent attribute automatically appears.

3 Scrubbing through the animation, we see that the ball now follows the platform, but stays there the entire time. Because Blend Parent is on (1), Maya ignores the keys and follows the constraint. We need to key it on at f41, but have it off up until then to see the animation.

HOT TIP

An "all or nothing" approach is usually best when working with constraints. If it's a more complex character animation, it's often easier to ignore any constraints until the animaton is in its polish phase. Then you can constrain props without worrying about having to shift frames around or make big changes to the movement.

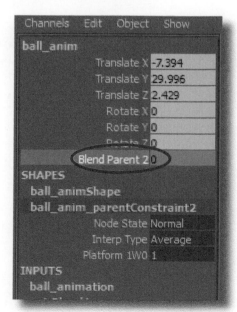

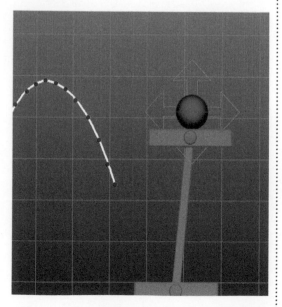

5 Go to the frame before, frame 40, and set Blend Parent to 0 (off). Right click it and key selected again. Since this will be the first key for Blend Parent, all the frames up to it will be off as well.

6 Scrub again and you'll see that the ball is once again animated until frame 41, where it follows the platform perfectly.

Animating w/ Constraints (cont'd)

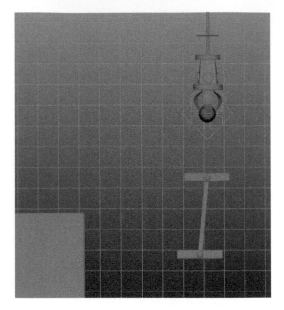

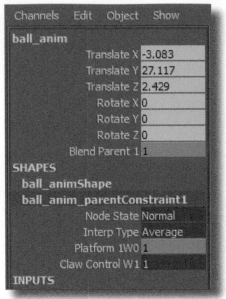

7 Open ballCourse_constraints2.ma. This file has everything we've just done, as well as the blocking animation to get the ball up to where the claw grabs it. Scrub through to frame 88.

8 Select the claw control, then the ball control and go to Constrain > Parent. Notice in the Channel Box that we get a Claw Control W1 attribute. Remember that these weight attributes tell Maya which constraint is currently active.

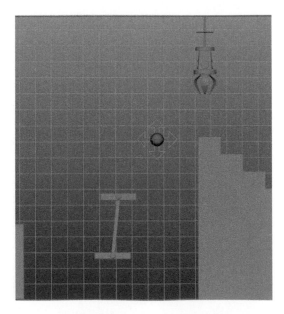

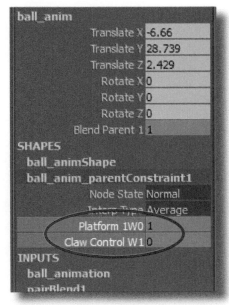

11 At frame 88, key the Blend Parent to 1. This makes it switch on over one frame, making our transition seamless. The ball still doesn't follow the constraints properly though, as we need to set keys on the weights to tell Maya which constraint we want active.

12 At frame 41, RMB > Key Selected to set a key with the Platform weight at 1, and the Claw Control at 0. The ball will snap back to the platform. However, it should follow the claw at frame 88, so the weights need to change there.

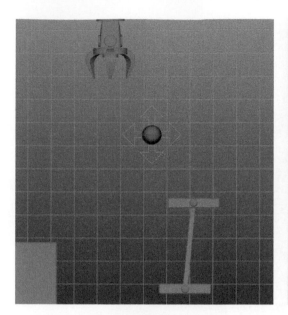

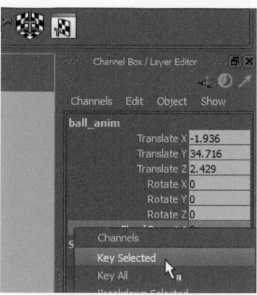

9 If you scrub, you'll notice the ball acting strangely at the constrained parts of the animation. This is because, since both constraint weights are on, they both pull at the ball equally.

10 Let's key the Blend Parent so the ball starts to follow the claw's constraint at frame 88. Go to frame 87, enter 0 in the Blend Parent attribute and RMB > Key Selected. At f75, key the Blend Parent at 0 as well. This will make the ball follow its keyed animation from frames 75-87.

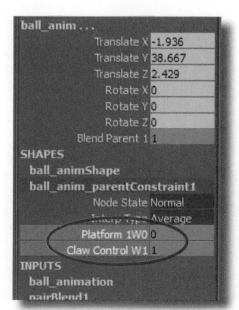

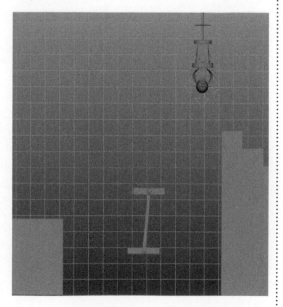

13 Set a key on both weights at frame 87 so this value holds through there. Then at frame 88 key the weights at the opposite values; the platform at 0 and the claw control at 1. Also key the Blend Parent back to 1 so it switches to following the constraint.

14 Now the ball stays with the platform when it's supposed to, jumps on its own from f75-f87, and follows the claw after frame 88.

Animating w/ Constraints (cont'd 2)

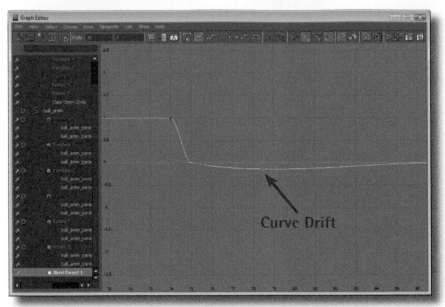

15 If you notice the ball behaving strangely during the constrained sections, check the Graph Editor. If the curves for the Blend Parent or weight attributes have any drift in them, they will mess up the constraints. Be sure to zoom in and check the curves closely, as they can look flat zoomed out.

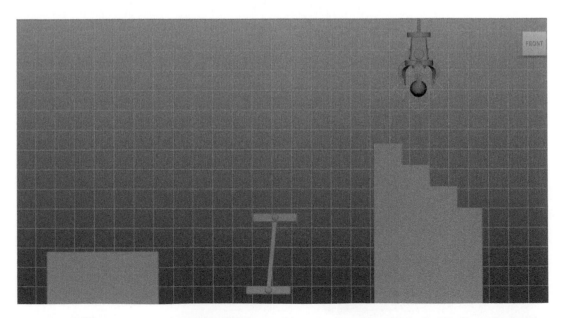

17 Open ballCourse_constraints3.ma and it will have everything we've done, along with the final blocking animation of the ball being released and bouncing down the stairs. We can't see it, however, because we need to key Blend Parent off once more, to tell Maya to once again use the keyframe data on the ball.

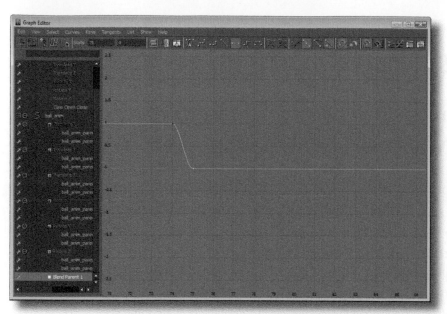

ballCourse_
constraints3.ma

16 If you find this happening, simply select the curves and set them to flat, linear, or stepped tangents using the buttons at the top of the Graph Editor. Any of these tangent types will work for this purpose. See Chapter 2 for more details on how the different tangent types work.

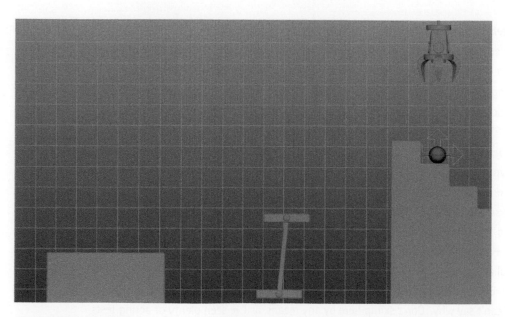

18 At frame 112, key Blend Parent to 1 to hold it through that frame, then key it to 0 at frame 113. Scrubbing through, you should see the ending blocking animation. We now have blocking of all the animation, including the constraints. If you have more constraints in an animation, remember to always have the active constraint's weight keyed at 1, and all others at 0. Always set a redundant key at the frame before the weights and Blend Parent change to hold the current state up to that point. Remembering those two steps will get you through using any number of constraints, no matter how many there are!

The Right Stuff:
Making sure shots on your reel have everything you need to get noticed
by Eric Luhta

ASSEMBLING SHOTS FOR YOUR DEMO REEL CAN BE TRICKY, particularly if you're trying to get your first animation gig. When thinking about what goes on a reel, every animator asks themselves, "What does the person judging my reel want to see?" But rather than give you an arbitrary checklist of types of shots to do, let me impart some ideas that I've come to see as much more important. While there are no surefire ways to make a reel that will guarantee you the job you apply for, here are some elements that will help you stand out from the crowd. If you work hard to incorporate these elements successfully in everything on your reel, getting a job will likely be much easier.

Entertainment The reason for doing any type of character animation at all is, in the end, to entertain. The word entertainment doesn't just mean "funny." Anything that engages us, makes us interested, makes us feel something, and that we want to keep watching is entertainment. A tragic, sorrowful acting scene is just as entertaining as a slapstick pantomime bit if it's successful. Look at every piece you've created and ask yourself "if this wasn't my own work and it came on TV or the movie screen, would I want to watch it or have it be part of something I paid to see?" Be honest with yourself, and if you decide (or others you trust tell you) it's not, rework it or create a new shot that is entertaining.

Physicality The physics and body mechanics of what you've animated have to be working in a believable way. If you're applying for professional animation work, the people evaluating your reel will see poor physicality instantly. If you struggle with physical animation (and many of us do, including myself), get lots of feedback from others! Even non-animators will often be able to say something doesn't feel right, even if they can't say why. Don't skimp here by any means, as I've seen plenty of acting tests that had really nice acting choices, but the unpolished physicality was distracting and ultimately hurt the work. Study live reference of the physical movement in your shot, and seek lots of feedback until everyone tells you it feels good. Correct physicality is the one aspect of animation that isn't subjective.

Believable Characters As a character animator, your job is to give things their personalities and souls! Even if you're doing a simple physical test, it should be done by a character you've created for yourself—one who has a past, a unique personality, likes and dislikes, different experiences that shaped who they currently are, and more. It may seem like overkill at first, but working a character's backstory out before you do a test will surprise you with the choices that it opens up to you. Creating a character will give you limits; things that this particular being would never do and approaches which they will gravitate towards. Limits are where creativity truly thrives.

Sincere Acting The acting of your characters should be carefully considered and worked out with much diligence. Every action should have a reason for being in there, from the broadest gesture to the smallest eye dart. Avoid theatrical, "animationy" cliche acting and use lots of reference to come up with fresh yet appropriate choices for your characters. Analyze the gestures you're using and ask yourself "Are these motions I see people doing in real life or in live action movies and not just in animation?" If not, work to find something better—it will set you apart more than you probably realize. Also, study subtext in life and film and make use of it whenever possible. Bland characters are doing and saying exactly what they are thinking inside, interesting characters are often contrasting their internal thought with their external action.

Story As much as possible, you should try to tell a little story with your shots. Have a twist or something that surprises, like an unexpected result of the character's actions or an interesting take on a line of dialogue you're animating to. Dialogue tests should imply a larger picture and story beyond what you've animated. Showing command over story crafting, even in simple terms, will get you very far indeed. Something with a good story to it and an interesting acting performance, even if it's not the most polished work, will be better received than amazingly polished animation that is boring to watch.

Those are the core elements I think every animator should work to have in their tests, and do your best to have all of them to some degree. So even if you're doing a shot to work on something very standard, like lifting a heavy object, you can easily incorporate character, story, entertainment, and physicality to create something that not only demonstrates your animation craft, but also your skill as a storyteller and filmmaker. Stop thinking only as an animator, and instead also as a storyteller and entertainer, and you'll soon create a reel that gets you in the door.

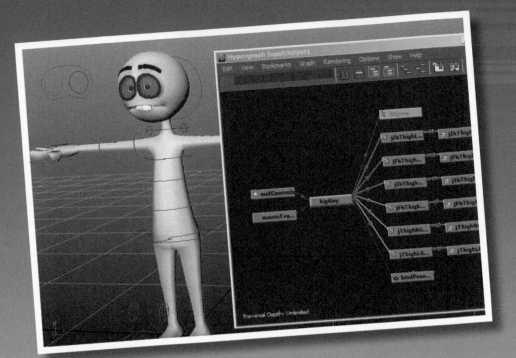

■ The most commonly sought-after skill in an animator besides animation skill is rigging knowledge. This is because animators with a little bit of awareness of the techniques behind the controls can solve production problems on the fly.

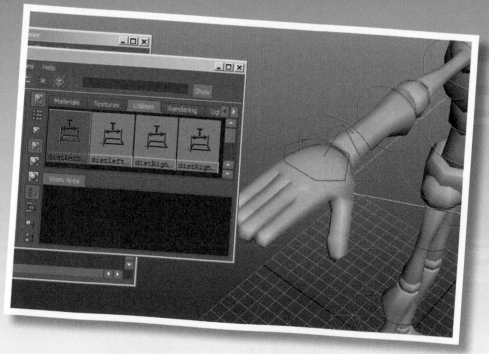

6

Rigging Cheats

EVERY ANIMATOR HAS RUN INTO PROBLEMS with a rig at some point in their career. Be it a hidden controller or bad weighting, a rig problem can ruin your day quickly. This is why knowing a few cheats about rigs is a good idea. In the latest version of Maya, these rig cheats are ultra-stable and time-saving. You'll (hopefully) never again be working on a scene only to be stopped in your tracks by a misbehaving skeleton. We've scoured the web to find a few new rigs to include with this edition of How to Cheat in Maya, so let's go ahead and dive into the best rigs the web has to offer and see what we can find...

Rig Testing

ET'S FIRST RUN THROUGH a few of the things you should identify in your rigs before you start working with them.

In an ideal production setting, you are given enough time to test your rigs before you have to animate shots. This is in an ideal setting. Not very many productions are ideal! Schedules sometimes demand that you are producing work on day 1. When the deadlines are that tight, we need to have a quick list of things to check to make sure our rigs are going to behave how we want them to.

Some of these cheats will reveal characteristics about a rig that aren't necessarily indications that the rig is broken or low quality. These characteristics might include scaling breaking after a certain point, IK/FK switch channels being on the same control that you are using for posing, or proxy meshes hidden in the rig. It would be quite a shame if you completed a shot using a new rig only to see later on that an attribute or parameter was set incorrectly.

Since all rigs are slightly different, the locations, names, and even geometry type of the controls we point out in the following cheats may not be the same in your production rigs. However, there is a certain amount of standardization inherent in rigging, and we'll expect you can always find the "IK hand controller" or the "FK head controller" no matter what character you're working with. To get used to this, in this chapter we'll use the semi-standardized names to describe the rigs.

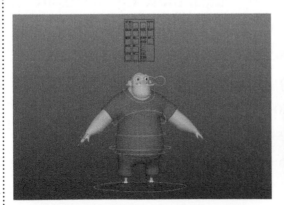

1 Open Groggy_Test.ma. We're going to test two things right now: controller symmetry, and controller object space.

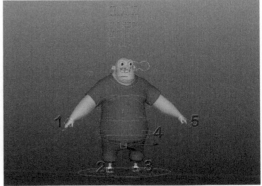

2 Select his IK hand controllers, his IK feet controllers, and his IK pelvis controller. The first thing you want to check is that all of the controllers move in the same world space, and that they are symmetrical.

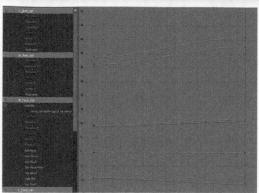

Groggy_Test.ma

3 Set a key on frame 1 with the controllers in place. On frame 40, move the controllers forward in world space substantially different from that of his master controller.

4 Now we check if the controllers are in world space. With the controllers still selected, open the Graph Editor. Uh oh. Look at all of the different translations on these controllers!

If you look closely, the arm's object space is not aligned with the feet or the pelvis. What this means is we need to be careful when we are posing the character, especially in cycles, because this rig was not set up with "FORWARD" being represented by only the Translate Z channel. Below, you can see that if we move the controllers in the Z channel alone, the results are totally unpredictable. This rig would be very unwieldy if we used IK arms in a walk cycle. If you must use this character with arms in IK mode, then it's easiest to pose the character using "WORLD" translation mode by holding down **W** and LMB dragging to the left on the marking menu that appears. Also, the infinity curve type will be "cycle with offset" for all three translation channels (not just Z as it would be normally) for a character like this. More on that in Chapter 9 on cycles.

HOT TIP

You can also check in the Channel Box to see if all world controllers are moving in world space by moving them, and then selecting each individually and seeing if the values change.

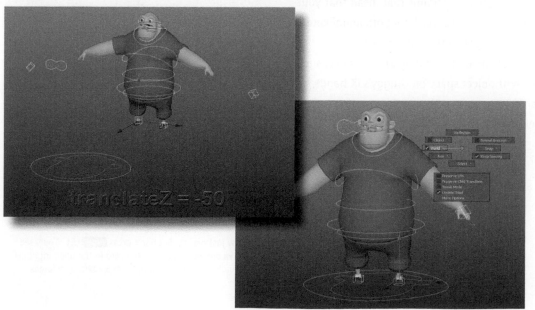

Rig Testing (cont'd)

RIGS CAN HAVE IDIOSYNCRASIES that you come to learn over time. We took a look at the Groggy rig in the last section and found that IK arms will require us to have a few extra steps to make our cycles perfect (again, more on that in the "Stride Length" section in Chapter 9). There are many reasons that rigs have different characteristics, though. Different proportions, the rigging pose, and the general use for the rig (some rigs are designed to be able to blend mocap data into a robust control system, for example). But there ARE a few things that pretty much all rigs should have under control, pun intended.

The first is that setting all of the controller's attributes to zero, or "zeroing," puts the rig back into the initial pose. This is vitally important for avoiding gimbal lock while animating; it is important for dealing with animation curves while you are polishing your scene; and it is vitally important for creating cycles with a set stride length.

The second requirement is that animation can be copied and pasted on the rig. With most rigs, this works fine. However, sometimes rigs have very complex hierarchies filled with connections and nested constraints that mean that your animation is not copied perfectly. We'll try both animExport and good ol' Copy Keys to get to the bottom of this.

While many of the quirks of a rig are workable, such as the slightly different object space on Groggy's IK hands, some things are show stoppers. Let's see how this rig stacks up on these two essential issues.

1 Open Groggy_Zero.ma. See how Groggy is in a pose? Let's try "zeroing" him out. Drag a selection around his whole rig to choose all of his controls.

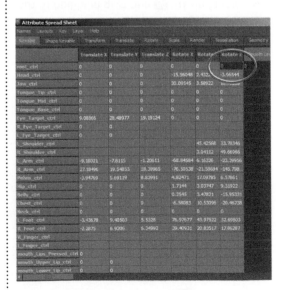

4 Now just type 0. But don't press *Enter* yet. You'll see Maya automatically puts the zero in the upper right cell when you have selected multiple cells, rows, or columns.

140

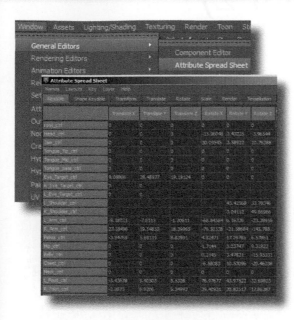

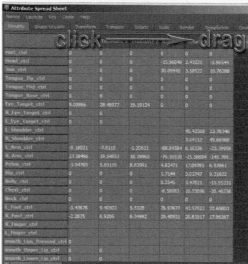

Groggy_Zero.ma

HOT TIP

The Attribute
Spreadsheet
is very under-
utilized. Spend
some time
making changes
to multiple
cells by shift
selecting them,
or by dragging
a selection box
on an area and
typing in values.

2 Now let's open the Attribute Spreadsheet. This is a very under-utilized panel in Maya. It displays in spreadsheet format ALL of the attributes for the selected objects. Nice!

3 Now to zero all of the controls back to their origins, we're going to select all of the Translate and Rotate Columns. LMB click and drag across the very top of the Attribute Spreadsheet, selecting all six columns.

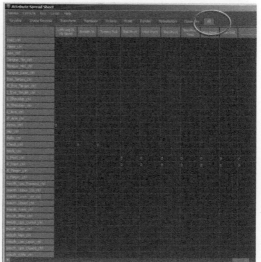

5 Now press *Enter*. Groggy passes the test! He snaps right back to his initial pose. This is great.

6 We only zeroed his Translate and Rotate channels. If there were other channels (IK switches, foot roll, etc.) you would have to find them in the All Keyable tab of the Attribute Spreadsheet.

Rig Testing (cont'd 2)

1 Open Groggy_Copy.ma. This is a completed animation scene; but what do we do if we need to copy the animation onto another rig? We're going to show you the normal way with animExport, and a great cheat using Copy Keys that works even faster.

2 First we need to enable the animExport plugin. Go to Window > Settings/Preferences > Plug-in Manager. Find animImportExport.mll and check both the Loaded and Auto Load boxes.

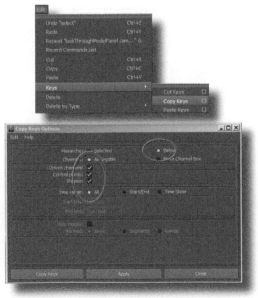

5 Let's try this using just the clipboard. This is much quicker and useful if you don't need to save the animation, just copy it fast. (Very common if there's a rig update in production.) Open Groggy_Copy.ma again and select Groggy:root_group in the outliner.

6 Go to Edit > Keys > Copy Keys □. This dialogue is the same as the animExport dialogue, because what you are doing is the same, except you are only copying keys to the clipboard and not saving them for later. Copy the settings above.

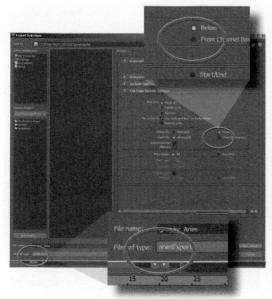

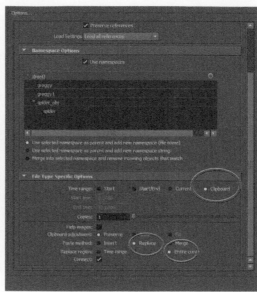

Groggy_Copy.ma

3 Now in the outliner, select the animated Groggy's rig group node, Groggy:root_group Go to File > Export Selected. In the Export dialogue, change the type to animExport and leave everything default, except change Hirearchy to Below. Name the file groggy_Anim.

4 Now we'll import that animation onto the static Groggy rig. Select his main rig group, groggy1:root_Group. Go to File > Import. Make sure the file type is set to animImport, and copy the rest of the settings circled above. The animation copies perfectly.

HOT TIP

At its core, Maya handles animExport and Copy Keys the same way. One just writes a file and the other stores it in your clipboard. The nice thing about Copy Keys is you don't have to hunt for the saved file, AND, you can copy keys from one scene and open another scene to paste them into – Maya keeps the curves in the clipboard.

7 When you press the Copy Keys button, the script editor returns "// Result: 281" in the Command Line. That means 281 curves were copied to the clipboard. Now select the static Groggy's rig group groggy1:root_Group.

8 Go to Edit > Keys > Paste Keys □. Copy my settings above and hit Paste Keys. Beautiful. The curves in the clipboard are pasted onto Groggy and he moves as expected. This is extremely useful if Replace Reference does not work and you need to copy animation onto a new rig!

143

Sprucing It Up

ONE OF THE BEST WAYS to cheat in animation is to take advantage of the fact that Maya interpolates motion for you. For example, in 2D animation done for TV, it is still typical for the animation to be done on "2s" – every other frame is held for two frames, giving you effectively 12 frames per second instead of the normal 24. Well, this looks choppy to the well-trained eye. In 3D, unless we are using stepped mode, there will ALWAYS be motion on every frame. When people say "on 2s" in Maya, what they mean is they have set key poses every two frames – but there is still motion on every frame.

The way we can cheat using this property of 3D is to "spruce up" a rig with some dynamic objects. We can get away with using far fewer poses and less movement, because the dynamic objects will be constantly moving. It will take away the choppy feeling and make it look like the "world" in which the character is living is smooth and continuous, even with staccato movement in the character itself.

We're going to take a scene that has VERY crude animation on Moom, and add a ponytail and earrings using two very different dynamic methods. You will then see, when we play back the animation, that the scene has taken on a more dynamic quality. The mere addition of these dynamic objects and the secondary motion they create helps us cheat the animation. When you are on extremely tight deadlines and can only afford the time to set a few key poses in a shot, this cheat will save you.

1 Open moom_Dynamics_Start.ma. I've done a lot of the work for you by setting up the earring and ponytail geometry and starting the process of creating the dynamics objects.

4 Select the curve and go to nHair > Make Selected Curves Dynamic. In the Attribute editor under the dynamics Tab of hairSystemShape1, change Bend Resistance to 10. Select follicleShape1 in the Outliner in the hairSystem1Follicles group, and change the Point Lock attribute to Base.

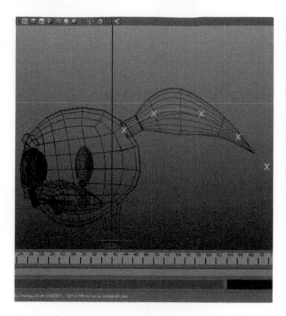

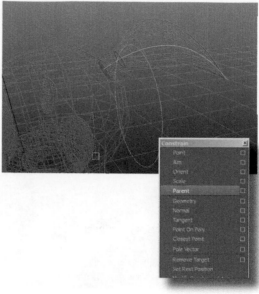

moom_Dynamics_
Start.ma
moom_Dynamics_
Finish.ma

HOT TIP

Depending on
your computer
performance,
you may not be
able to watch
the dynamics
play at speed.
Maya solves
dynamics in
real time,
so normally
every frame
must play. To
watch complex
dynamics or
to watch on a
slower machine,
change your
playback to
Every Frame in
the Time slider
preferences.

2 Let's first create the ponytail dynamics. We're going to
use a simple hair curve and wrap the geo to it. Switch
to the Side View and draw a nurbs curve through the
ponytail using the EP curve tool.

3 Now select Moom's head control, and shift select the
new curve you created. Hit F2 to bring up the Animation
menu set, and choose Constrain > Parent. Hit F5 to switch
to the Dynamics menu set for the next step.

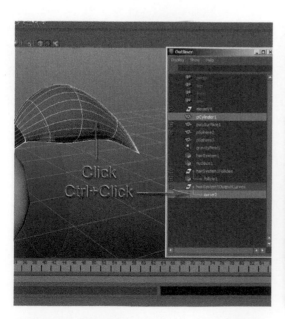

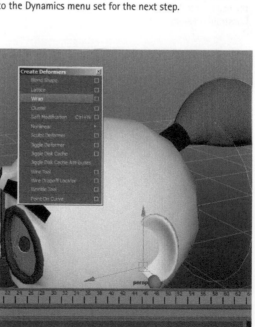

5 On frame 1, select the ponytail mesh. In the Outliner,
find the newly created hairSystem1OutputCurves group.
Curve2 inside is the result of the dynamics applied to curve1
that you created. *ctrl* click curve2.

6 Hit F2 to bring up the Animation menu set again and
go to Create Deformers > Wrap. Press play and see the
ponytail whipping back and forth. See how the scene has a
sense of fluidity even though the animation is really rough?
You cheater you.

145

Sprucing It Up (cont'd)

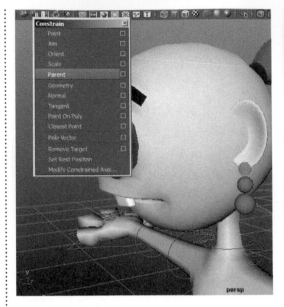

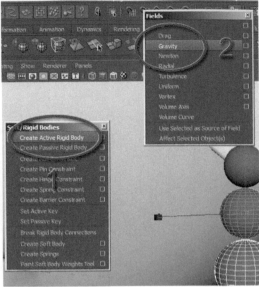

1 Hair curves are a quick solution but are not ideal for meshes that shouldn't deform. We're going to use rigid bodies to make the earrings dynamic . On frame 1 select the head control, *Shift* select the top of the earring, and go Constrain > Parent.

2 Now let's make the two other spheres rigid bodies. Select both of them, and hit F5 to switch to dynamics. Go to Soft/Rigid Bodies > Create Active Rigid Body. With both of them still selected, click on Fields > Gravity.

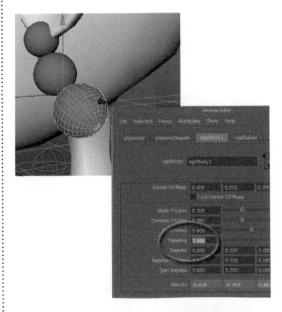

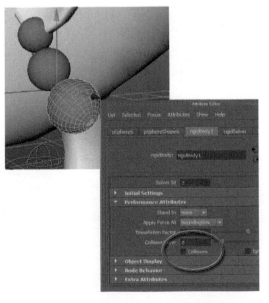

5 There are a few settings we need to change to make the earrings move correctly. First in the rigidBody1 tab, with the bottom sphere selected, find the Rigid Body Attributes section and change Damping to 5.

6 Next, scroll down in the attribute editor to find the Performance Attributes section. Turn off collisions. Select the middle sphere, navigate to the rigidBody2 tab and repeat the last two steps.

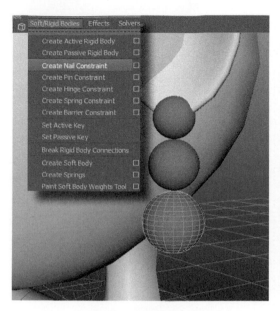

3 We need to set up these spheres to move with each other. The Nail Constraint is perfect for this. Select the bottom sphere and go to Soft/Rigid Bodies > Create Nail Constraint.

4 Move the new Nail Constraint to the bottom of the middle sphere, *Shift* select the middle sphere and hit *P* to parent it. Now repeat the last two steps for the middle sphere, creating a Nail Constraint and then parenting it to the top sphere.

moom_Dynamics_
Start.ma
moom_Dynamics_
Finish.ma

HOT TIP

The Nail Constraint is the perfect dynamic constraint for swinging objects like earrings. There are many other types of dynamic constraints and I encourage you to try them all. Hinge Constraints are like Nail Constraints but they only rotate on one axis, and Spring Constraints are like Nail Constraints but they stretch!

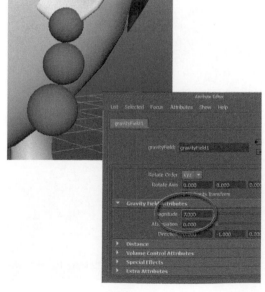

7 Select gravityField1 in the outliner and change the Magnitude attribute to 7.

8 Now hit the play button! Watch how the ponytail flops around with the head movement, and how the earrings swing nicely from Moom's ears. As crude as the motion is in the scene, there's something soothing to the eye to see nice smooth dynamic movement.

Visual Switches

ADDING SWITCHES TO YOUR PANEL is a great way to cheat the normal method of having to select hidden controls and adjust multiple channels. It can be cumbersome, unintuitive, and simply take much longer to hunt down the right channel when working with switches. Let's simplify this whole process and give you a simple, easy-to-use, easy-to-read switch that you control in panel. Once again I've done a lot of the work for you, by creating the switch and output nodes you'll need to hook this into any IK/FK system. In fact, you can actually use the files included in this cheat with any rig and in any scene you are working on in production; I'll show you how.

This cheat assumes that you do all of your switching across one frame. Although the issue of single-frame switching or multi-frame switching is still out to jury, this cheat more than makes up for the advantages of switching across multiple frames with the visual feedback you get.

We'll first import the switch and familiarize ourselves with its control. We'll then constrain it to the wrist of our character and hook up the correct channels. Then we'll create some animation on the arm and practice switching using our new switch. You'll be amazed how nice it is to have the visual feedback on your FK/IK switches, and I'm sure you'll be applying this cheat to all of your rigs in the future.

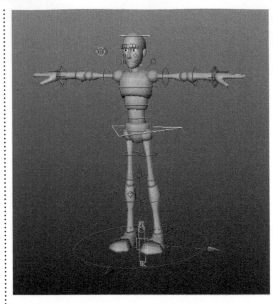

1 Open goon_Switch.ma. Here we see Goon with his arm out, ready for our handy little switch to be added to his rig. Go to File > Import and choose switch.ma. The switch will load into the scene at the world origin.

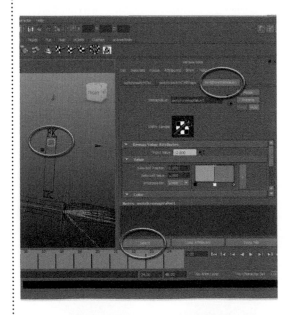

4 Now we hook up the switch. Select the nurbs circle switchCtrl. In the Attribute Editor (*ctrl*+*A*) switch to the remapValue1 tab and hit Select at the bottom of the Attribute Editor.

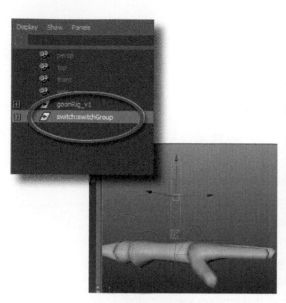

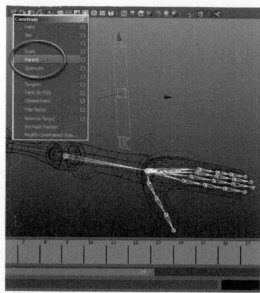

goon_Switch.ma
goon_Switch_End.
ma

2 In the outliner, select switchGroup and in the panel move the group to be up somewhere near his left wrist. Scale the group down a bit to be a nice size.

3 Let's first constrain the control to the wrist bone, so that it moves with the wrist regardless of which system is being used. Select the joint in his forearm, LowerArm_ Left, *ctrl* select the switchGroup in the outliner, hit F2 to switch to Animation, and click on Constrain > Parent.

HOT TIP

The remapValue node changes one value range into another with less scene overhead than expressions, or driven keys. I chose "None" for interpolation in the remapValue node because I want to change immediately between FK and IK, but the other interpolation types give you very detailed control over the blending. Open it up and see for yourself.

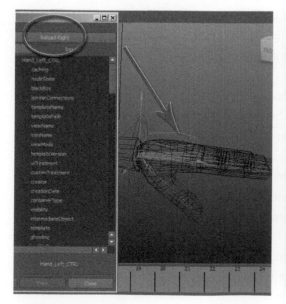

5 Go to Window > General Editors > Connection editor. The left column will already have your remapValue node's attributes loaded. Select Goon's Hand_Left_CTRL in the panel, and in the connection editor, hit Reload Right, at the top.

6 In the left column, select outValue. In the right column, scroll down until you find ik_Weight, and select it. These two attributes are now connected. Move the arm a bit and test it out! Your switch now changes the arm control system from FK to IK, and does so in a very visual way.

Holding Your Own

by Kenny Roy

IN TODAY'S ANIMATION MARKET, there is a high probability you will be working at small to mid-sized studios for the majority of your career. Simply put, even if you had all of the animator positions at the top ten animation and visual effects studios in the world (Pixar, ILM, etc.) put together you are still only talking about 1000 or so jobs. This is not meant to discourage you from trying to be an animator at the top studios in the world, rather to prepare you for the career opportunities you WILL have.

It is undeniable that animation is the CG task that requires specialization above all others. Animation combines the most technique with the most artistry in CG. Modelers and lighters might complain at this statement, but it's true. All you have to do is look at the salaries and you'll see that animators do the best out of all CG artists. The reason I'm bringing this up is because you are presumably on your way to becoming a marketable animator in the animation industry, ergo you are specializing. But while your supervisors and producers are hardly ever going to call on the modelers to pitch in on animation, in both slow times and crunch times animators are often called upon to pitch in on other tasks.

How do you know if you know enough about the other disciplines of CG to not be a burden when the deadline looms? I'll tell you here, in this short guide. I'll list the disciplines and then a good minimum amount of knowledge you should have regarding each one.

Design, Storyboards - Drawing skill is coming back in style. In the early days of CG it was enough if you could "learn the computer." Now many art students take up the mouse and can draw amazingly as well. Keep a sketchpad with you at all times, because stick figures won't cut it.

Modeling - You should know your way around a model, be able to fix problems like open edges, five-sided faces, asymmetry, flipped normals, etc. You should understand how pivot relates to blendshapes and bind pose. You should be able to model (cleanly) simple objects and props.

UV/Texturing - You might not have the best techniques for laying out UVs, but you should know a problem when you see it, like overlapping UVs or UVs outside the normalized range. Be able to switch UV sets and apply textures to different sets. Be able to load textures and assign them to materials.

Materials/Shading - Know the difference between the common material types. Be able to create some simple shader looks like glossy plastic, matte paper, a mirror, and skin. Not necessarily final materials, but enough that if the production is in a pinch, the client won't freak out when they see your materials as placeholders.

Rigging - Know how to rig props correctly, with a controller, pivots centered on the origin, geometry with no history, clean hierarchies, and frozen transforms. Know how to diagnose common rig problems, including double transforms, weighting issues, poor rotation order selection. Know all of the common rig properties that will lead to difficulties in animation, like the ones described in this chapter regarding controller symmetry and object space.

Lighting - Know how to place and choose simple lighting setups. Know how to create shadow-mapped or raytraced shadows. Know how to place objects and lights into render layers.

Rendering - Understand common file formats and common output dimensions for TV and film. Understand the different renderers and their qualities. Be able to set up a scene to batch render with the correct output path.

Compositing - Know what an alpha channel is and how to make a garbage matte for use in your Maya scenes. Know generally what the different blending modes (multiply, screen, for example) will produce when compositing layers.

I know this list seems long. And while you will definitely get a job as an animator without knowing any of these skills, it is better to know these things than to be clueless when your studio needs help on the spot. All of the things I mentioned above are easily researched and learned through the Maya help, online forums, and other training resources readily available to those who want to learn. As animators we need to have a few more skills in our wheelhouse because when a deadline quickly approaches, you do not want to be seen as the person who "ONLY knows how to animate."

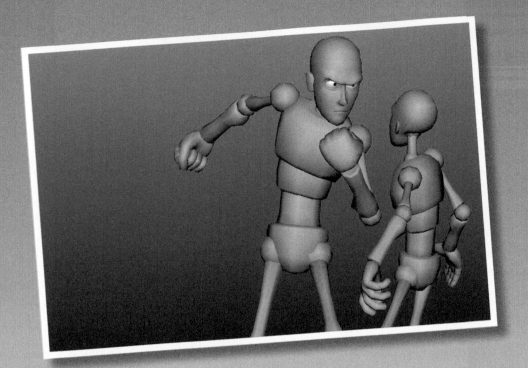

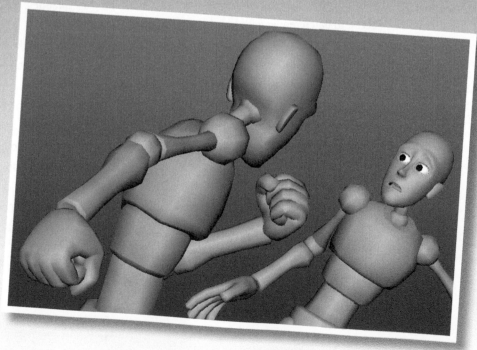

A brilliant animation doesn't look like one if it's not filmed effectively. This chapter contains everything from animating cameras to composition to the camera tools in Maya 2013.

7 Cameras and Layout

AT ITS HEART, animation is about storytelling. And not too long after the camera was invented master storytellers started using them to craft films. As animators, our primary job is to create performances within a scene. However, as the craft becomes more widespread and animators need to be more well rounded, knowing how to manipulate cameras in Maya will become required for the job. Animators wishing to create short films or test animations for their demo reels also have to familiarize themselves with camera work to be able to compete for the top positions at major studios. Finally, knowing a little about film directing, editing, and composition will only help you integrate your performance choices better within the scenes you are given. Let's look at the tools in Maya 2013 that give you true filmmaking power in creating animated performances.

Framing and Lenses

ANIMATORS WORKING WITH MAYA 2013 will find that the camera tools are second to none. They have to be! Maya is the de facto standard of visual effects studios around the world. Visual effects supervisors need to work closely with cinematographers and be able to use the same terminology. If you are planning on a career in visual effects, it will behoove you to understand the fundamentals of camera work, and know how to frame your shot for the greatest impact.

Don't forget your staging! In all scenes it is imperative to make sure your action is staged nicely in order to allow for dynamic camera angles and lenses. Take the time to really practice interesting staging, with dynamic poses and compositions. A lot of times, experimentation will lead to the best choice; time spent "feeling around" the scene will pay dividends when your animation starts coming to life.

When your staging is complete, it's time to pick angles and lenses. Remember that a low angle can make a character seem formidable and aggressive. A high angle can make a character seem small and unassuming. Wide angle lenses distort perspective to an extreme degree, and are good for establishing the scene layout, moving through the scene, and for when you want perspective to play a role in composition. Narrow or "long" lenses remove the effect of perspective on your composition, are great for flattening the scene layout, and are generally not used for moving cameras because of the lack of depth.

Let's apply these principles in a scene that has been staged for us. It is a scene where a bully is about to clobber a smaller student at school. The poses have been set, and now it's time for us to create some cameras to get the right feeling in this scene.

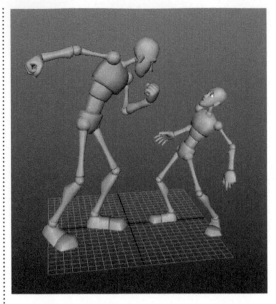

1 Open framing_start.ma. Our characters have been posed, and it's time to set up this shot to get some dynamic camera angles.

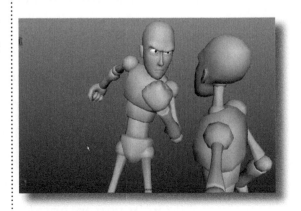

4 This is a good start. We've recognized that the bully should be seen from a low angle so that he looks very forebidding, and the little kid is being pushed close to the frame edge so he feels cornered. However, since the little kid is in between the camera and the bully, he's actually almost as big as the bully in composition.

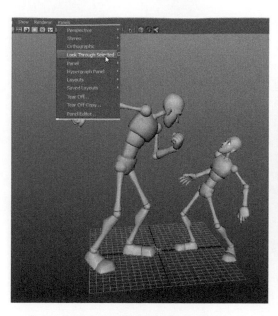

2 Create a camera by going to the Create menu, and selecting Cameras > Camera. A camera will appear at the world origin. Let's switch to this camera by going to the Panels menu, and choosing Look Through Selected.

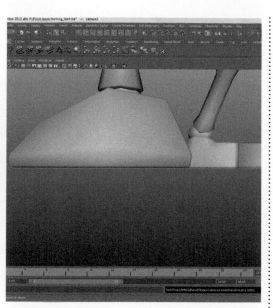

3 Our view changes to the new camera's perspective, and we're staring right into the bully's foot. Charming. Now let's move this camera to an angle facing the bully, and try to make it so that it shows off how big he is.

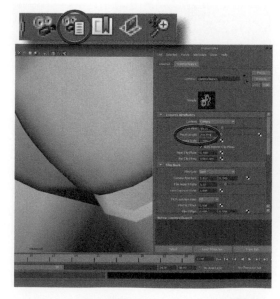

5 Open up the camera's attributes by clicking the small Camera Attributes button in the top left of the panel. In the Focal Length attribute, put in 200. This makes the camera a 200 mm lens, far more telephoto and zoomed in than Maya's default 35 mm.

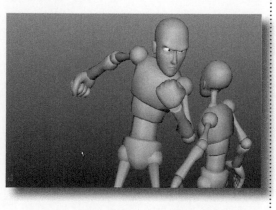

6 Now dolly the camera backwards by *alt* RMB dragging. Notice how the bully is bigger in composition, even though he's farther away? With this nice zoomed lens, the effect of perspective has been diminished and we've flattened the scene to keep the bully larger in composition.

framing_start.ma
framing_finish.ma

HOT TIP

When working with multiple cameras in a scene, choosing with the Outliner and using Look Through Selected is the fastest way to move between them.

Framing and Lenses (cont'd)

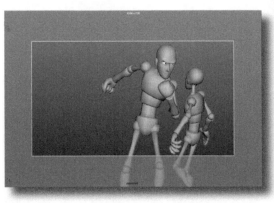

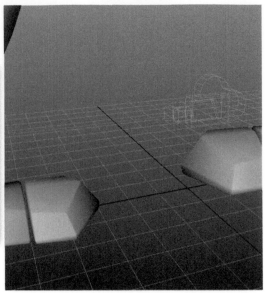

7 But we're still not ready to animate; we have to check what the scene is going to look like once rendered. Hit the Resolution Gate button in the camera panel. The box that appears is our render area, and I'm not happy with the bottom being cut off. Adjust the camera to get their hands in frame.

8 Now let's frame the "reverse" (a camera facing the other character in a scene). Switch back to the Persp view and create another camera, but this time create a Camera, Aim, and Up. This camera type has handles that allow us to keep its orientation well under our control.

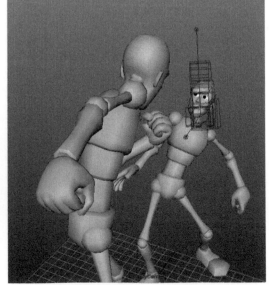

11 In reality ALL cameras have aims, and ups. When you dolly a camera around in Maya, you are actually moving that camera's aim. In fact, it's possible to get this aim so far away from where it needs to be it causes trouble. In the Persp panel, select Look Through crazyCam.

12 It's almost the same angle as our other camera, so what's wrong? Orbit the camera and watch as it behaves totally unpredictably. Its center of interest is very far away, which can happen without you knowing it. The fastest way to get a camera to return to normal is to hit **F** to Frame Selected, and then reframe the shot.

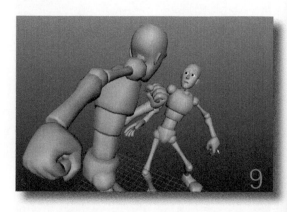

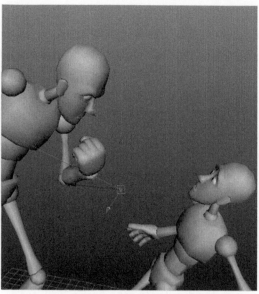

9 Look through the new camera, and use the normal camera tools to frame the shot as above. You'll notice that the aim moves with your camera when you dolly, and that the camera rotates around it when you orbit, (*alt*+LMB).

10 As I said before, the nice thing about a Camera, Aim, and Up, is that you are given controls to precisely control the orientation of your camera. Fine tune the framing of the shot by switching to a two-panel layout and moving the new camera's aim in a Persp panel.

HOT TIP

Pros can spot a default 35 mm camera from a mile away. Using a default camera homogenizes student work. In your personal work, distinguish yourself right away by choosing a new lens for your shots. It might even be a good idea to open the Create > Camera > Camera options box and set your default focal length to 50 or 60 just to be sure you won't accidentally follow the crowd!

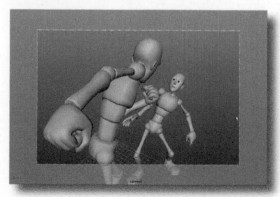

13 Switch back to camera2, and let's make the shot a little bit wider, to emphasize the bully's fist in composition. Set camera2's focal length to 25 and then dolly and pan to frame the shot like above. Don't forget that your cameras have their own undo buffer. ■ and ■ undo and redo camera movements.

14 Every once in a while we'll happen upon a framing that we love, but "Oh no!" we're looking through the Persp camera! No problem! Create a new camera, then Parent Constrain the new camera to the Persp camera with Maintain Offset unchecked. Voila, camera saved!

Camera Sequencer

ONE OF THE BEST WAYS to create and manage a multi-shot sequence is using the Camera Sequencer tool. Introduced in Maya 2011, this tool has become rock solid in stability in Maya 2013. The idea behind this tool is to make it so that complex scenes with multiple cameras can be visualized all within a single Maya panel. In production, it is quite common for a sequence with very complex "hookups" (the animation that continues across an edit from one shot to the next) to be blocked in a single Maya scene and then sliced up into component shots. Certainly at the previz stage, when the director has to make camera placement and editorial choices with very little to go on, this tool will be extremely helpful. Now animators can create an entire sequence within a single scene file, and even do some basic editing with the director to get a better "feel" for a sequence as early in the film as possible.

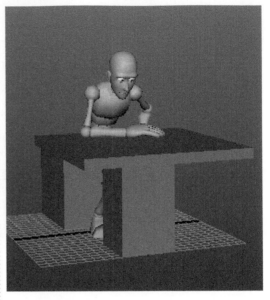

1 Open up sequencer_start.ma. This scene looks familiar! I've extended the timeline just a little bit to give us more frames to work with.

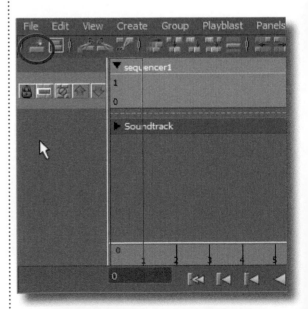

3 Let's now add all of the cameras to the sequence. Click on the Create Shot button in the top left corner of the Camera Sequencer. A shot will appear and its length will match the time slider.

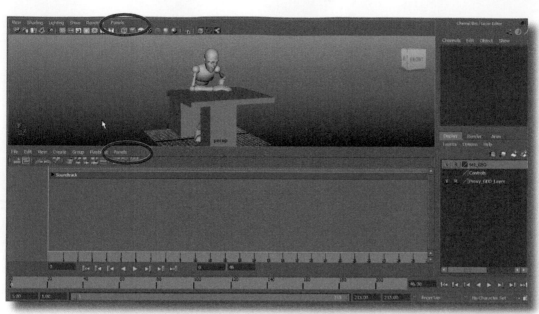

sequencer_start.ma
sequencer_finish.
ma

2 Set your panel layout by going to Panels > Layout > Two Panes Stacked in the viewport menu. Now, in the bottom panel, choose Panels > Panel > Camera Sequencer. The Camera Sequencer will load in the bottom panel.

HOT TIP

You can export the edits you do in the camera sequencer as XML files to use in other software packages, like Final Cut. Just go to File > Export Editorial.

4 Now right click on the added shot and click on Change Camera > camera1. This will designate camera1 as the camera for this shot in the Sequencer.

5 Create two more shots using the Create Shot button, and change their cameras the same way we just did, to camera2 and camera3, respectively. Your Camera Sequencer should look like this. Note that the traditional panel zoom and move tools work the same in this panel.

Camera Sequencer (cont'd)

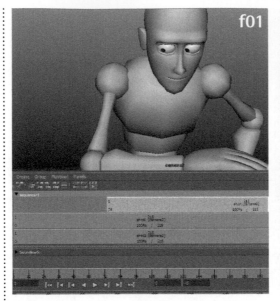

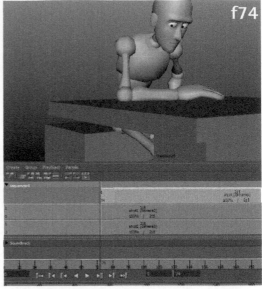

6 So, what exactly is going on? Just like layers in Photoshop, the shot that is on top of the Camera Sequencer will display. Move the top shot to the right by LMB clicking in the middle of it and dragging it to the right. Hit play on the bottom of the Camera Sequencer.

7 You may notice that camera2 is displaying up until the timeline gets to the beginning of shot1 in the Camera Sequencer, at which point it goes to camera1. BUT! Also notice that it goes back to frame 1 as well! We'll fix this now.

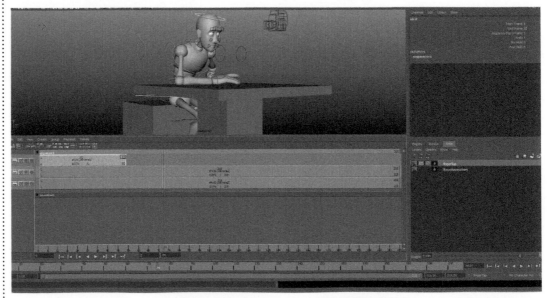

9 Unless you want to render multiple angles and takes of the same motion (called "coverage" in filmmaking) you are most likely going to want to keep linear time in your sequences. Manipulate the shots by grabbing the top row of numbers instead. Drag the top right number to 52 and hit play. The camera switches from camera1 at frame 52 and camera2 picks up the action.

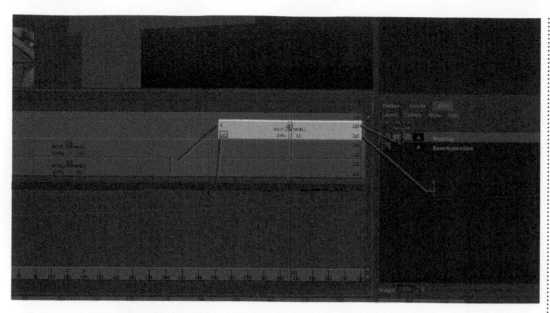

8 There are four numbers on a shot in the Camera Sequencer. The top row corresponds to the start and end frame in the scene file itself. If you move or scale a shot in the Sequencer, you are effectively editing non-linearly in time. The bottom row of numbers corresponds to the sequence you are creating. Hence in our shot right now, at f163 in our sequence, Maya is switching to camera1 and playing all of frames 1-215 at fast speed until the end of the sequence.

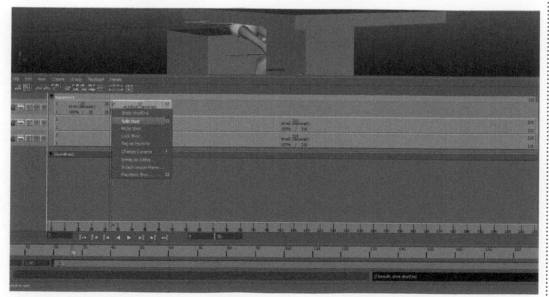

10 We're going to lay out this sequence cinematically, but first let's split shot1 so that we can go back to our "master" shot at the end of the sequence. Drag the timeline in the Camera Sequencer to frame 26. Right click on shot1 and choose Split Shot.

161

Camera Sequencer (cont'd 2)

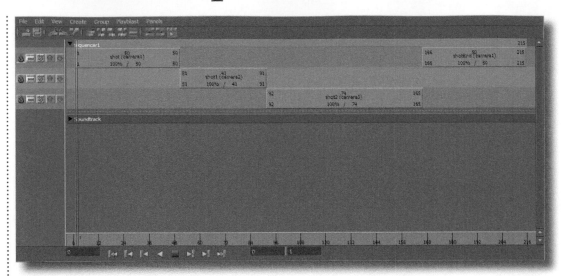

11 Lay out the scene like I have here. We go from camera1 to camera2 when Goon notices the person off-screen. Then we cut to the close-up of his eyes as he watches them pass. Finally back to the wide shot, camera1, to finish the scene. Make sure your shot and sequence frame numbers line up.

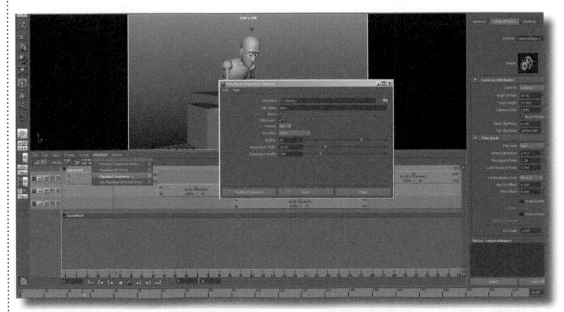

13 If we want to submit this edit choice as its own movie file, it's simple and easy with Maya 2013. Click on Playblast in the Camera Sequencer Panel, and choose Playblast Sequence. Notice how Maya can now playblast Offscreen, meaning program windows that get in the way of the main Maya window will not interrupt the playblasting. Convenient!

12 We need to get a feel for how the shot is going to render, so let's apply the Resolution Gate. Select camera1 in the outliner and open up the attribute editor. Change Fit Resolution Gate to Vertical. In the Display Options tab, check both Display Resolution and Display Gate Mask. Change the Gate Mask Opacity to 1, and Gate Mask Color to black, and change Overscan to 1.0.

HOT TIP

When you are working in the Sequencer, you can not only time your sequence, but also strengthen the framing and composition of your shot by adjusting the camera live. Work with the attribute editor open, and manipulate the camera as it is loaded by the Sequencer. You could even create multiple cameras to start with and then wait to frame them until after they're in sequence.

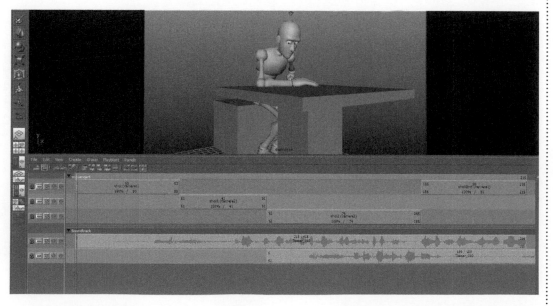

14 A final update to this tool comes in the area of audio. You can add multiple tracks of audio in the Camera Sequencer itself. Just click on File > Import Sequencer Audio and choose a file. Another nice feature is the ability to link audio to a shot. Select a piece of audio and *Shift* select a shot. Right click on the audio and choose Link Audio. Now the audio will match the edit of that shot.

7 Cameras and Layout

UberCam

THE UBERCAM IS A BRAND-NEW addition to the Camera Sequencer that allows you to create a single camera that follows all of the edits of your sequence. This has a lot of potential for production purposes. First, having an animated camera means that you can watch your sequence without having to use the play controls in the Camera Sequencer; you can simply have the UberCam loaded as one of your panels and work this way. Second, rather than render multiple sequences at rendertime, the single UberCam can be chosen as your renderable camera, saving you time when it comes time to composite a sequence. The last benefit is scene overhead and manageability. In a very long sequence you may have a dozen cameras and 20 to 30 edits. With the ability to use this new tool to bake all of this data onto a single camera you can unclutter the outliner and get back to creating compelling performances with your characters.

We'll use the sequence we just finished to practice creating and manipulating UberCams.

1 Open ubercam_start.ma. Change a panel to the Camera Sequencer and hit the Frame All button in the top left corner of the panel. Remember, the normal Maya zoom and move controls work in the Camera Sequencer too.

4 The UberCam is not updated live, however. Change your panel layout to Four Panes in Panels > Layouts. Make the top left panel your UberCam, the top right panel camera3, and the Outliner one of the bottom panels.

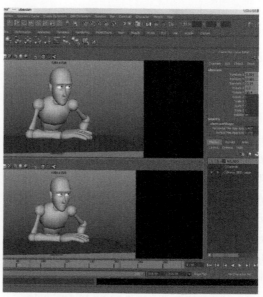

ubercam_start.ma
ubercam_finish.ma

2 Creating the UberCam itself is very simple. In the Camera Sequencer Panel, click on Create > UberCam. Maya will create the camera and it will show up in the Outliner.

3 Change the bottom pane from Camera Sequencer to UberCam. You can either select the UberCam in the Outliner and click on Panels > Look Through Selected, or simply click on Panels > Perspective > ubercam. Now you can watch the sequence playback in this panel while making changes to the animation.

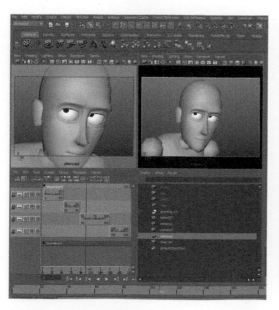

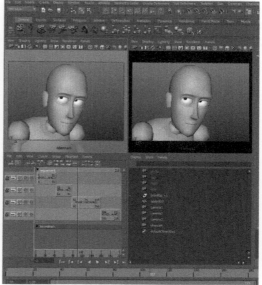

5 Select camera3 and open the attribute editor. Change the focal length attribute to 120. Camera3's focal length changes, but the UberCam's does not. Since it is not a live connection, we have to recreate it.

6 Whenever you make a change to a camera position, focal length, or any animatable attribute, you must recreate the UberCam. Select and delete the UberCam from the Outliner. Change the bottom panel back to the Camera Sequencer and do Create > UberCam. Back in business.

Animating Cameras

NOW THAT YOU ARE FAMILIAR with static cameras, it's time to learn some cheats on animated cameras. You will quickly discover that animated cameras really are a totally different animal.

For starters, audiences have become very savvy and you can't get away with unrealistic movement in your camera work. It stands out badly, and for potential employers demonstrates a lack of understanding of filmmaking. So we'll take a look at animating a camera in a realistic way, as if a person is holding it.

In live-action filmmaking, camera movement has been taken to some extremes; with helicopter cameras, underwater cameras, Steadicam, motion-controlled cameras, huge cranes and boom shots, directors have never stopped searching for new ways to move the camera. Our second scene is going to deal with animating a camera moving in an extreme way.

Within both these scenes, and all of your animation, you should bear a few rules in mind. First, know what kind of camera movement you are trying to recreate. Second, key the camera as little as possible. No matter what kind of effect you are trying to achieve, camera animation looks very choppy very quickly. Last, only move the camera with a purpose. Staging, composition, and story dictate whether or not the camera should be moving.

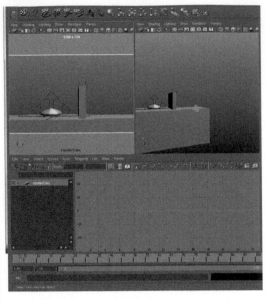

1 Open anim_hand_start.ma. Our familiar bouncing ball animation is going to benefit from an animated camera, as if the camera is hand-held. Prepare the scene by opening three panels, renderCam, Persp view, and the Graph Editor, and the renderCam's attributes.

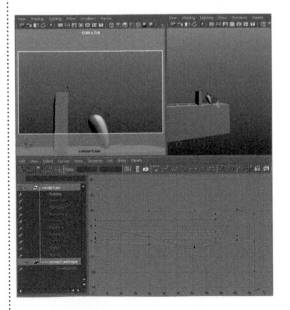

4 Another thing that really makes a camera feel hand-held is it lagging behind the action a little bit. Key the camera again on frame 61 and 68, and make sure the ball is leading the frame.

anim_hand_start.
ma
anim_hand_finish.
ma

2 One of the quickest cheats to make a camera look hand-held is to make it look like the camera operator "notices" the action. Let's achieve this with an animated zoom. Key the Focal Length at 35 on frame 1, and then key it at 60 on frame 36. Flat the tangents in the Graph Editor.

3 Now let's key a little bit of pan and tilt in the camera. Hit **S** to key the camera on frame 1. Then on frame 24, frame the ball in the center of the camera by rotating the camera in the Persp window. Set a key again on frame 36, 43, and 52, with a VERY small amount of random rotation.

HOT TIP

We flattened the tangent on keys set on Focal Length because on a real camera the zoom ring doesn't move unless it's being touched. When we flat the tangent, we are creating the illusion that the camera operator is letting go of the zoom ring.

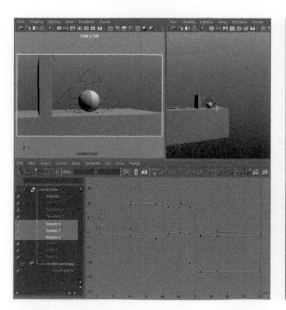

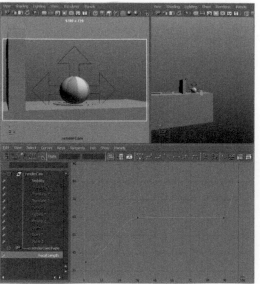

5 Set two more keys on 76 and 88, and settle the camera. Then one more key frame on 120. Do not flat this last tangent; animated cameras should never come to a complete stop, and certainly not right at the last frame.

6 Let's key one more quick zoom in. Key the Focal Length on frame 95. Now on Frame 105, key it at a value of 80. Flat this tangent.

Animating Cameras (cont'd)

7 Open anim_motion_start.ma. We're going to animate a dramatic camera move that is seemingly created by a camera on dolly tracks. First we need to set up a camera made for this kind of movement.

8 We'll need a camera with an aim to keep everything easy to control. Go to the Create menu, and choose Cameras > Camera, Aim and Up.

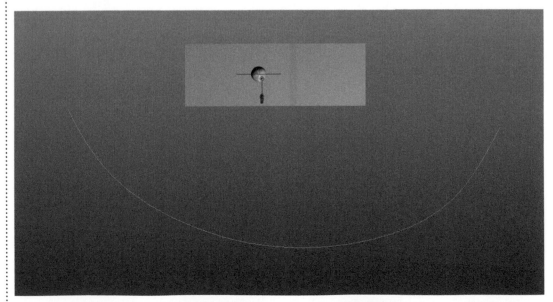

10 Next switch to the top panel, and select the EP Curve tool in the Curves Shelf. We are creating our camera's path, so create a nice half-circle curve like the one here by clicking points in the view. Finish your curve by hitting *Enter*.

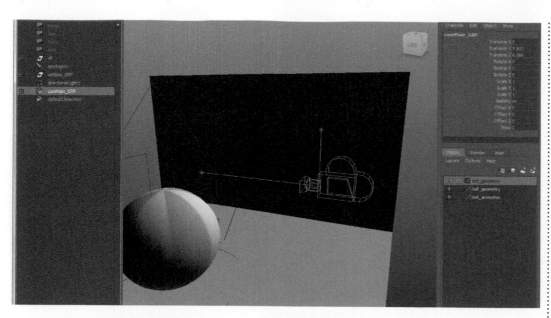

anim_motion_start.
ma
anim_motion_
finish.ma

9 Our camera needs to move with its Up control, so let's group them together. Select the Camera and Up control, and press **ctrl** + **G** to group them. Rename the group camMain_GRP, and center the pivot by selecting Modify > Center Pivot.

HOT TIP

Grouping is a great way to add multiple layers of pivot points to an object for easier animating. See the pages 108–111 for a cheat on multiple pivot points.

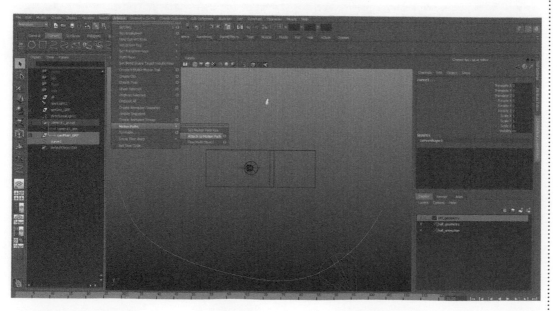

11 Now we attach the camera to the motion path. Select the camMain_GRP in the Outliner and then **ctrl** click the newly created curve1. Now click Animate > Motion Paths > Attach to Motion Path.

Animating Cameras (cont'd 2)

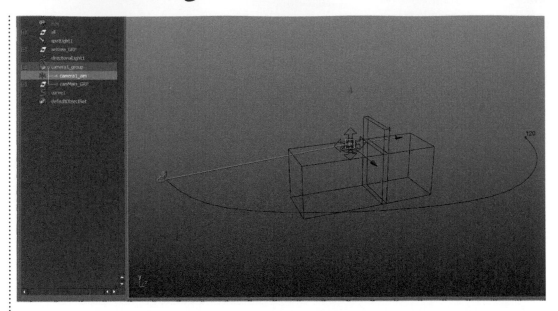

12 Let's frame up the bouncing ball. Select curve1 and translate it upwards in Y to 3.0. Also select the camera Aim and center it on the ball on frame 1.

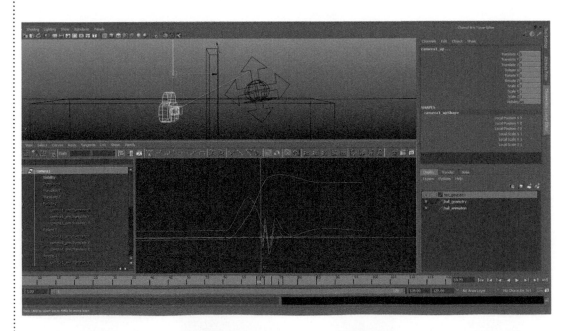

14 We were wise to group the camera before: now we can add a bit of camera shake on top of the path animation. Select the camera and, starting on f69, animate some camera shake, straight ahead, by moving the camera Up control subtly upwards and then downwards for a few frames.

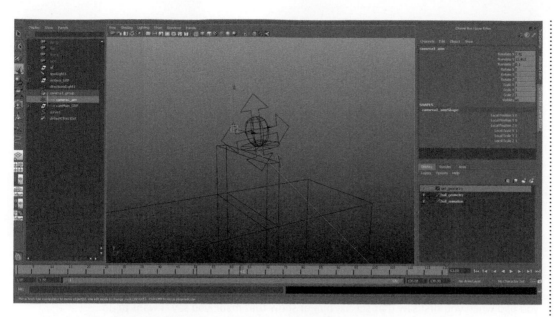

13 Now let's follow the motion of the ball. Just like in the hand-held scene, we want to key the aim a little bit behind the ball. I have a key on frames 1, 51, 63, 73, 99, and 120. The fewer the better.

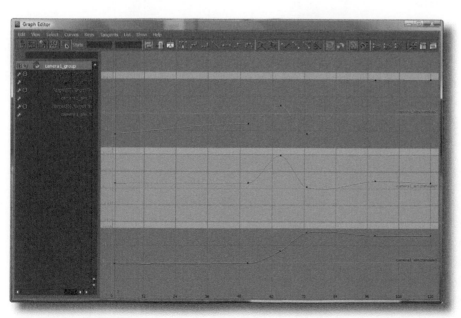

15 Here is a closer look at the curves for the main camera movement.

HOT TIP

For very dramatic camera moves, a path is a great way to go. The ability to visualize and edit the path is invaluable when doing sweeping movement. However, using Maya 2013's editable motion trails, you can technically recreate the same kind of feedback we saw using paths with keyframes alone. It will be interesting to see this new animation paradigm give rise to new ideas!

171

Finding Inspiration

by Eric Luhta

EVERY ANIMATOR KNOWS WHAT IT'S LIKE to get that "fire in your belly" feeling. After seeing something that you found so cool and awesome, you want nothing more than to run to your computer and create something just like it. Whether it's a film, book, TV show, piece of art, whatever, inspiration can come from many sources. As artists, we can fall into a rut where we forget what made us want to animate in the first place. Experience is a catalyst for growth, but it can also erode the wide-eyed wonderment you had when you first saw that special film or show that made you say "I want to do THAT!" But staying inspired isn't difficult; it's just something that needs some attention every once in awhile. If creating is starting to feel commonplace and uninspired (and it happens to everyone at some point), then perhaps seeking out some of the following will help rekindle the flame.

Inspiration by:

Top 10

Everyone has a top ten list of their favorite animated films. When's the last time you watched one? What was it about them that made you so excited to animate? The films and TV shows that define the art form for you should never be more than an arm's length away from your desk.

Films

Any film, from animated to live action to everything in between can serve to inspire your creative flow. It's true that many animated films are made for a specific audience range, but many animators fantasize about creating work outside the typical "family scope." Documentaries, art films, sci-fi epics, slasher movies, anything outside the box for animation can give you new ideas and things to try. Looking beyond genre, perhaps it's the way a film was shot that inspires new staging and composition ideas, or how it uses a soundtrack. Leave no film-related discipline unturned when searching for something unique.

Other art forms

Move away from the time-based visual element we work in. Books, music, museums, graphic design, theater—any creative discipline can give you ideas that make for refreshing animation work. Different mediums engage your brain in different ways. If you haven't been reading much, you may find that a book opens some new doors for you, or that listening to some music you're unfamiliar with gives you visual ideas you wouldn't have had otherwise.

Process

You can be inspired by a particular artistic process or challenge. Never did stop motion? Set up your digital camera, grab some action figures and give it a try! Create interesting limitations and see if you can meet their challenges... can you make a simple ball rig emote? Make a cool animated gif with photographs from your family reunion? Animate only characters in the Wingdings font and tell a story? Anything that pushes you out of your comfort zone or initially seems unreasonable is great process fodder.

Other artists

With the multitude of blogs, websites, artist sketchbooks, *Art of* books, interviews, DVD extras, and more, we have more information and inspiration available to us than any past society. Make use of it! Having an hour set aside each week to seek out new things you haven't heard of is a wise idea. You can watch shorts on YouTube, read blogs, look through artist websites and communities, view photographs, watch other reels, anything that shows you what everybody else is doing. Keep a folder or hard drive that functions as your personal inspiration library, and archive anything you find that you like. When you're not feeling your work, start browsing through your library and see where it leads you.

These are just a few of the ways you can keep your creative desire fresh and always hungry for more. Maintain a steady flow of inspiration, and you'll never tire of challenging yourself and becoming a better artist. And who knows, you just may come up with the thing that inspires everyone else to keep on going. Best of luck, and happy animating!

When you have a process that you repeat over and over, the inefficiencies are eliminated very quickly. Shots like the one pictured here just "come together."

174

8

Workflow

YOU'VE READ THE INTERLUDE, so you know: simply put, workflow is the step-by-step process that you follow every time you create animation. It is your go-to guide. It is your savior when things go wrong, it is the ever-evolving and improving rubric for success that you depend on.

No? Still not sold on workflow? Fine, maybe this chapter will change your mind. We're going to walk through a shot and demonstrate all of the great cheats that repeatedly make an appearance in a professional's workflow. If by the end you are still not convinced, then consider this: before I started committing myself to improving my workflow, this shot would have taken me over a week to complete. With workflow? This shot took three afternoons without a single headache!

Planning/Reference

THE BEST WORKFLOWS START with a strong foundation. This means thoroughly planning out your scene. There are a lot of planning methods but the most common and beneficial planning tools are definitely thumbnails and reference video.

With thumbnails, it's important to your workflow that the drawings are very strong. Focus primarily on the body positioning and pose, and less on the staging and camera. You want these drawings to be your guide through the entire shot, so getting too caught up in the staging and direction of the shot at the thumbnail stage will get in the way.

Reference video is easy to gather on YouTube. Spend some good time finding as many related clips as you can. The more the merrier. You should also be creating your own reference footage. For this shot, the animation needed to be very cartoony. I've found the best way to make a reference video for really cartoony actions is to "puppet" your hands around and create a "sound effects track" by making noises with your voice. It may seem a little silly to be yelling and screeching at your desk, walking your fingers around like legs, but when you see how closely the animation was timed to my reference video I think you'll see the benefits outweigh the embarrassment.

We're going to go through a few cheats that are great for making sure your drawings and reference video are at your fingertips. We're then going to import your reference video as well and keep it handy.

1 Open 01 - Cartoony_Start.ma. This scene has been laid out with the character and set, and is ready for our awesome planning to be imported in a way that will keep it at our fingertips.

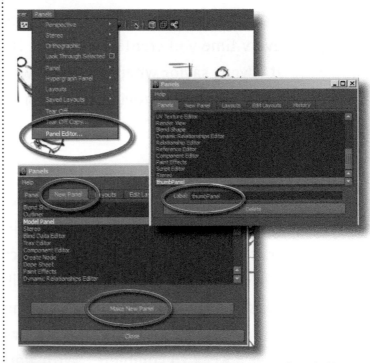

4 Let's save this view for later. Go to Panels > Panel Editor... Go to the New Panel tab, select Model Panel in the list and hit Make New Panel. In the Panel Editor go back to the Panels tab, select the new panel you just made (at the bottom of the list), name it thumbPanel, and press *Enter*.

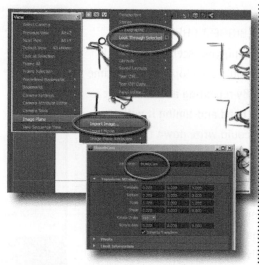

01 - Cartoony_
Start.ma

2 You can simply view a file. Go to File > View
Image. Select Thumbs.tif. Maya opens the
image with FCHECK by default. The only advantage
of using this method is Maya remembers the file
path in case you close it accidentally. Instead let's
make sure that isn't an issue.

3 Go to Create > Cameras > Camera. Name your new
camera "ThumbCam." In any panel go to Panels > Look
Through Selected. In the panel go to View > Image Plane
> Import Image. Select Thumbs.tif. Very nice. The image is
now loaded into this Maya camera.

If you ever
accidentally
close this
panel, get it
back by going
into any panel,
switching to
the thumbPanel
you created,
and tearing off
the panel for
easy use. Your
thumbs are
never far away...

5 Maya may change your panel back to camera1.
Go to Panels > Panel > thumbPanel. In the Panel
menu go to Show > None, then Show > Cameras.
Lastly turn off the grid by hitting the Grid button at
the top of the panel.

6 Now go to Panels > Tear off... . The panel now floats
and you can move, minimize, and maximize it. This
is a great way to work with your thumbnails right at your
fingertips.

Planning/Reference (cont'd)

ONE OF THE BIGGEST CHEATS of all involves timing your scene. In the old days, animators would use stopwatches to time their animation. By repeating an action over and over in their head and timing it with the stopwatch, they could write down the specific frame numbers and always have this timing reference close by. I find it alarming that now that we've moved into the digital age, this cheat hasn't been updated as well! We are going to use a piece of video reference created specifically to give us really high-energy timing to our scene.

Maya 2013 imports all kinds of movie files now, making video reference accessible and valuable deep into the production of your shot. With multiple codecs and formats supported, you will always have your video reference at your fingertips.

The movie file we're going to load was created to give a very specific sense of timing that could not be acted out. Hence the reason why I use my hands and sound effects (whistles and screams) to get a feel for the energy. "Acting out" your scenes like this, especially when they are cartoony-styled shots, is an invaluable piece of reference. Don't be shy, the more energy you put into this "timing reference," the better the shot will turn out!

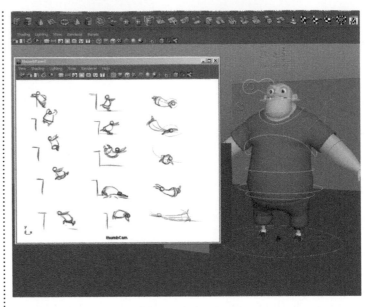

1 Open 02 - Cartoony_Timing_Start.ma. Here is our scene with the thumbnails loaded that we created in the last cheat. In order to nail the timing and energy, let's load the reference video.

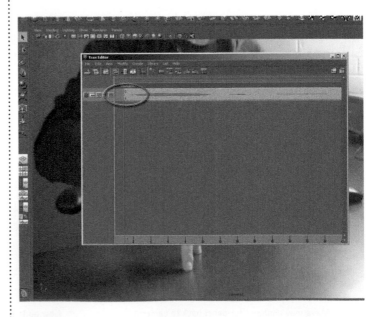

4 Slide the audio to the right in the Trax Editor so that it starts on frame 1. Retrace the steps in the previous cheat to create a new model panel so that you can always get back to the refVideoCam in case you close it.

02 - Cartoony_
Timing_Start.ma

2 Create a new camera, name it refVideoCam, and look through this new camera. In the panel select View > Image Plane > Import Movie. Select shot_Ref.mov in this chapter's scenes directory.

3 Open the Trax Editor by going to Windows > Animation Editors > Trax Editor. We want to see the footage in a camera, but also the audio in the Trax Editor for timing. In the Trax Editor go to File > Import Audio, and choose shot_ref.wav.

HOT TIP

If you go into the Panels > Saved Layouts > Edit Layouts you can save this panel layout as well, and get even more time-saving customization in Maya.

5 Look how awesome we are set up if we open the thumbCam and the refVideoCam alongside our Perspective and Camera panels! Ready to Block and Roll!

FCheck Trick

W E ARE ALWAYS LOOKING FOR ways to cheat our timing. Any visual cues we can give ourselves to help the timing should be employed whenever we can use them. We've already checked out how the timing can be helped by using an audio file. Let's see what we can get out of a little trick using FCheck.

If you aren't aware, FCheck is the tool that ships with Maya for playing back .iff streams (or any supported file format). Commonly, you watch your playblasts in FCheck if you haven't changed the output file format.

One little-known thing about FCheck is that you can draw on any frame using the right mouse button. And, if you hit play, it will actually 'capture' your mouse gesture for some visual cues. We'll use this to get even more helpful reference for the energy of this scene.

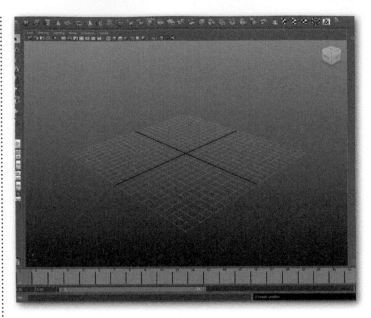

1 Create a new scene in Maya. It's best to start with a blank scene with this trick so there's nothing distracting you. Make the frame length 200.

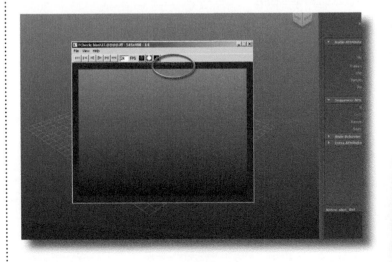

4 When it is done, the playblast will load up in Fcheck. The sound will play too, and this is what we want. Let it play through once so that the files all load into RAM. It will change from displaying dsk to displaying mem at the top when this is done.

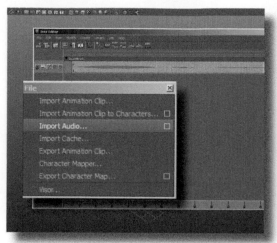

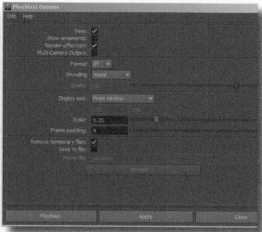

2 Add our sound file to the scene by going to the Trax Editor, and then click File > Import Audio... Don't forget to slide the audio to start on frame 1.

3 Let's create a playblast. Copy my settings here. Now, the output settings will depend on your computer specs: if you see the playback is choppy, reduce the image size and try again.

You can save this playblast with your gestures on it by going to File > Save Animation. Save it to a new folder and then load it into your Maya scene on a new camera for even MORE visual reference right at your fingertips!

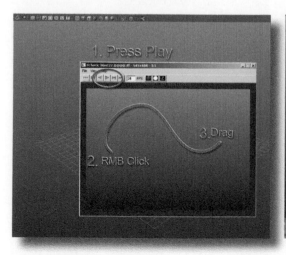

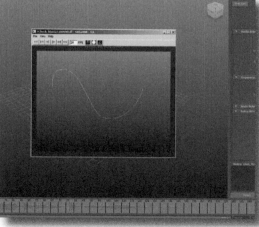

5 Now, take a deep breath and feel the energy of the audio. When you are ready, click play. Click anywhere in the FCheck window with your RMB and drag it around. Use gestures of your hand to "sketch" the energy.

6 When the sound file is done playing, let go of the RMB and watch your gestures play back on screen. What a great visual guide for analyzing the rises and falls of the energy of the scene.

Stepped Keys

W E KNOW FROM THE GRAPH EDITOR **CHAPTER** that stepped keys give us instantaneous transitions between values. When you key all of the body's controls in stepped mode, you could say that the resulting key frames are almost like "images" that you can retime at will to give yourself the best result.

Workflow-wise, blocking is the most efficient stage to be doing this retiming. Maya 2013 has awesome tools for retiming keys. We'll practice this by using both the brand new Retime Tool in the Graph Editor, as well as the Dope Sheet.

With the Retime Tool, our goal is to retime whole sections so that they line up with the energy of the beats much better. This is achieved easily because the retime tool is intuitive and rock solid.

With the Dope Sheet, a very underutilized tool in Maya, we get a top-level view of the distribution of the keys in our scene. It's very important to make sure you are hitting your beats exactly at the blocking stage. We'll use the Dope Sheet to make sure the impacts of the feet are right on the same frames as the sound, and the impact of the body on the ground also matches the audio we've recorded.

Many novices think that the best animators create perfect timing on their first try. Quite the contrary! The best animators are normally really good at quickly RETIMING and adjusting their animation. If you can go through a dozen iterations in the time it takes another animator to do just one version, you will be far ahead of the pack. Some might say it looks like you're cheating...

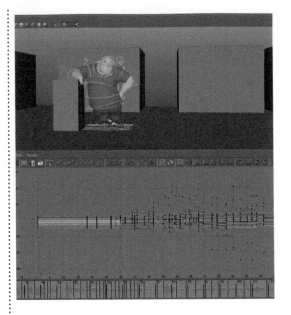

1 Open up 03 – Cartoony_blocking_start.ma. This is our stepped-key blocking. Hit play and see how, although the key poses are all there, the timing is off. Now select all of Groggy's controls and see how tidy stepped keys look in the Graph Editor.

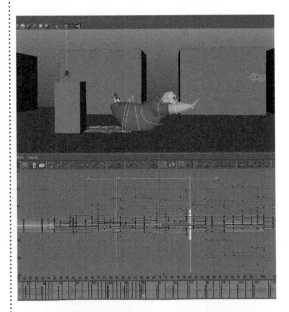

4 Now let's find the moment of impact in the audio. It seems to be somewhere around frame 80. Drag the middle of the right retime handle to the right until it's sitting above frame 80.

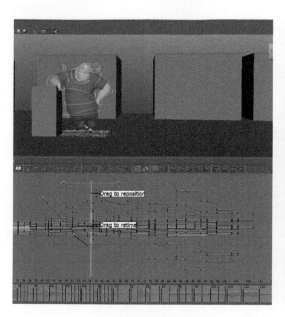

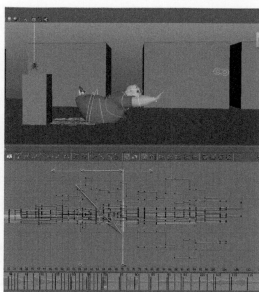

03 - cartoony_
Blocking_Start.ma
03 - cartoony_
Blocking_Finish.ma

2 The section of Groggy running and falling is timed too quickly. The Retime Tool is perfect for retiming sections of keys and preserving the rest. Select the Retime Tool and Double click on frame 56 in the Graph Editor.

3 We need to choose a moment that is easy to pick out from the audio file. The moment of impact when he falls is a good choice. It is currently happening on frame 70. Let's create another retime handle there by double clicking on frame 70.

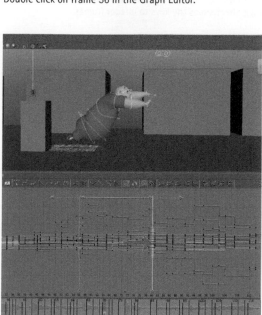

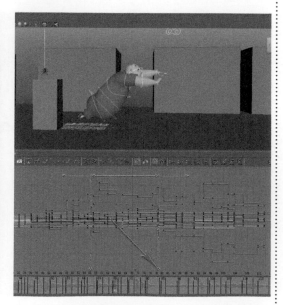

5 It's a good idea to snap your keys to frames, so let's do that. Go Edit > Snap. Play the animation and see how much better the timing is working now.

6 The retime handles are preserved. To delete them, click on the little "x" at the bottom of the handle. You will want to put your handles on integer frame values if you do more retiming from here on out.

183

Stepped Keys (cont'd)

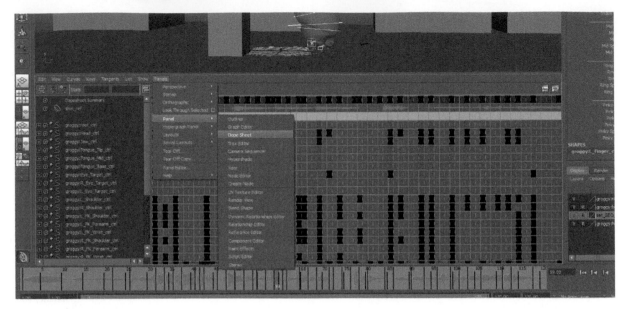

1 Now let's switch to the Dope Sheet. The Dope Sheet is the highest-level view of the keys in your scene that we have in Maya. While it can be cumbersome once you get too far into the progress of your shot, the Dope Sheet offers some very quick keyframe editing capabilities. Specifically, the ability to slide around all of the keys on a frame by selecting only a single block in the Dopesheet Summary row is a great way to cheat having to select multiple keys in the Graph Editor, or even more time consuming, shift click a range of keys in the timeline. Another little cheat is that moving the keys around in the Dope Sheet snaps the keys to integer frames.

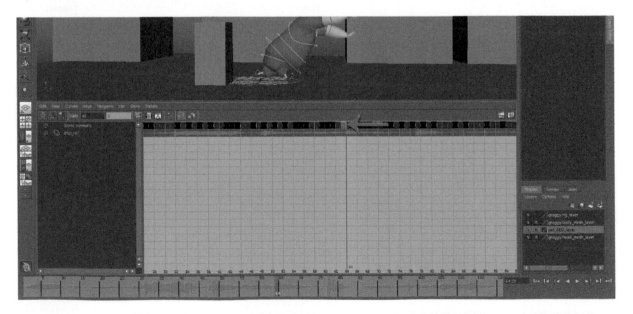

4 The third hit in the audio is happening on frame 64, but our keyframe is only on frame 65. Select it and move it one frame to the left.

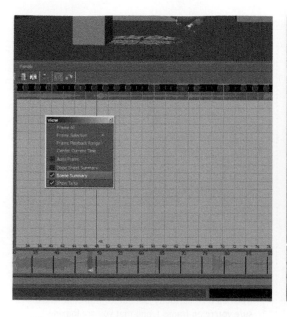

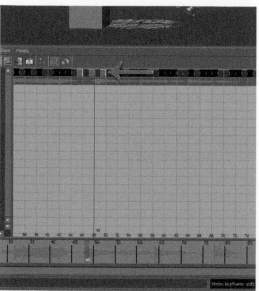

03 - cartoony_
Blocking_Start.ma
03 - cartoony_
Blocking_Finish.ma

2 Let's unclutter our workspace. Deselect everything and in the Dope Sheet uncheck View > Dope Sheet Summary, and check View > Scene Summary. Now we see all of the keys in the scene.

3 Let's use this top-level view to improve our timing. Select the keys on frames 46, 48, and 50, and hit **W** to switch to the move tool. These keys are a touch late: move them a frame to the left by dragging with the MMB.

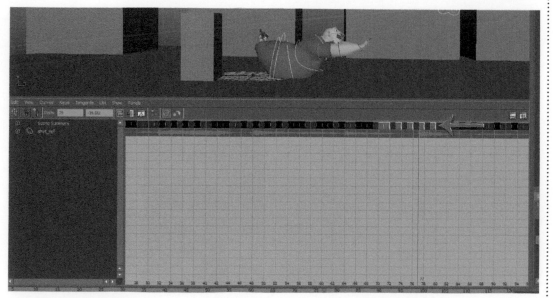

5 The last moment is the big splat on the ground. Let's fix the timing there too. Select all the keys from frames 71 to 81 and move them a frame to the left. Play it back and see how these small changes make all the difference.

185

Checking Silhouette

AS WE MOVE THROUGH BLOCKING, it's imperative we are also sticking close to our workflow. Deviations at this stage can mean we get so off track that we can struggle to regain control of our scene. Indeed, as the scene gets more and more complex, it will be our workflow that keeps things manageable. In blocking, what tends to happen is that, as we add breakdowns, the silhouettes get muddy. Posing tends to sacrifice itself to timing as a scene comes together.

It's a great idea to continuously check your silhouette as you work. Everyone knows the good old "seven" trick (we'll go over that one too just in case), but this cheat gives you an even better way to check silhouette. Using render layers, we can set up a silhouette check that still allows you to add lights to your scene (which negates the "seven" trick), and also allows you to compare the silhouette with and without the environment geometry.

Keep a constant eye on silhouette through the blocking phase and your poses will not go astray.

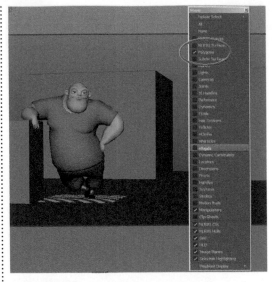

1 Open up 04 - cartoony_Silhouette_start.ma. Make sure you're on frame 1, and that you are looking through camera1. In the camera1 panel go to the Show menu and turn off everything but polygons.

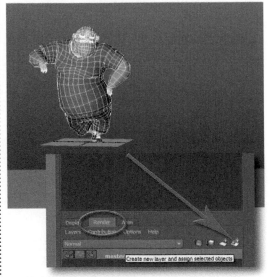

4 No big deal. Let's make a render layer for checking silhouette. Select all of Groggy's geoemetry and over in the channel editor switch to the Render tab. Then click the New Layer from Selected button.

04 - cartoony_
Silhouette_start.
ma
04 - cartoony_
Silhouette_finish.
ma

HOT TIP

You can even
unhide the
set_GEO_layer
and it won't
show up in
your silhouette
checker.
You always have
to manually
add objects and
groups to render
layers in Maya.
You can change
the sets,
characters,
lights...
everything,
and this layer
will remain the
same.

2 Turn off the visibility of the set_GEO_layer in the
display layers. Hit the **7** key on your keyboard and the
panel turns to Lit mode. With no lights in the scene, you
get a good look at the silhouette.

3 This is nice and all, but it doesn't always work. I had to
change the textures (turn off incandescence) for this
to work in this scene. And it doesn't work if there's lights!
Click Create > Lights > Directional Light. Oops. No worky.

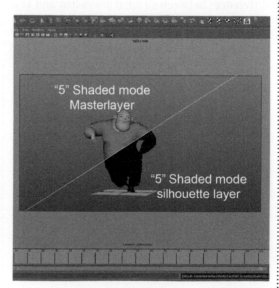

"5" Shaded mode
Masterlayer

"5" Shaded mode
silhouette layer

5 Rename the new layer "silhouette" and press _Enter_.
Right click on the silhouette layer and choose Overrides
> Create New Material Override > Surface Shader.

6 Now check out your new silhouette checker. Even if
you hit **5** (flat lighting shaded mode), you still get
a silhouette. Add as many lights as you want, change the
textures at will! Click back and forth from masterLayer and
the silhouette layer and see!

Moving Holds When Splining

THE SPLINING STAGE IS SO TERRIFYING: it's very hard to know what you are going to get! When you are done adding essential breakdowns in stepped mode, most animators hold their breath, close their eyes, and click Spline in the Graph Editor, only to fret when the resulting mush doesn't carry any of the old appeal of the stepped version. Transitions seem slow and floaty, the character cruises "through" poses without any of the snap that you imagined in stepped, and overall it seems that all of your amazing timing choices have all changed.

This is fine and normal, but it won't do for production. Pros know that when you are going through your workflow, you can't have a step that basically leaves the success of your shot up to chance! And one of the most striking differences between stepped animation and keys that have been freshly splined is the absence of any moving holds.

In the last edition of *How To Cheat in Maya* we showed you how to do copied pairs. This cheat is an expansion on that thought; we'll start with a copied pair but this time in stepped mode. Then we'll use a fancy cheat I've devised to give just the right amount of movement on a character in a moving hold. It's the best kind of cheat – one that you can and should use over and over in your workflow, but more importantly one that takes all the guesswork out of a scary stage in your shot!

1 Open 05 - cartoony_Moving_Holds_start.ma. This scene has only the two poses that represent the beginning of the animation. Select all of Groggy's controls and in the Graph Editor you'll see the keys are in stepped mode.

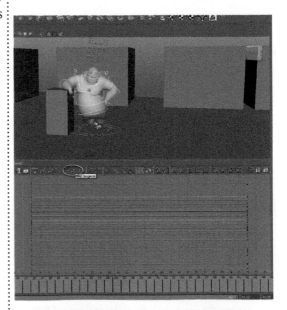

3 Click Stepped again to get us back to stepped keys. We'll now build the pose that gives us a good moving hold.

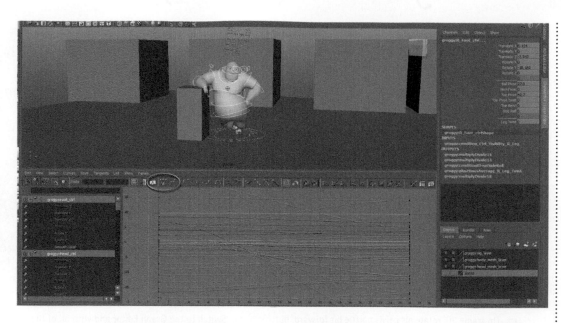

05 – cartoony_
Moving_Holds_
start.ma
05 – cartoony_
Moving_Holds_
finish.ma

HOT TIP

Remember
from Chapter
2 that clamped
tangents give
us flat tangents
when there's not
much change
in value, and
spline when
there is a big
change in value.
We can use
this knowledge
to predict the
results of going
from stepped to
spline.

2 Now let's take a close look in the Graph Editor at what happens when we spline the animation. Press `alt`+`Shift`+RMB and drag upwards to zoom in vertically a bit in the Graph Editor. With all the controls still selected, hit the AutoTangent button and see what happens to your curves. This is expected. Maya thinks you want to ease each of these keys, so it chose flat tangents for you.

4 Let's build a relaxed pose. With this cheat, we try to imagine the character after he's been holding the pose for ten minutes. To do this, imagine the big muscles like his legs and shoulders relaxing the most, and the smaller muscles like the neck and fingers relaxing least. You'll see why in a second.

Moving Holds (cont'd)

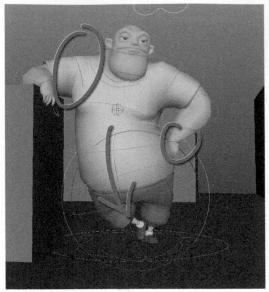

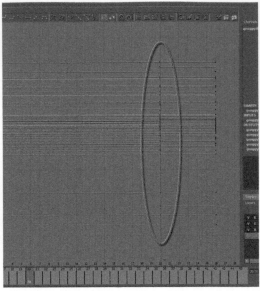

5 On frame 20, rotate his pelvis a little bit forward, but straighten his legs a tad by moving his pelvis upwards slightly in Y. Rotate the rest of his spine to straighten him up a bit too. Adjust the arms to be back in their resting positions.

6 Switch to the Graph Editor and with all of the controls selected hit **S**. Make sure a key is placed on all of the curves.

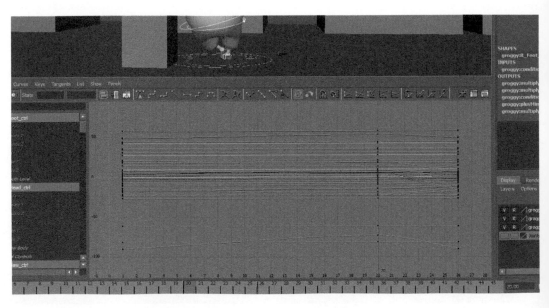

9 Now we're going to use a little cheat to adjust the amount of movement that is happening in our moving hold. Switch to the panel configuration of Persp/Graph as above and play the animation. He's moving too much!

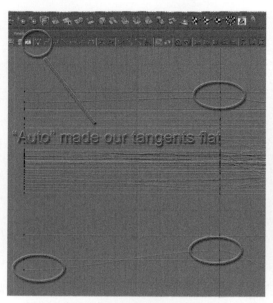

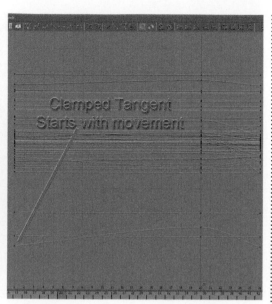

7 Now hit the AutoTangent button and look at the result. All of the tangents are flat. Maya thinks we need an ease in and out of all of the keys right now. But we don't want Groggy to start from a dead halt on frame 1.

8 Let's try clamped instead. Clamped will give us much more predictable results when creating moving holds WITHIN stepped mode. I recommend you convert from stepped to clamped as part of your workflow.

HOT TIP

If you go halfway between two keys, you get roughly 50% change, but for more fine-tuned adjustment, you can copy a key only a frame or two before your last frame and get a 5% adjustment. It's common to do a 50% copy and then a couple smaller copies to get a finely tuned result.

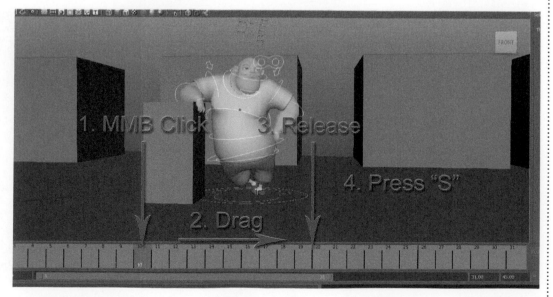

10 To reduce the amount of movement, we're going to use a tried-and-true cheat, of middle mouse copying the keys on the timeline. MMB click on the timeline on frame 10, and drag your mouse to frame 20. Release your mouse and press Ⓢ.

191

Moving Holds (cont'd 2)

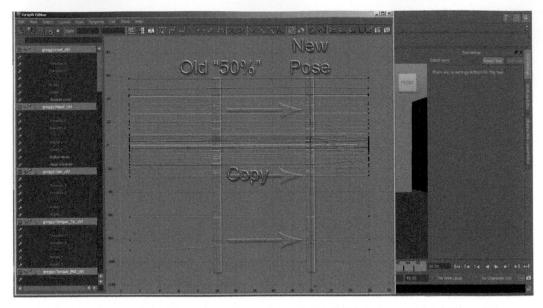

11 What just happened? Since we went about halfway between our two splined keys, when we paste the keys on frame 20 we get roughly 50% of the movement we had before.

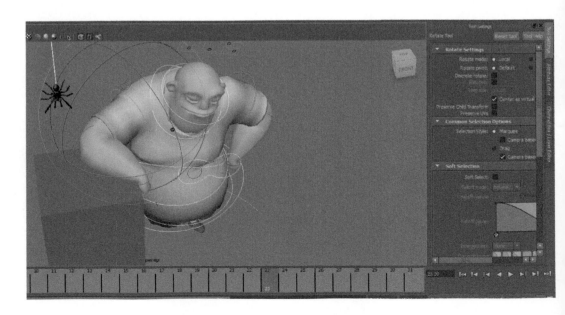

13 Don't forget the arms. On frame 23 check that his right arm is staying generally still by rotating the shoulder and elbow. Flip back and forth between the three keys (20, 23, and 26) using the comma (,), and period ⬛ keys.

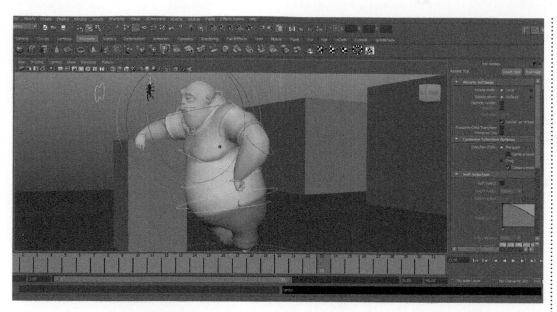

12 If it seems like there's still too much movement, then repeat the last step. Let's add a breakdown in between the end of the moving hold and the final pose. On frame 23, rotate his spine forward a bit as well has his head.

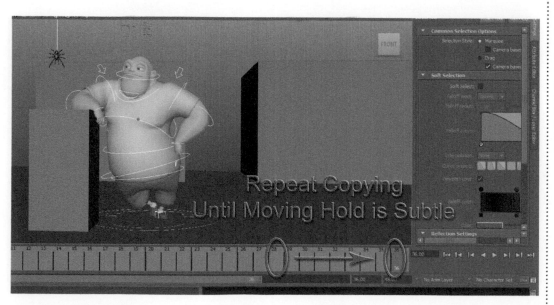

14 Now we create another hold until frame 36. Create a slightly relaxed pose on frame 36 the same way we did before. Middle Mouse Copy over and over until you've watered down the pose change enough that it's barely visible. Now the first part of this animation is almost done.

HOT TIP

Converting your stepped keys to clamped when splining gives the most predictable results if you create your holds using this method. But change your default tangent to AutoTangent after converting everything to clamped to get the most help from Maya as you move on.

193

Moving Holds w/ Retime Tool

THE BRAND NEW RETIME TOOL OFFERS a brand new paradigm for manipulating and creating keys in the Graph Editor. We can make broad adjustments to timing, or in this case repeat the copy-paste method of moving hold creation in a snap.

Most professionals know that the best way to cheat in Maya is to find quick, effective methods of doing tasks that you must do repeatedly throughout the workday. And while Maya offers very powerful scripting capabilities, rarely will a script come in handy when it comes to something like a moving hold.

Instead we must use all of the new tools Maya has to offer to refine and perfect our workflow. In the end, your workflow should take full advantage of the aggregate improvements added to Maya every new version. To ignore these awesome new tools is to ignore cheats that could save your shot!

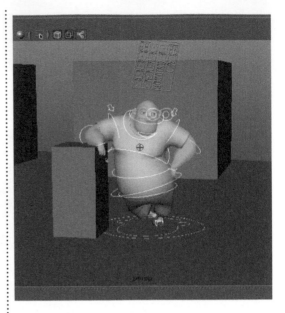

1 Open 06 - cartoony_retime_Holds_start.ma. This is the same scene as before, only this time we're going to use the Retime Tool to create the moving holds. Open the Graph Editor and familiarize yourself with the keys again.

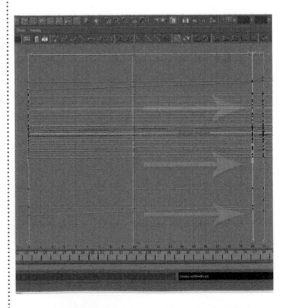

3 Double click on frame 20 to add a retime handle there too. Now drag the retime handle from frame 10 to frame 20. The retime handle we just created will shift over to near frame 21.

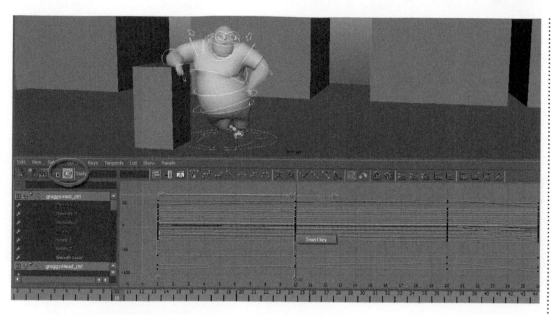

06 - cartoony_
retime_Holds_
start.ma
06 - cartoony_
retime_Holds_
finish.ma

HOT TIP

Remember
Retime
Handles are
not saved into
a scene. You
need to make
your timing
adjustments
before you close
your file or you
will lose the
handles you've
created.

2   In the Graph Editor, click on the Retime Tool in the upper left, and double click on frame 1 and frame 10. This creates
retime handles on those keys. Now right click on the retime handle on frame 10 and choose Insert Key. Now we have
a key that represents our 50% point in the animation again.

4   Hit **Q** to switch to the select tool. Select the keys on frame 21 and hit *Delete*. Go Edit > Snap to make sure your
newly retimed moving hold is firmly on an integer frame. Moving hold, done!

195

Refining Arcs in Polish

B Y THE TIME YOU HAVE WORKED THROUGH your entire workflow and have made it to the polish phase, you are most likely dealing with an amount of keyframes that is unwieldy, to put it lightly. To make even the slightest adjustments can take hours of deleting, redoing, tweaking, and frustration.

Arcs are such an important fundamental that we need to make sure at this point in our workflow that we double-check our arcs look great. However, like I mentioned before, finalizing your arcs in the polish phase means navigating a rat's nest of curves in the Graph Editor.

Fortunately for us, the Editable Motion Trail tool is good not just for creating and defining motion, but also for keeping arcs manageable in this time of super-dense keys. We took a look at how to use Editable Motion Trails in Chapter 1 and Chapter 4 so you should be pretty familiar with creating them by now. But unlike in those chapters in which we created smooth motion, we will now be using them to finalize arcs among very dense keys. Maya 2013's Editable Motion Trails are rock solid and very stable now.

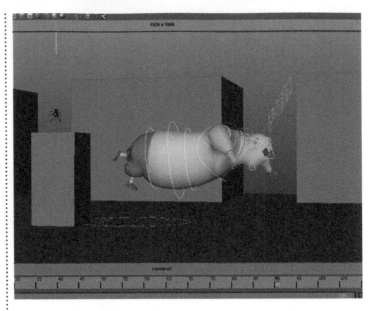

1 Open 07 - cartoony_Arcs_start.ma. This scene is at the end of "blocking plus" and is ready for polish in the arcs. Play a few times through and see if you can pick out the problems.

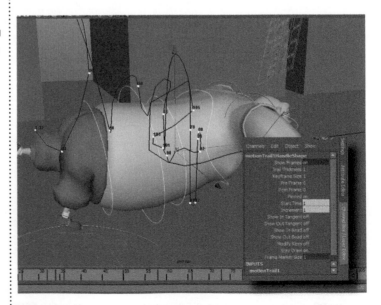

3 By default our trail shows no tangents nor influences on the keys; we'll show those later when it's time to refine. Select one of the keys in the panel and move it to test it.

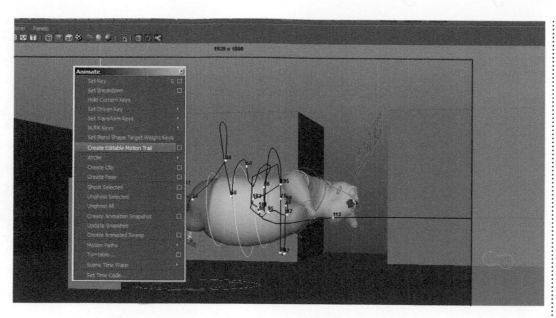

07 - cartoony_
Arcs_start.ma
07 - cartoony_
Arcs_finish.ma

2 We're going to focus on the chest in the frame range 90–102. In these twelve frames, there is a lot of popping and movement. Select his chest control and in the Animation menu set (F2) go to Animate > Create Editable Motion Trail.

HOT TIP

Remember that an Editable Motion Trail is most useful on controllers that have translation keys on them. You get much less predictable results if you add a motion trail to a controller that is in an FK Chain.

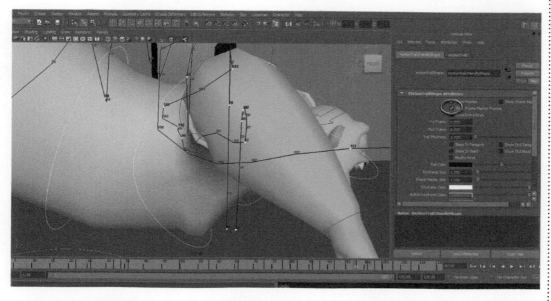

4 Things are easier to follow if you can see all of the frame markers and not just frames with keys on them. Turn them on by checking Show Frame Marker Frames in the attribute panel with the motion trail selected.

197

Refining Arcs (cont'd)

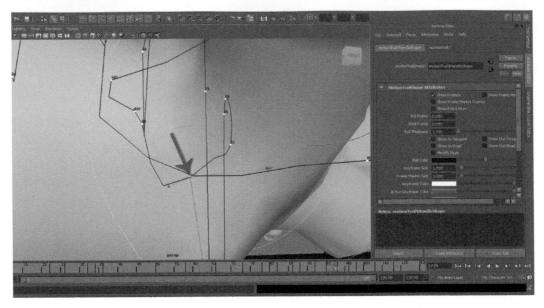

5 Move the key that is labeled "95" down to bring it into more of an arc shape. You'll notice the Editable Motion Trail stays kind of ragged no matter how you move this key. Time to play with the tangents.

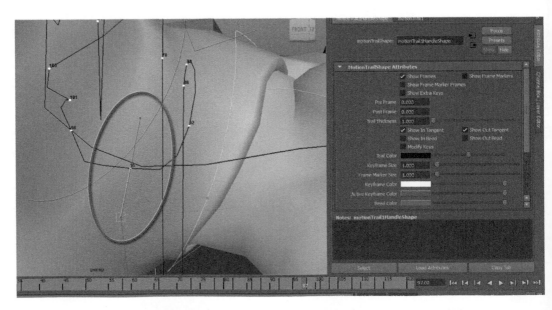

7 Click again on the key labeled "95". The tangents will be selected and you can middle mouse drag them around in the panel and see their influence. Adjust the keyframe's position and tangents' influence until the arc looks smoother.

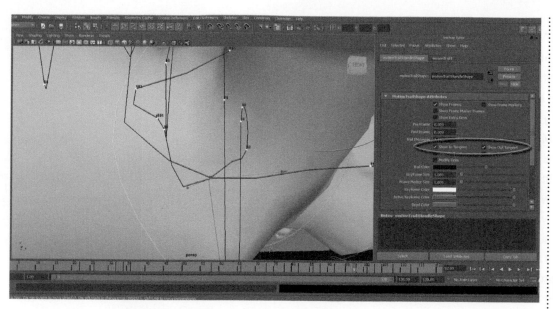

6 In the attribute editor check Show In Tangent and Show Out Tangent. This enables influence editing in panel on the entire Motion Trail, not just the selected key.

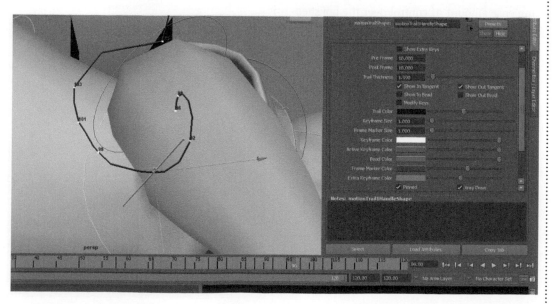

8 Now do the same adjustment to the position and the tangents on the other frames between frame 90 and 102. Don't stop until you have a nice clean arc in this chest movement.

HOT TIP

Our final check of any arc is looking through the main camera. An arc may look great in perspective but until you see what it looks like to camera, you are not finished finessing.

Final Texture

THE VERY LAST THING YOU SHOULD HAVE in your workflow is adding final details like little bits of texture to your scene. This is called non-performance texture: these little details aren't contributing to the performance choices you've made. Instead they are making the scene feel full of detail and real.

With Maya 2013's animation layers, adding texture to your polished scene means that you can non-destructively experiment with ideas. It is crucial that you understand the importance of workflow at this point; animation layers need to be planned for very carefully. If, halfway through working on your shot, you suddenly decide to do some of the animation on a layer, chances are you will get horribly off track. Instead, you must either plan on your animation being done in layers (a walk cycle on the legs on one layer, for example, and adding torso movement on a new layer), or you must wait to add very fine details at the end.

By adhering to our strict workflow, we are safeguarding our scene against unforeseen problems later on. Animation layers give us an immense amount of control over the polished scene, without any destructive effects on the keys we already have.

1 Open 08 - cartoony_Texture_start.ma. We are going to add a little breath at the beginning of the scene. Turn off all the selection masks except curves and then drag a selection box around Groggy. You will select all of his controls.

4 Set another key on frame 30.

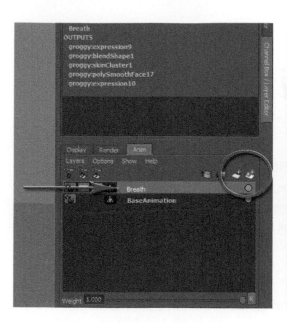

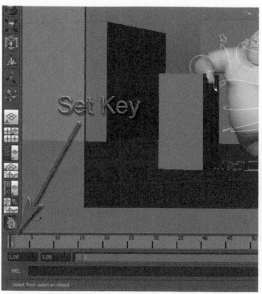

08 – cartoony_
Texture_start.ma
08 – cartoony_
Texture_finish.ma

2 In the Channel Box or Layer Editor, click on the Create Layer From Selected button, and rename the new layer "Breath".

3 Click on the Breath animation layer to make it the active layer. Nothing you do now will affect keys on the BaseAnimation layer. Select all of Groggy's controls. On frame 1 hit ⑤ to set a key for the beginning of the breath.

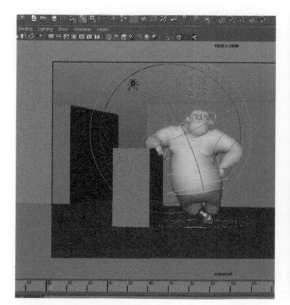

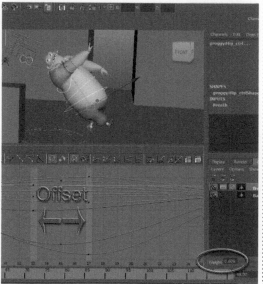

5 On frame 15, create a pose with Groggy's spine bent backwards slightly, like he's taking a breath. Don't forget to adjust his arms back into position. Include the pelvis, belly, chest, and head controls when you are making this pose.

6 Now you have a breath in the animation. You can adjust the amount that this animation is added to the BaseAnimation layer by adjusting the weight value in the Layer Editor. You may even want to offset the keys of the spine to have the pelvis move first and the head last.

8

Spotlight - Özgür Aydoğdu

OZGUR AYDOGDU IS A 3D GENERALIST at 1000 VOLT Post
Production, Istanbul, where he has worked on a variety of
commercials for Coca Cola, Vodafone, Turkish Airlines, Danone
and feature films *The Ottoman Cowboys* and *The Breath*.

TELL US A LITTLE ABOUT YOUR CENK RIG. WHERE DID YOUR INSPIRATION COME FROM?

As you could imagine, the daily work in a studio might easily fall into a routine,
especially when the works are mostly commercials. At this point, I believe in the
importance of personal projects as a tool to try different things and develop yourself.
I was looking for a challenging task to improve my rigging and character animation
skills; where I would carry out each step by myself, starting from design, model, texture
to rig and animation. I was already sketching some characters; and what I had in my
mind for my project was kind of a fat character instead of a stereotypical cute one.
I imagined him as a goofy character who would get into a series of funny situations due
to his physical appearance. My aim was to try some new techniques and I experienced a
lot more than I imagined throughout the project.

WE SEE ON YOUR INTRO VIDEO FOR CENK THAT YOU INITIALLY SKETCHED HIM OUT
BEFORE PROCEEDING WITH THE MODELING AND RIGGING. DO YOU FEEL THIS IS
IMPORTANT FOR CREATING ANY GOOD RIG?

I think it's an essential step, not only for creating a good rig but also for modeling
and animation as well. It provides a quick end vision in your mind before you actually
sit in front of the computer. It helps you better explore the character, its volume and
expressions so that you can easily see the limits of the design or any other pitfalls
beforehand. So, you start playing with the character to see how much you can push

the design. But, apart from all these benefits I should admit that I enjoy sketching itself. I also enjoy looking at other people's drawings. Most of the time, I like the character exploration sketches in the *Art of* books more than the final 3D versions of the characters on the film.

DID YOU GO TO SCHOOL TO RECEIVE YOUR ANIMATION AND RIGGING EDUCATION, OR DID YOU TEACH YOURSELF THOSE ASPECTS OF THE PIPELINE?

I received my bachelors degree in computer science and did not receive an animation or rigging education. However, I was growing up in a family where I was very much exposed to various art disciplines – mostly due to my father's being a painter – since my childhood. I always had an interest in drawing and technology as long as I can remember. When I was a child, I used to fill my school notebooks with drawings and flip book animations like many other animators. Later, I started to try basic scripts with my first computer, a Commodore 64. Then I met 3D with early versions of 3D Studio on PC and started modeling any stuff that I see around. Throughout my university years, I pursued my interest in 3D modeling via various freelance projects. Upon graduation, I started to work in a company developing simulation software. But soon I understood that the work was not really for me and started to work on some personal projects mostly on modeling and rigging, at home. With one of these projects I applied to a post production company and since then I have been working as a 3D generalist where I mostly do character rigging and animation.

But, apart from these, I am kind of obsessed to find solutions when I come across something which I do not have much clue about. That's why I read, watch and search a lot. Whenever I see a fascinating piece of character animation, I dig into it and watch over and over again to understand timing, acting and the deformations of the character. And I enjoy trying new things that would be challenging for me. Maybe these contributed to me developing my animation and rigging skills and teaching myself throughout the pipeline.

WHAT ARE THREE QUALITIES YOU FEEL ARE NECESSARY FOR A GOOD CHARACTER ANIMATION RIG?

The first thing that comes to my mind is stability. The rig must be robust enough in terms of its technical structure. The IF/FK and dynamic calculations, transferring animation keys, caches, reference updates, new features, and component additions during the production should all work properly and as expected so that the animators could focus on their animation without having to deal with technical problems which they are not responsible for. A robust rig would maximize the efficiency.

Flexibility is another important quality. The rig should be flexible enough so that the animators would work freely and reach poses that they have in their mind easily. Even, the flexibility of the rig might give them an opportunity to try a different pose that they did not imagine at first. By this way, the animators would not be limited to the rig but the rig itself would push the animator. For instance, the flat and soulless look of CG characters due to their symmetric structure seems to be a problem for me so I tend to solve it by adding secondary deformation points on the face which let animators make finer tweaks on the pose and get more natural expressions. Besides, the ability to squash and stretch adds a lot. There would always be some other things to try.

To me simplicity is another important aspect of a good rig. It should not take a lot of time for an animator to achieve a nice pose after digging into numerous controllers. In fact, putting too many controllers may sometimes freak the animators out, and it can even become cumbersome to animate. The rigger should take the story and concept drawings into account and should not define controllers more than needed. I also prefer making my controllers visually appealing and colorful, which make them shout like "come play with me!"

AS AN ANIMATOR, YOU ARE ALWAYS THINKING OF THE MOTION YOU WILL GET OUT OF A RIG. HOW DID YOU DECIDE ON THE CONTROLS YOU PUT INTO CENK REGARDING ANIMATION YOU WANTED TO DO WITH HIM?

As he does not have a body, he had to give out his mood and feelings via using his head only. I was looking for a way to be able to easily define line of action on the head, that's where the IK controls come in. The free deformations like he has in the eyes and nose also adds to the candid expressions I guess. The shape of his head when he bounces was also important as he would move from somewhere to another by bouncing up and down, so I thought to keep this motion as realistic as it can be. Since the character has a very round design, I added the ground collision feature, making his bottom flat and bulge when he sits on the ground, which makes the audience feel his weight.

DID YOU ALWAYS PLAN ON MAKING HIM A FLOATING HEAD, OR WAS HE ORIGINALLY A FULL BIPED?

To tell the truth, I thought him a fully biped at the beginning. However, it seemed to me that it would take a lot of time for me to incorporate the level of details I imagined into the full body. So, at some point, the project kind of stopped for me. Then while I was watching Miyazaki's *Spirited Away* for the hundredth time, when I bumped into the three floating heads in the Yu-Baaba's room, I thought why can he not be a floating head at all? I would still be able to tell a short with a head and it might even be more interesting to watch. But I made some changes in the design, for instance he did not have a helmet when he was a full body but the sketches which I made with the head looked too neat for my taste so I added the helmet to corrupt the symmetry and tried to make the design more appealing.

I imagined a series of funny events that he would experience thanks to his physical shape. Like, he was trying to get rid of a fly on his head, but he cannot as he does not have hands. He bounces up down, gets eager and angry, his head falls down and the fly seems to be getting all the pleasure that it can out of this; or I imagined him while listening to an iPod, then one of the earphones falls out and he tries all his best to put it again into his ear. And he cannot actually. I'm looking forward to see him in these hilarious situations.

ANY ADVICE FOR COMPLETING A PERSONAL PROJECT OF THIS SIZE AND QUALITY?

For rigs, the quality of the result is directly proportional to how well you organize the project from start to end. I can recommend the philosophy of "divide and conquer" as a technique for handling a large, complex problem by breaking down it into smaller, solvable problems which in fact can be applied to any other issue in real life. In my case I layered all of the deformations, which helped me focus on each feature individually. I had my rig hierarchy and layers clearly sketched on a sheet of paper all the time, because the deeper you go into the details (which in fact make the difference) the more likely you get out of line and lose control on the project. This might also happen if you are too much focused on the project for long days. I find keeping my mind always busy with the project in daily course (in the bed, on the subway, etc.) useful but sometimes you would need to move away from the project for a couple of days to refresh your mind. This would help to see things differently and you might even spot a problem in a second which did not take your attention before. Eventually it's really a challenge to balance things as you don't actually have a deadline in personal projects. I tried to overcome this by setting deadlines to myself and trying hard not to be too self-critical.

Last but not the least, is that you should really enjoy what you are doing. It takes a lot of work and real passion to achieve in this field. The pace of development and change is incredible and new things to learn always fly around. One should be eager and passionate enough to keep up to date and then be able to make a difference. This could only happen if you really love it I guess.

HOW DID YOU DECIDE ON WHAT FEATURES TO PUT INTO CENK'S FINAL DESIGN? DID YOU LEAVE ANYTHING OUT?

Although Cenk has been taking attention mostly due to its rigging features, I always had the idea of animating him in a series of vignettes to tell different stories. That's why the features I had are the ones that I would like to use when I animate him by myself.

To fulfill the needs of an exaggerated style of animation, I added IK and FK controls with volume, preserving squash and stretch. Since there are a lot of dynamics going on around the face and on the helmet, I decided to add a geometry cache importer/exporter into the rig. For the mouth, I added a sticky lips feature as I had a couple of stories where he was supposed to be eating. It helped me get some nice smiling expressions, too. Other than these, I was planning to add a camera-based lattice deformer on the overall mesh, which would let me enhance the silhouette of a particular pose by moving the lattice points. I hope I can do it next time!

WHAT ARE SOME OF YOUR HOBBIES OUTSIDE OF ANIMATION AND RIGGING?

Photography is kind of a passion to me. I take photos of artworks and portraits of artists to be used in their exhibition catalogues and art books. But actually I love street photography and taking photos for myself, reflecting my confusions and documenting lives around me. I enjoy sharing them on my blog, which keeps growing as a visual diary of my personal life. I am interested in black-and-white film photography. Hanging out in the dark room developing and printing photos literally takes me out of this world. Besides, I believe that the art of photography is a very influential medium for anyone dealing with CG, in terms of cinematography and lighting.

Apart from that, I am interested in watching exhibitions and seeing what other artists are doing. I might say that cinema is another passion for me.

WHAT IS YOUR FAVORITE FEATURE THAT YOU INCORPORATED INTO THE FINAL RIG?

I love the IK controls best. I think that the IK spline applied on a full mesh with a combination of convincing squash and stretch really adds value to the character. Think of a head shaped with a curve, when you make it concave towards the audience, the character has a timid expression who is not willing to communicate. And he turns out to be an extravert person when you make the curve convex. I can give an instant clue about the mood of the character very easily by using this feature.

■ Having skill in efficient cycle creation is a requirement of every professional animator.

9
Cycles

CYCLES, or animation meant to loop or repeat, are a mainstay of the animation industry. From games to film to TV, cycles will most certainly be a part of your career in animation. The ability to quickly create realistic and appealing cycles is the hallmark of the experienced animator. To do this you must be familiar with all of the tools that Maya 2013 has to offer. In production it is common for an entire animation team to share cycles, and so having cheats to avoid little technical problems can have a large impact on a project.

We're going to look at the technical aspects of creating a cycle. Then we'll manipulate a walk cycle and create a flying cycle. With both of these cycles the plan is to use the simplest method to get the best results; with cycles, that cheat is called "offsets."

9 Cycles

Cycle Basics

WHEN WE TALK ABOUT cycling in animation, there are a few terms and technical rules you should be aware of. We'll run through them here.

First of all, when dealing with cycles where a character moves "forward," the Z axis is the axis that is used to show forward movement.

Next, you will be dealing extensively with Maya's Pre and Post Infinity curve types. Maya uses these settings to determine how to cycle animation before your first and after your last keyframe. We'll test out all of the different types here.

Another rule is that all of the controls of your animation need to have the same number of frames between the first and last frame of the cycle. They don't necessarily have to be the same frames, however. For instance, your head could be animated between frames 1 and 24, and your arms could be animated from frames 18 to 41.

Also, it is typical to counter-animate a master control against the Translate Z to make it so that the cycling animation stays centered over the world origin, as if it's on a treadmill. This is extremely handy when you are working with a cycle that covers a lot of distance, like a run cycle. It is easy to create this treadmill; simply cycle the master controller backwards the same stride length and frame range as the character cycle.

Finally, cycling is a lot more manageable when you are familiar with the idea of "offsetting" your keyframes in the Graph Editor. The basic idea is to create animation on controllers within your set frame range (1–24 for example), and then move the keyframes backwards or forwards in time. These new offset keys have the same total duration of the cycle, but you don't have to worry about getting some hard-to-create curves cycling on the same frames as your base animation. An example of this is if there is an extremely wobbly antenna on your character; it's hard to imagine at exactly what point in the overall motion that antenna should be started at on frame 1, whereas it's easy to key the entire flopping motion and then offset it.

1 Open cycle_basics_start.ma. In this scene we're going to have this ball move up and down, and tilt left and right. You'll see two keys are already created for you. Our cycle length is 24 frames, and there are keys on frames 1 and 12.

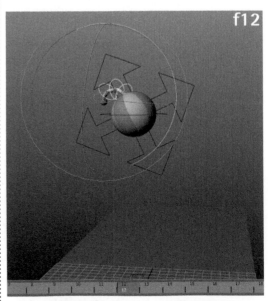

4 Expand the timeline to 48 frames and watch how nicely the animation loops. Now let's key the antenna flopping over from the left to the right. On frame 1, key the antenna bent over to the right, and on frame 12 key the antenna bent over to the left.

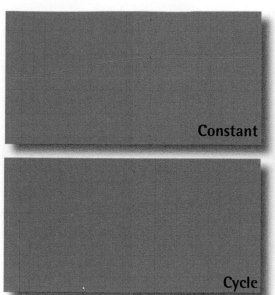

Constant

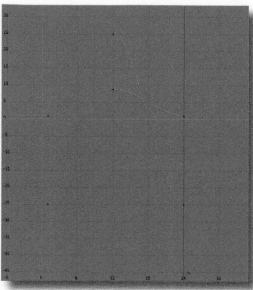

Cycle

cycle_basics_start.
ma
cycle_basics_finish.
ma

2 Let's look at the different cycle types. Select the ball_ anim control, and open the Graph Editor. Click on View > Infinity. As you can see, the value is constant before the first and after the last keyframe, by default. Select the Ty and Rz curves and go to Curves > Post Infinity > Cycle.

3 "Cycle" means that when it gets to the last keyframe, Maya will loop the animation by going back to the first keyframe. In order for the cycle to work, the first and last keyframes need to be identical! In the timeline, MMB drag frame 1 to frame 24 and hit **S** to paste the key at the end of the animation. Flat all tangents.

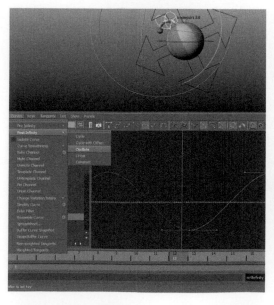

5 In the Graph Editor, select the antenna control's rotation channels. Go to Curves > Post Infinity > Oscillate. Also go to Curves > Pre Infinity > Oscillate. This infinity curve type tells maya to "bounce" backwards and forwards through the animation when it gets to the first and last key.

6 Now let's make the character move forward. Set a key in Translate Z on the ball_anim control at frame 1. On frame 24, move him forward in Z about 10 units.

Cycle Basics (cont'd)

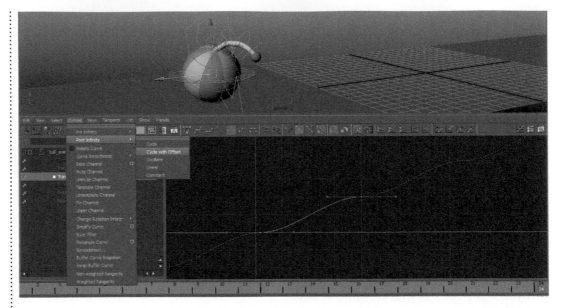

7 The rule of thumb is that Translate Z channels on your MAIN character controls (body, feet, etc.) should be Cycle With Offset. Set the Translate Z curve to this type in the Graph Editor. Flat the tangents on the Z channel and notice that Maya takes the last frame as the "new" start frame and "goes from there."

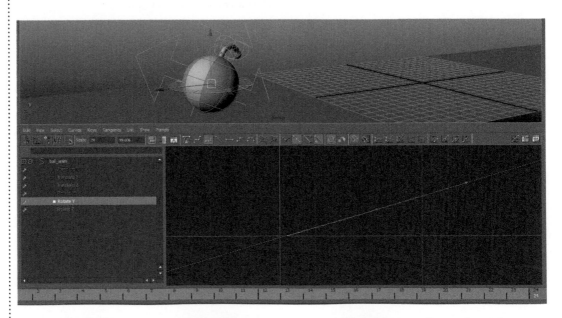

9 Now set the Rotate Y curve Pre- and Post-Infinity type to Linear and see the resulting curve. The rotation continues linearly forwards and backwards to infinity. Let's do our first offset. Remember, offsetting animation is a great way to build layers in a cycle.

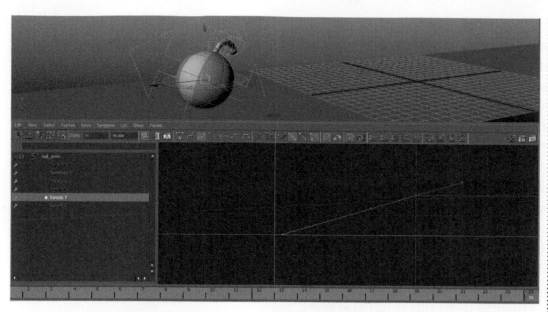

8 The Linear Infinity type extends the animation as if a linear tangent were applied to the keys. Select the ball_anim control and hit **S** on frame 24 to make sure there is a key on the Rotate Y there. In the Graph Editor, select the key on frame 24 on the Rotate Y channel, and move it up to a value of 100.

HOT TIP

Now that you know all the cycle types, be aware of the simplest way to get the motion you need. Pros are always using offset animation curves to build complex motion that would be immensely difficult to create working only within a set frame range.

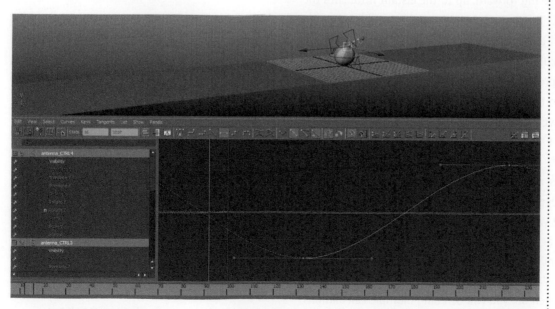

10 Select the controls of the antenna. In the Graph Editor, select the rotation curves and move them forward four frames to make the motion more overlapped. Notice how the curve retains its shape, but also how hard it would be to create the curve shape that exists between frames 1 and 24 from scratch.

Stride Length

W HEN CREATING ANIMATED CYCLES, we'll first want to quickly sort out a few decisions, namely cycle length (frame count) and stride length (how far one complete cycle "travels" in space). These two decisions are essentially the principles of timing and spacing applied to walk cycles. However, unlike a performance shot in which these decisions can be eyeballed and changed, you'll want to be sure you are working within your set standards so that the result is predictable, manageable, and most importantly, usable.

What is stride length? Simply put, stride length is the distance that a character travels in one complete cycle. If you are animating a biped, one stride would be two steps. If you are animating a quadruped like a dog or a cat, the stride length is the distance the character covers after all four paws have stepped. Another way to think about stride length is as the distance the character travels in the time it takes for any one of its feet to complete one cycle (go from being on the ground, to lifting, to moving forward, up to the instant it touches the ground again). This way of thinking about it works no matter how many feet a character has.

Why is calculating stride length so important? If you are working on a project with many animators who are all going to share cycles on the project, then it is extremely important that you create a cycle that will loop perfectly to infinity. Without knowing your EXACT stride length, it is impossible to truly create a perfect cycle. This is one of the most overlooked aspects of creating cycles, and you'll see when we get into this cheat how problematic "eyeballing" a cycle can actually be.

The easiest way to calculate stride length for a walk cycle is to pose a character taking a (comfortable) step using just the root control and one foot. Then simply observe the value in the foot's Translate Z channel, and double it to get your stride length. From then on, you will be doing multiple calculations with this number, confident that, armed with stride length, your cycle will loop perfectly for eternity.

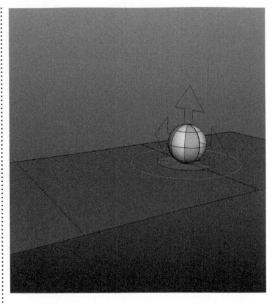

1 Open stride_start.ma. This is a bouncing ball animation, in which the ball is taking leaps forward. A good way to think of this for the purposes of stride length is that the ball is a uniped (one footed), and the "foot" is the entire character.

4 Play back the animation. Looks great? Right? Now expand the timeline to 480 frames. Play back again. Still looks fine, so what's the problem? Go to f1. Select the ball_Master_CTRL, and right click on the Translate Z channel. Choose Unmute Selected.

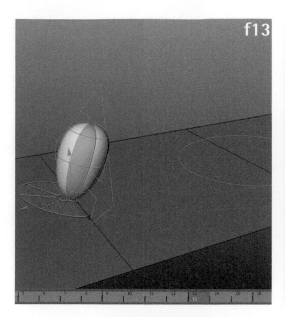

f13

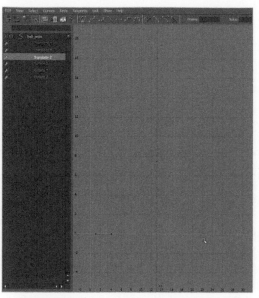

stride_start.ma
stride_finish.ma

2 He does one complete leap and landing every 24
frames. All that's left is animating the Translate Z
channel to give him forward motion. Select the ball_anim
control. On f13, translate it forward to about where the
next edge in the ground plane is showing. (If the edges are
not showing click on Shading > Wireframe on Shaded.)

3 On f24, with the ball_anim control still selected, hit **S**
to set a key. Open the Graph Editor and change your
Translate Z to linear interpolation, like the one above. Now
select the curve and change the Post Infinity interpolation
type to Cycle With Offset.

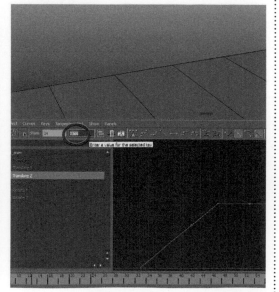

5 The master control is counter-animated against the
ball_anim control to keep it in place while we work. It is
moving backwards according to a set stride length, but since
we eyeballed the ball's Z movement, it moves further away
from its home position every cycle that goes by.

6 Let's investigate why our cycle is getting off center.
Select the ball_anim control and open the Graph Editor.
Select the two keyframes on the Translate Z channel that are
on frames 13 and 24. Look up at the value box to see what
value is on these frames. Mine is 7.365.

HOT TIP

The stride
length method
presented here
is the simplest,
but it's also
possible to
animate stride
length with an
inverse method:
by translating
the Root
control forward,
countering a
cycle that has
been animated
in-place. See
the additional
content on the
*How to Cheat in
Maya* website
for a chapter
on walks where
that method is
demonstrated.

Stride Length (cont'd)

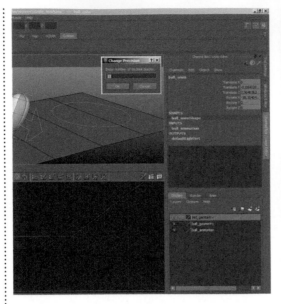

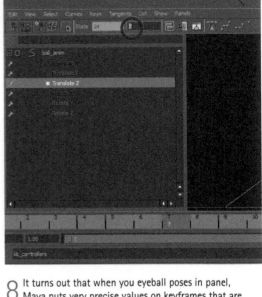

7 Is it really 7.365? Go to f13 in the time slider and then in the Edit menu in the Channel Box, click Settings > Change Precision. Type in "15" (the maximum) in the box and hit enter. Now look at the Z value. Mine is 7.364636278760326!

8 It turns out that when you eyeball poses in panel, Maya puts very precise values on keyframes that are nowhere near clean, integer values. Since our stride length is supposed to be 7 units, in the Graph Editor select the Translate Z keys on frames 13 and 24, type "7" in the value box and hit *Enter*.

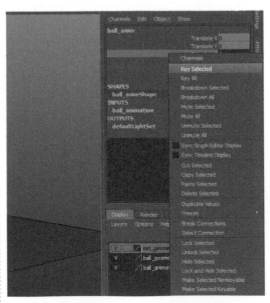

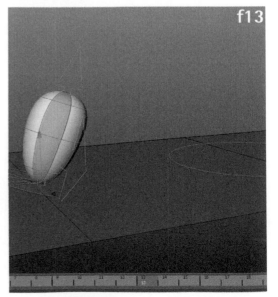

f13

11 Now let's set some keys. On f1, type in "0" on the ball_anim control's Translate Z channel. Right click on the Translate Z channel and choose Key Selected. We're going to be careful not to add any keys on channels that we don't need to.

12 Advance to f4. Right click on the Translate Z channel and choose Key Selected. On f13, move the ball forward using only the Z axis on the translate tool, and try again to line it up with the edge on the ground plane ahead of the start position.

9 Now the stride length is perfect. If this were a character, all of the legs would cycle correctly, knowing the stride length. Let's be totally sure: expand your timeline to 50,000 frames. Notice how the ball is still cycling perfectly in place.

10 A more common workflow is to eyeball the stride length in panel and correct it later. Select the ball_ anim control and right click on the Translate Z channel in the channel box. Choose Delete Selected. On f1, select the ball_Master_CTRL Translate Z channel, right click and choose Mute Selected.

Making your stride length close to an integer value makes keeping the stride equal on all controls easy. But you may have to do a little bit of math: if the stride is 8 units, and the root starts at Translate Z=0, then it obviously moves to 8. But if one foot's Translate Z starts at –3 and the other at 6, then they need to finish at 5 and 14, respectively.

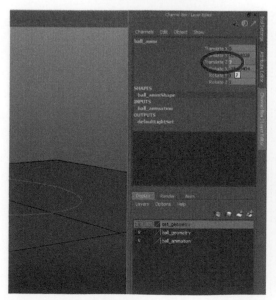

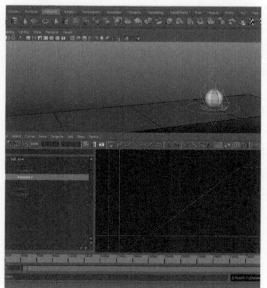

13 Pros will eyeball a pose and then choose nice, round numbers for their stride lengths. After you've set a controller's position, type a value in the Channel Box. Notice that even with 15 decimal places of precision, when you type it in, it is EXACTLY the value you chose. Type in 7 in TZ, right click on the TZ channel and choose Key Selected.

14 Set another key on f24. In the Graph Editor, make the TZ curve interpolation linear, and the Post Infinity curve type Cycle With Offset. By eyeballing and then correcting, we have a workflow that gives us fast, accurate stride lengths. Unmute the TZ channel on the ball_Master_ CTRL and check the animation on frame 50,000 for fun!

217

9 Cycles
Walk Cycle

W E ARE GOING TO LEARN how to find the stride length of a walk cycle quickly. This will be invaluable to your workflow, because a good animator should know how to put together an accurate, looping walk cycle in a short amount of time. Use this cheat whenever you start any looping animation that needs to travel in Z; for walk cycles that stay in place without having a master control counter-animated against the world IK controls (like in games), you need only make sure that, as the animation cycles, there are no visible pops in the animation.

Remember, the stride length is the distance that a character travels in one complete cycle. For a biped, this means two steps. We are going to assume a 20-frame walk cycle, meaning ten frames per step. Also, the first and last frame need to be the same so we're going to be doing a lot of copying keys, and a lot of math input in the Graph Editor's stat boxes (see the Graph Editor chapter, Chapter 3, for detailed info on the math operations). However, knowing our stride length, this is a simple process and will quickly become an indispensible part of your workflow.

We are not going to animate the full cycle, only find the stride length and animate the feet accurately (see the additional content at www.howtocheatinmaya.com for a complete walk cycle tutorial). The rest of the animation on the body, that doesn't travel in Z, is very simple to make cycle: copy the first frame to the last frame of the cycle, and make sure the Post-Infinity curve type is just cycle! Let's give it a shot.

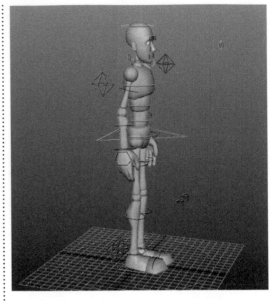

1 Open walk_start.ma. Goon is standing still, ready to animate. Remember that we're going to be using a lot of math operators in the Graph Editor, so open it up in preparation for this.

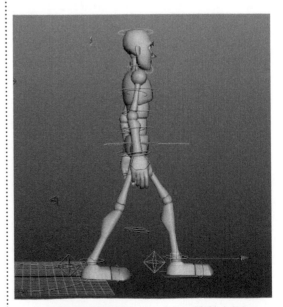

4 Go to frame 10, and now pose Goon with his left foot forward, along with the root moving forward as well. Keeping everything exact is not important because we're going to be typing in the Z values once we've found our stride length.

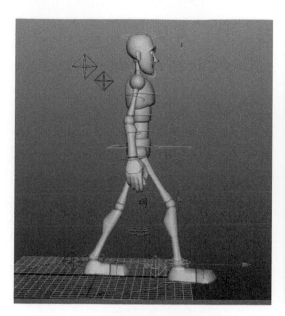

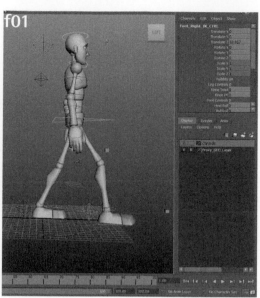

f01

walk_start.ma
walk_finish.ma

2 Pose Goon with his right foot forward, his root comfortably between his feet and a little bit downwards in Y. We normally make a "milestone" frame 1 of a cycle, like the foot planting, as we've done here.

3 Set a key at f01 on all of the world IK controllers that are moving in Z. These are his left and right feet controls, and his root. Take note of what the value is on Goon's right foot. Mine is 10.967.

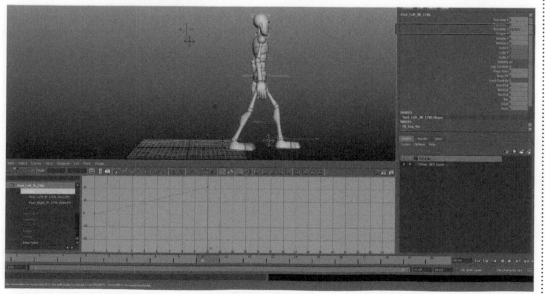

5 Now look at the Translate Z value on the left foot. Mine is 21.96. Hey! That is roughly double the first value we had. We can now approximate our stride length. The nearest nice integer value is 22. Voila! We have our stride length.

Walk Cycle (cont'd)

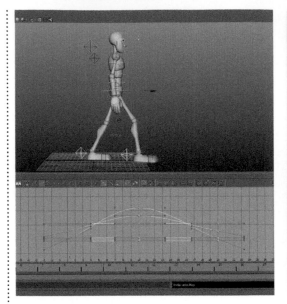

6 On the timeline, middle mouse drag and copy frame 1 to frame 20, with both feet and the root selected.

7 Now select the Translate Z channel in the Graph Editor on all three controllers (both feet and the root). In the value stats box, type in "+=22". The last key has now been adjusted to reflect our stride length. Using a math operator means we know the values are exact.

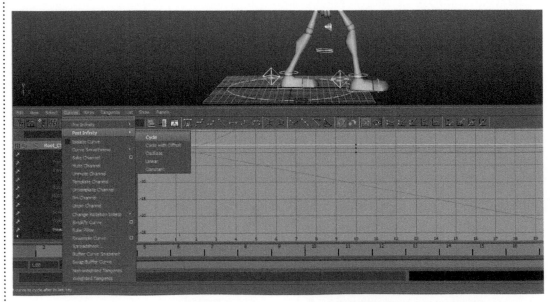

9 Now let's make sure these keys have the right cycle type. Select all of Goon's controls and, in the Graph Editor, go to Curves > Post Infinity > Cycle.

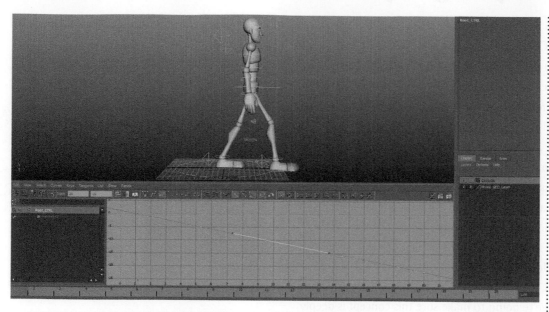

8 Flat all tangents in the Graph Editor. Now select the root_ctrl on the ground at Goon's feet. Set a key on frame 1 and then on frame 20, set a key on Translate Z on -22.

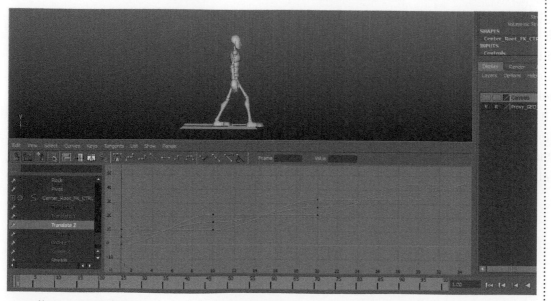

10 Now select both foot controls, the center root, and the ground root control. In the Graph Editor, select only the Translate Z channels. Go to Curves > Post Infinity > Cycle with Offset. Expand your timeline and watch Goon cycle perfectly in place! The rest of the cycle now comes easy.

9 Cycles
Flying Cycle

FLYING CREATURES are a popular item in games, a major portion of the animation industry. Flying characters also find their way into popular feature films, TV shows, and commercials. From cartoony characters to the ultra-realistic, a flying cycle is an interesting exercise in the art of offsets. To cycle a flying creature, we are going to be taking advantage of some of Maya's great tools that we learned about in Chapter 3, on the Graph Editor. We're going to want to be able to see immediate results in the panel from making minor adjustments in the Graph Editor.

The first and best thing for an animator to realize about a flying cycle is that downward motion (thrust) of the wings will produce upwards motion in the body. It seems common sense, but we're going to make sure this concept is deeply engrained in your process by creating the wing motion and body motion together, then practicing offsetting again.

We'll start with a demon version of Goon, with horns and bat-like wings added to our familiar rig to demonstrate fly cycles. It's worth mentioning that a hovering fly cycle like the one we are going to create has applications in many different situations, from butterflies to dragons. However, you will quickly find that the principles of bird flight (simply put, forward motion creates the lift in the wings) are wildly different. It will take very extensive research and reference gathering to accurately create any realistic flying cycle. That said, though, the workflow cheats presented here will serve you with all your flying animation.

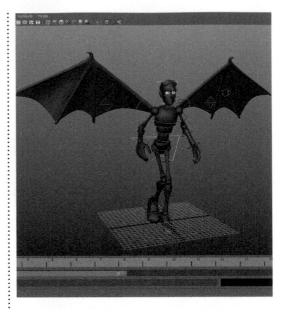

1 Open flyCycle_start.ma. With flying cycles, keying the extremes and offsetting is a quick and easy way to get the motion you want. We will create poses for the up and down wing positions, and then offset the keys on the different controls to get a more natural bend on the wings.

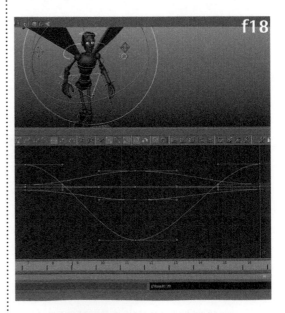

4 Remember that a cycle needs the same first and last frame. Select all of the wing controls, and from f1 on the timeline, MMB drag to copy the key to frame 18. Let go of the MMB, and hit **S**. Open the Graph Editor and make sure the frame was copied; then flat all tangents.

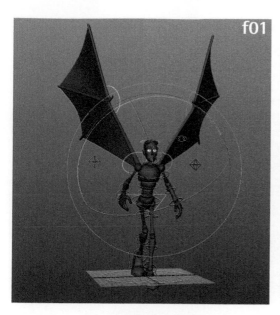

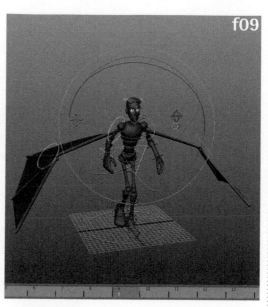

flyCycle_start.ma
flyCycle_finish.ma

2 First make a pose with the wings up. This can be done entirely in panel. Using the round controls on the wings, set a key on frame 1 with the wings in an upward position. I like this.

3 Now let's make the down pose. It looks really cool if the wings are curled under the body for big creatures. Key the wings down on frame 9 (we're making an 18-frame fly cycle.)

5 To make the breakdown poses for flapping wings, we need to remember that the wings are not flapping in a vacuum–they're pushing air! So on frame 4 key the tips of the wings bending upwards as if they are being pushed, and on frame 13 key the tips down.

6 Now it's time to key the up and down motion of the character. We're going to get some great practice doing offsets here. Go back to frame 1 (we're going to create all of our poses on frame 1 and 9 and then offset). Key the root_CTRL at Translate Y=5.

223

Flying Cycle (cont'd)

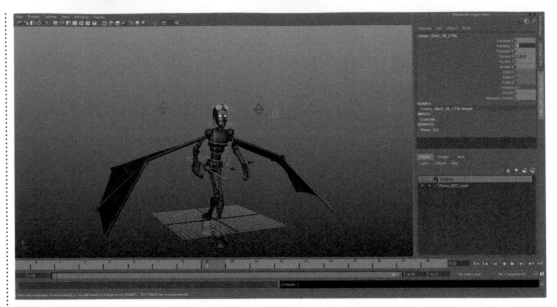

7 Select all of the controls in the body and set another key on frame 9. Translate the root control down in Y to about -5.

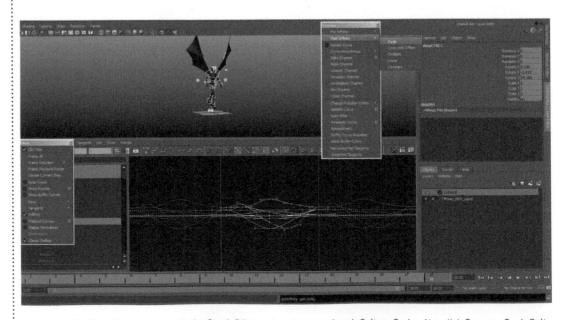

9 Select all of Goon's controls, and in the Graph Editor, select Curves > Post Infinity > Cycle. Also click Curves > Pre Infinity > Cycle. Remember, this setting tells Maya to cycle the animation on any frame before our first and after our last set keyframe. View these curves by clicking View > Infinity in the Graph Editor.

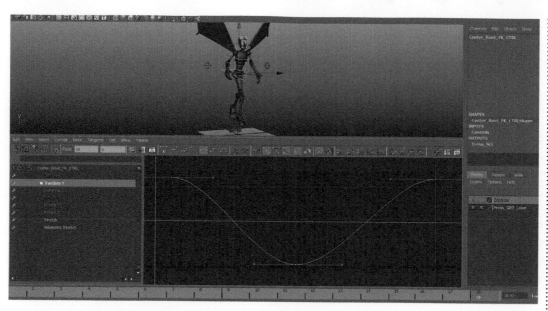

8 Middle mouse drag and copy frame 1 to frame 18 in the time slider, open the Graph Editor, and flat all tangents. Noticing a pattern in the workflow yet?

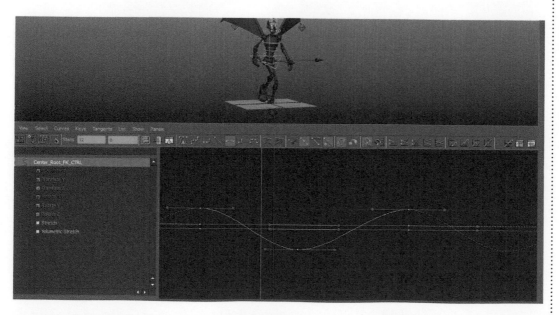

10 Let's offset! Select Goon's root control, and select all of the curves in the Graph Editor. One awesome feature of Maya is that you can make a change in the Graph Editor while the animation is playing and watch the result. Hit play on the timeline and move the selected curves backwards six frames in the Graph Editor.

HOT TIP

When creating cycles, experiment with making sections of the cycle slightly different lengths to get a more organic feel. For instance, sometimes in a walk you can make the right foot's step take 9 frames and the left foot 10 frames. Small differences that you imperceptibly feel but don't see can make an animation more lifelike.

225

Flying Cycle (cont'd 2)

11 Cool! It now looks like his wings are thrusting through the air! Let's build another layer of offset animation. Since we'll be selecting Goon's spine and legs a lot, let's make a quick select button. Select his spine and leg controls, and click Create > Sets > Quick Select Set. Name it SPLEG and click Add to Shelf.

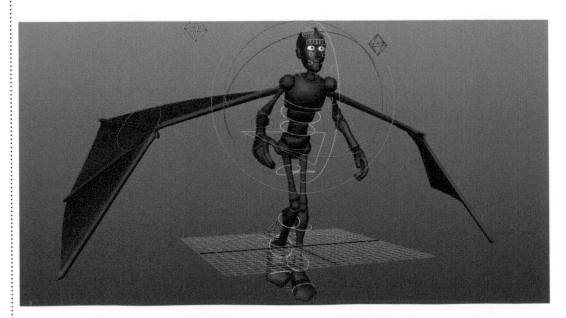

13 On frame 9, key Goon's spine bent forwards, and his legs slightly extended. Click the SPLEG shelf button, and copy frame 1 to frame 18 by MMB dragging in the time slider like we've become used to. We have our timing engrained in our mind by now, so creating animation on set intervals and offsetting is super-easy!

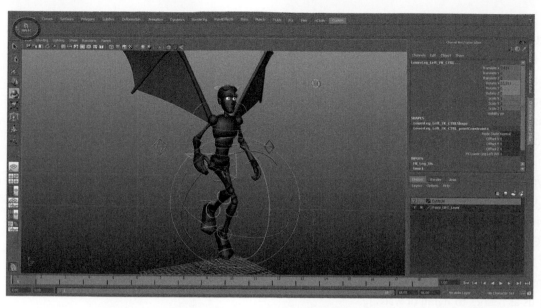

12 Now you have a handy button that selects these controls for you. Deselect everything, then click on the SPLEG button. Now, on frame 1, key Goon's spine bent slightly backwards, and his knees slightly bent, as above.

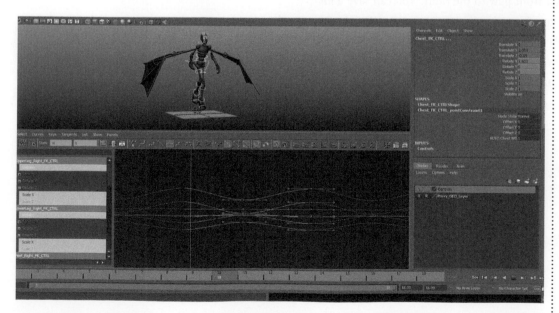

14 In the Graph Editor, set the Pre and Post Infinity curve types to Cycle as before. Select all the curves, flat all tangents, and offset! Drag his spine and leg curves backwards two frames. Play back your animation and adjust if necessary. Awesome!

HOT TIP

Don't stop working with your offsets after sliding the curves around. Keep subtly working more in by having the wings flap a frame or two apart from each other. Then use the tangent handles to give each wing a slightly different spacing through their individual flaps. Lots of little tweaks will add up to a big difference!

227

Quad Cycles

QUADRUPEDS ARE PREVALENT in games and feature VFX. Knowing how to quickly block a walk cycle is an important skill for an animator. Finding stride length is an extremely important cheat to have mastered when it comes to quads; any trouble you can get into with two legs is doubled for four!

While teaching a full quad walk is outside the scope of a cheat, you will clearly be able to see the use of offsets throughout the body of this quad walk presented here. Take a few moments to click on a few different controls and go into the Graph Editor. You will see that the animation is cycled for 24 frames on all controls, but offset greatly. This is the fastest way to cheat a cycle, and it applies just as much to quads as it does to flying or walking.

We're going to do another kind of offsetting with this cycle: offsetting VALUES instead of offsetting TIME. We need to do this because we are going to copy the animation from the left front paw to the right. You can save a lot of time by copying animation across a character's body, but as you'll see, we need to offset the values to make the animation work. We will be using the "Nico" Rig, which is an awesome quadruped rig.

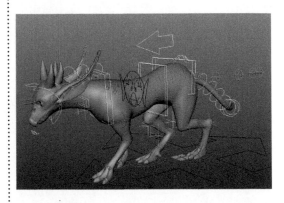

1 Open quad_Start.ma. We have a blocked quad cycle that you can look through later, but for now we're going to take a look at copying the animation from the front left paw to the front right.

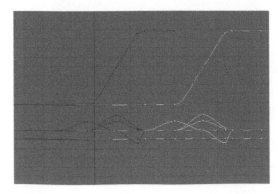

4 Let's offset the right paw. In the Graph Editor, select all of the curves, and slide them 12 frames forward in time. With the curves still selected, go to Curves > Pre Infinity > Cycle. Also select the frontLeg_CON Translate Z channel and go Curves > Pre Infinity > Cycle with Offset.

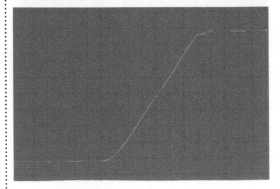

5 Now let's offset the value of the Translate Z channel. Putting the right paw 12 frames behind put it HALF A STRIDE behind. Select the curve, and in the type-in transform box put in "+=80". (Half of 160—our stride length). Now the right paw is moving where it should.

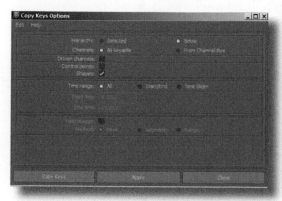

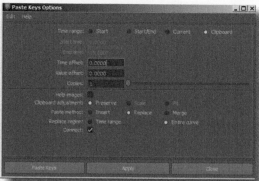

quad_Start.ma
quad_Finish.ma

2 Select the front right paw and go to Edit > Keys > Copy Keys ☐. Make sure your settings match mine.

3 Select the front left paw and go to Edit > Keys > Paste Keys ☐. Copy my settings once again. Now the front paws (and toes) have identical animation. Select the front right paw and all of the toes for the next step.

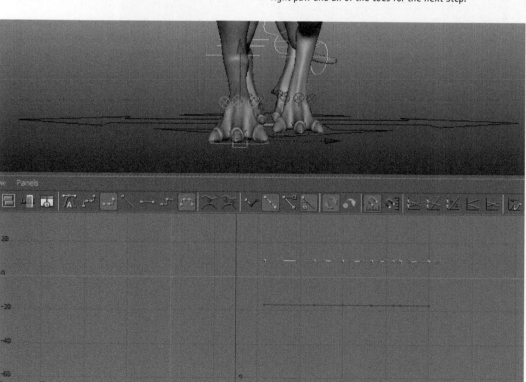

6 Finally, you'll notice that the right paw is sticking out to the side. This is the same X translation that is on the left paw. Select the Translate X curve in the Graph Editor and, watching the result in the panel, drag it upwards until the two paws look the same.

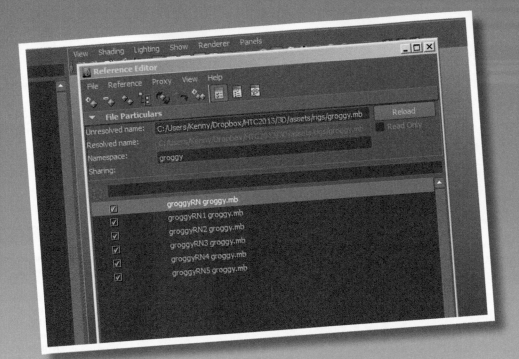

■ Referencing is a major part of a studio pipeline. Knowing how it works and ways to make it work better are essential to a professional workflow.

10

Referencing

UP UNTIL THIS POINT, WE'VE BEEN USING scene files that have all of the rigs imported into the shot. The reason we've done that is to make sure that you are focusing solely on the cheat at hand, and not trying to overcome any technical hurdles unrelated to the chapter.

Now, we're going to dive right into referencing, and hopefully we'll be able to use referenced scene files from now on without leaving any readers behind. Our referencing cheats will make your animation a lot more efficient (at the very least) and possibly save your entire project. It's time to take advantage of the power of referencing!

Referencing Basics

REFERENCING HAS BEEN A PART OF MAYA for many versions, and even before the system was perfected, artists and technicians realized the value of re-using assets in multiple scenes. The concept is simple: instead of having unique copies of frequently used assets in every single scene, create links instead to the source files. This way, changes to the original file will propagate down to the multiple scene files, and you will save immensely on scene overhead and file size. It is not uncommon for an animation file with dozens of referenced rigs (all between 20–50MB) to still be only 1–2MB or so when finished.

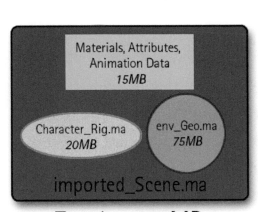

Materials, Attributes, Animation Data
15MB

Character_Rig.ma
20MB

env_Geo.ma
75MB

imported_Scene.ma

Total = 110MB
(Without Ability to Propagate Changes)

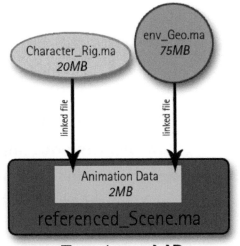

Character_Rig.ma
20MB

env_Geo.ma
75MB

linked file

linked file

Animation Data
2MB

referenced_Scene.ma

Total = 2MB
(WITH Ability to Propagate Changes)

1 Instead of importing characters and sets into a scene, we're going to reference from now on. In an imported scene, the data from all of the imported scenes combines to create a lot of scene overhead. In the referenced scene, the only data that is saved is changes to attributes, like animation curves for instance. The result is a far slimmer scene with less overhead, smaller file size, and the ability to make changes to assets and have those changes propagate into all of your referenced scenes.

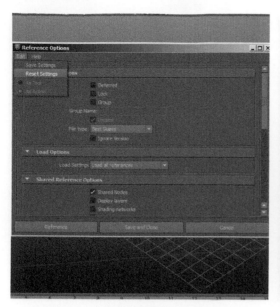

blank_Scene.ma
blank_Scene_finish.
ma

2 Open blank_Scene.ma. Go to File > Create Reference
□. In the options box scroll down and make sure
Shared Nodes and Display Layers are both checked. Click
Reference.

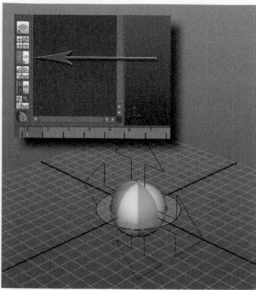

3 Choose ball_Rig.ma in the file dialogue that appears.
Maya will load the file as a reference and bring you
back to your panel. It looks like it's imported but let's take a
closer look. Open the Outliner/Persp panel layout by clicking
its icon in the toolbox.

HOT TIP

You can change
the namespace
in the Reference
Editor, which is
recommended
if your filename
is very long –
shorten the
namespace to
something more
manageable.

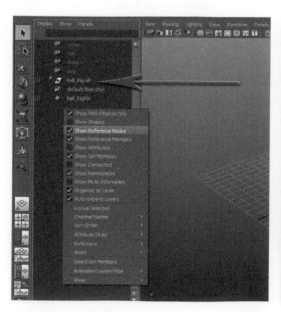

4 See the blue diamond next to the ball_Rig:all group?
That means the node is referenced. You can see all of
the reference nodes by right clicking in the Outliner and
checking the Show Reference Nodes box.

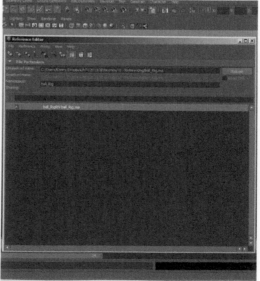

5 Go to File > Reference Editor. This box will give
you control over adding, substituting, and removing
references from your scene. It is also where you might go to
troubleshoot a reference.

Referencing Basics (cont'd)

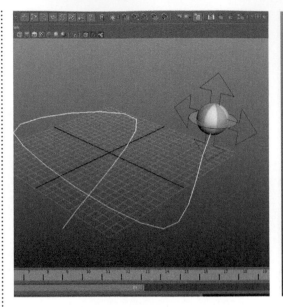

6 Close the Reference Editor, and select the ball rig's ball_Anim control. Set some random keyframes, moving the ball around the scene between frames 1 and 24.

7 Open the Reference Editor. Uncheck the box of the reference node. This unloads the reference, so the ball disappears. The reference is still there, it's just temporarily not in the scene. Check the box again and play back your animation.

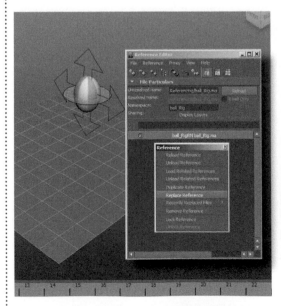

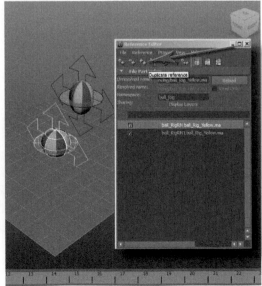

10 Let's replace this reference with a ball with a different color. Go to File > Reference Editor, select the rig, and click File > Replace Reference. Choose ball_Rig_Yellow.ma. Since the naming and hierarchy is the same, the animation stays intact.

11 In the Reference Editor, click the Duplicate Reference button. This is handy if you want to populate a scene with multiple references of the same file, but as you'll notice, animation isn't copied because it is considered an "edit" done in this scene.

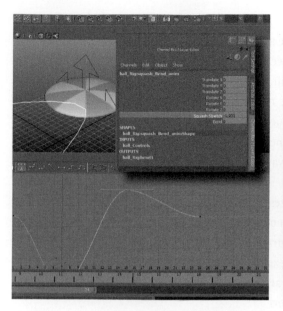

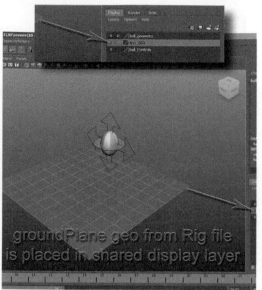

8 Notice that the squash and stretch attribute is animated. This animation is in the rig file itself. Up until now, you were unable to make any changes to animation curves on referenced objects. Now you can! In Window > Settings / Preferences > Preferences, under the Animation tab, check "Allow Referenced Animation Curves to be Edited".

9 blank_Scene.ma has a display layer called env_GEO. Our rig file has the same layer, and so objects in the referenced file are loaded into this layer when you check Display Layers in the reference options. Turn the visibility of this layer on and see.

HOT TIP

Come up with a standardized naming convention for your display layers and you'll find that you can get away with having as few as four or five that will allow you to handle hiding and showing all the objects in your scene!

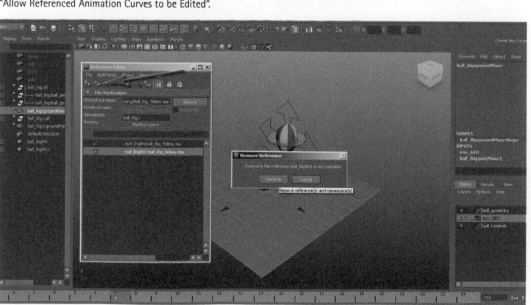

12 Notice how the display layers are still shared even when you duplicate a reference. You want to make sure your reference settings are correct before you duplicate anything. In the Reference Editor, select this new reference and remove it by hitting the Remove Reference button.

Offline Edits

T HE REFERENCE PIPELINE IS DESIGNED to give artists the ability to manage a massive number of scenes, first and foremost. Most of the functionality built into referencing is geared towards this goal. Even the tool we're going to use now, Export to Offline File, is geared towards being able to make edits to multiple scenes. We're going to cheat by using it as yet another way to export animation.

Reference edits come in all shapes in sizes, literally. Modifying an object's components, changing a texture's color, scaling the rig, even setting a keyframe is considered an edit. By allowing animators to export reference edits to an offline file, Maya 2013 has actually created a new, robust, and rock solid way to export animation. In fact, this new method is by FAR the most full-featured and fool proof method to export animation in Maya now.

Why? Exporting animation via AnimExport, Copy keys, even the brand new AtomExport only exports channels that have keys on them. Since changing ANYTHING is considered a reference edit, this offline file you export from the Reference Editor contains all attributes that have changed in your scene, even if there are no keyframes on it. I can't tell you how many times I've tried to import animation from an animator's scene only to discover they did not put any keyframes on the master control. I then have to go into the animation file, put a keyframe on all controllers (even unchanging ones) to be fully sure I am importing the entire performance. Not any more. In fact, this offline file will even recreate nodes that are related to the changes to your reference file, meaning constraints, layers, EVERYTHING.

1 Open ref_Offline_start.ma. You will recognize this file, as we just made it! Select the ballAnim control and notice there are no keyframes on the rotation channels. In Rotation X, Y, and Z, put values of 1, 2, and 3, respectively.

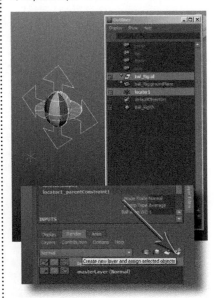

3 Let's also add the locator and the ball rig to a new render layer. In the Outliner select locator1 and ball_Rig:all group. In the Layer Editor's Render tab, click the New Layer from Selected button. Name this layer "testLayer".

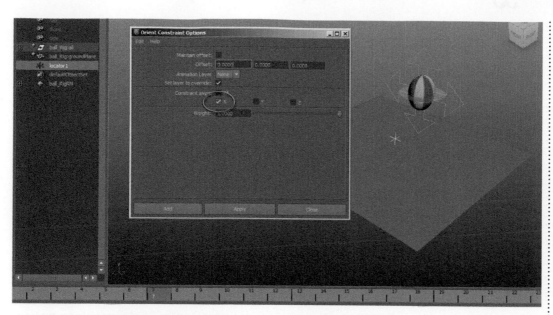

ref_Offline_start.
ma
ref_Offline_finish.
ma

2 Now we're going to get fancy. Go to Create > Locator. Hit F2 to get to the Animation menu set. Select locator1,
Shift select the ballAnim control, and go to Constrain> Orient ☐. Make sure just X is checked, and hit Add. We want
to see if exporting the edits includes these new nodes.

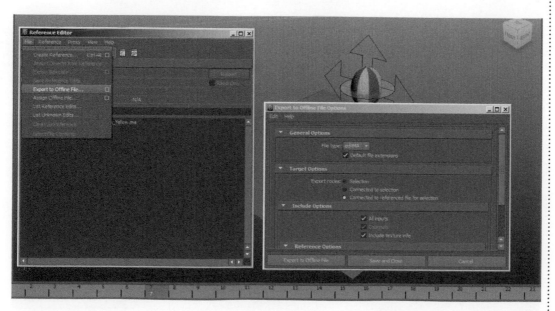

4 Now we export the reference edits.. Open the Reference Editor, select the ball rig reference, and go to File > Export to
Offline File... ☐. In the export dialogue go to Edit > Reset Settings. Hit Export to Offline File, and name it "ball_anim.
editMA".

237

Offline Edits (cont'd)

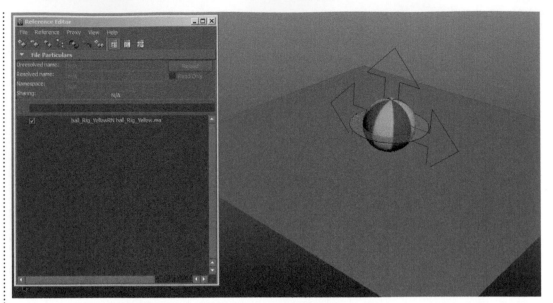

5 Remember we're hoping that not only the animation was exported, but the relating nodes like render layers, the locator, and the parent constraint. Create a new scene, and hit **ctrl**+**R** to load a reference. Choose ball_Rig_Yellow.ma.

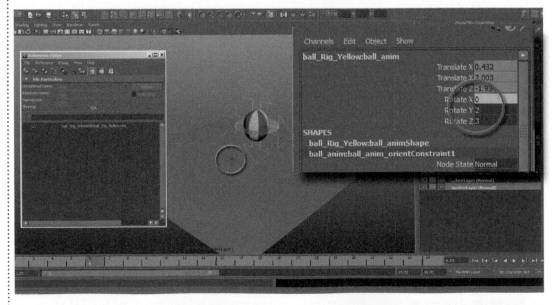

7 Check it out! First play back the animation and you'll see the animation has transferred. Also notice the locator1 has been brought into the scene as well. Select the ballAnim control. The constraint is in place, and the values of 2 and 3 in Y and Z rotation have come through too, even though there are no keyframes on those channels.

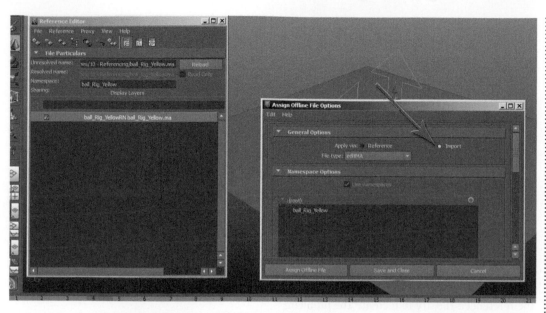

6 Now select the ball_rig_Yellow reference in the Reference Editor, and go to File > Assign Offline File ☐. Change the setting Apply via from Reference to Import. We don't want to load another reference of the edits themselves, we want the animation and nodes imported into this scene. Hit Assign Offline File and choose ball_anim.editMA.

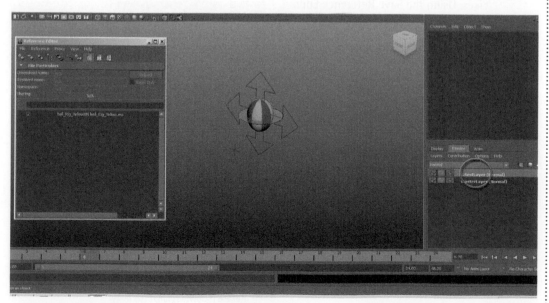

8 Select the render layer testLayer. See how the locator1 and the ball rig are loaded into this render layer? Excellent. Absolutely every single reference edit, modified attribute, animation curve, even render layer has been exported and imported perfectly. This tool may have been intended to propagate changes to many files, but we're going to cheat and use it to copy animation from now on!

239

Saving Reference Edits

W'RE IN THE HOME STRETCH of a project, and a change needs to be made to a referenced asset. But maybe the fix needs to be done in an animation scene and not the referenced file itself.

What kind of change would that be? Any problem that only presents itself in an animated scene, like a weighting issue, a rig issue, a material change, etc. It could be quite possible that we'd only see this kind of problem as we animate our character. The normal workflow would be to note the change you want to make, save and close the file, open up the referenced file, try to recreate the problem, make the change, save the file, open up the animation scene, see if the change you made in the referenced file actually solves the problem, and repeat as necessary.

Yikes. Using the Save Reference Edits command we can fix problems much more efficiently.

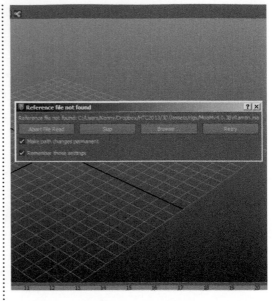

1 Open edits_Start.ma. The reference file is not found. No big deal. Navigate to the Chapter 10 folder and find Moom.ma. Check both Make path changes permanent and Remember these settings.

3 Rotate it down against his body.

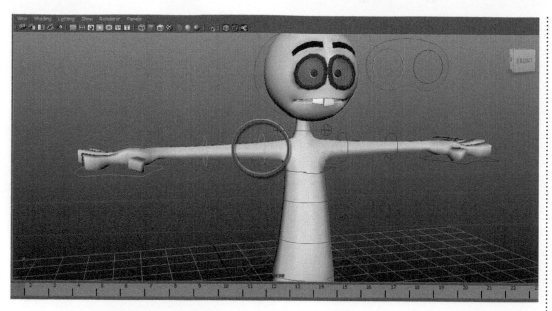

edits_Start.ma

2 Now that Moom is in the scene, we're going to select his controls and make sure the rig is working correctly. Select his right upper arm FK control.

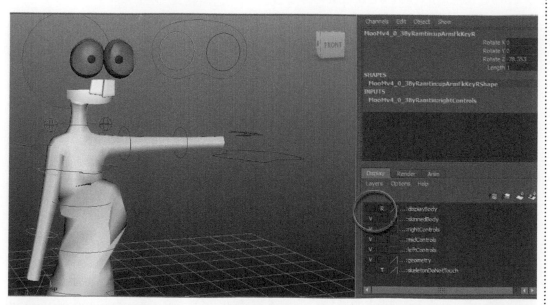

4 Yikes. He clearly has some weighting issues. Let's work these out and save the edits back into the rig file. Hide the display layer named displayBody and show the layer named skinnedBody. This geometry is the one we'll do the weight painting on.

HOT TIP

We normally check weighting in as many poses as possible when skinning. A great way to check if your weights are good is to use a modular rig system and to load animation onto your rig in the rig file itself. This saves being surprised later on.

Saving Reference Edits (cont'd)

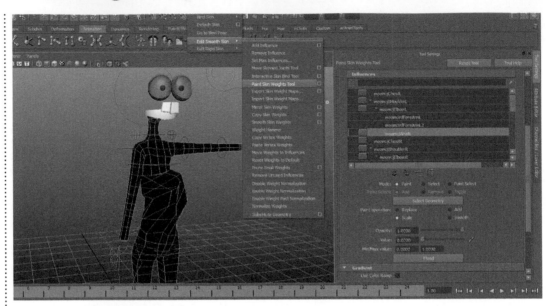

5 Select the body geometry and in the Animation menu set (F2), go to Skin > Edit Smooth Skin > Paint Skin Weights Tool.

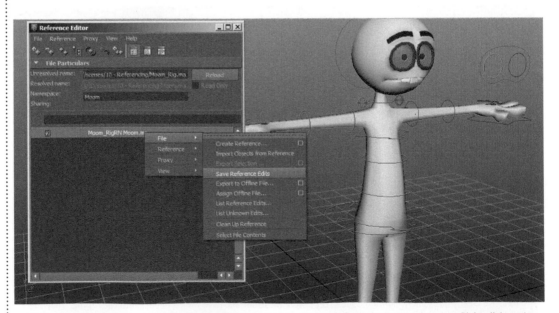

8 Turn off the display layer skinnedBody and turn the displayBody back on. Open the Reference Editor. Right click on the Moom reference and choose File > Save Reference Edits. It will inform you that you cannot undo this change. Choose Save.

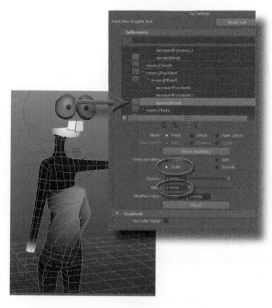

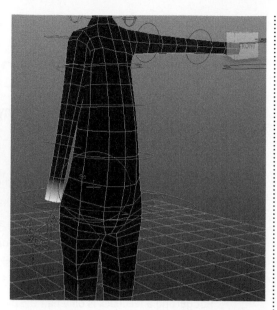

6 In the Tool Settings panel, select the influence named moom:jWristR. You will know it's the right one if the wrist AND the body turn grey to show there is influence on it. Change your paint tool to Scale and the value to 0.

7 Paint the zero weight on the body to remove the wrist's influence. Once all of the influence is removed from the body, select the upper arm control and rotate it around to check and see. If you see body vertices moving, repeat steps 5–7.

HOT TIP

You have to make sure you are not sharing any layers when you load your references, if you want to be able to save reference edits. A good idea might be to load references without anything shared to begin with, then switch to shared layers when you are sure you are finished making edits.

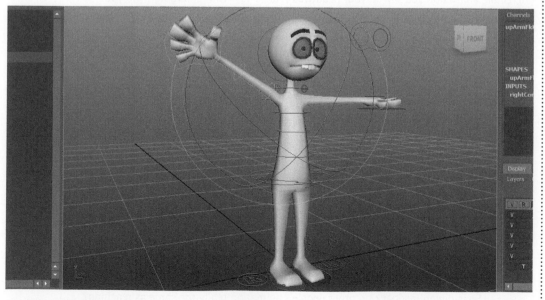

9 Let's test it! Open up Moom.ma in this chapter's scene folder. Grab his arm control and move it all around – the skin weights are now working correctly!

Giving Feedback

by Kenny Roy

IN THE LAST EDITION OF *HOW TO CHEAT IN MAYA* there was an interlude about getting feedback. Feedback is an essential part of the animation process. Indeed, we are creating experiences that are not meant to exist in a vacuum, they are meant to be enjoyed by audiences! To summarize the last edition's interlude, feedback is how you know you are improving not only your animation skills but your appeal and storytelling sensibilities.

But getting a feedback is only half the picture. You have to GIVE feedback as well. In short, while very helpful to the animator receiving your comments, giving feedback is actually a VERY self-serving gesture. Let's talk about why.

When you first started in animation, doubtless you were driven by performance and a zest for awesome motion. You quickly found out, however, that the incredible animation you saw in your head was years away from emerging from your fingertips. Animation takes a lot of time and effort to learn. But you persevered! You found resources like this book and you are taking learning animation with Maya very seriously. You get feedback on your work constantly, and always strive to incorporate the best suggestions in a way that will fit nicely into your established workflow.

What's missing?

It has been often said that you only retain 10% of what you hear, 25% of what you see demonstrated, 75% of what you practice, and 90% of what you teach. To put it simply, the best way to really solidify a concept is to teach that concept to someone else. In doing so, you are simplifying the concept in a way that YOU understand. This is different from memorizing a concept explained in SOMEONE ELSE'S way. Rather than just remembering a word-for-word regurgitation of an idea, you internalize the idea for simple explanation to others.

So is giving feedback on other people's animation really the same as teaching? Absolutely. You are first watching the animation to spot anything that doesn't appeal to your ever-improving eye. Once you've picked out a part of the animation that needs improvement, you must dive into the animation "vault" in your head and start retrieving the concepts that will allow you to voice your opinion clearly and thoroughly. Repetition of this process can mean the difference between knowing a concept, and really understanding a concept.

There is YET ANOTHER benefit to giving feedback that occurs after you have done it for a while. I'm often asked by my students for tricks on how to keep a critical eye your own animation. They are right to ask: the ability to be self-critical deep into the progress of a shot can be almost lifesaving in crunch time. Well, besides the normal tricks, like watching your animation in a mirror, playing the animation backwards, taking a break, etc., giving lots of feedback carries a nice side effect. After you've critiqued hundreds and thousands of pieces of animation you can easily switch into "critique mode"–a state of mind where you can actually look at your own animation as if it is someone else's, and as if you are seeing it for the first time. This ability doesn't come until after you've given feedback on at least a thousand shots. While that may seem like a LOT of animation, there's nothing stopping you from getting started today!

So go right now to an online forum and start being selfish: give feedback like there's no tomorrow! Here are some of my favorites if you need suggestions on where to start:

www.11secondclub.com

www.cghub.com

www.forums.cgsociety.org

www.cgchannel.com

www.3dbuzz.com

forums.awn.com

www.cgarena.com

www.itsartmag.com

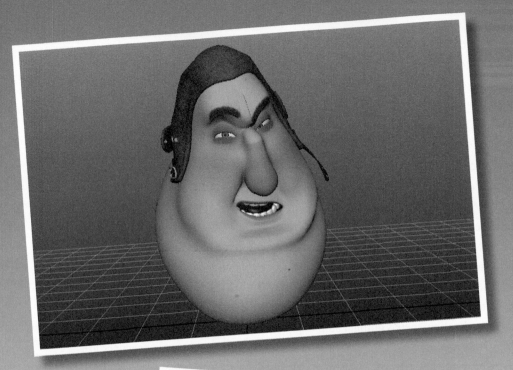

■ What's his
motivation? The
face is a huge
part of conveying
this clearly and
convincingly
through a
performance.

11
Facial Animation

ANIMATING A CHARACTER'S face is one of the most interesting and enjoyable parts of the animation process. We can convey much with the body poses, but this is the really good stuff: the detail that breathes life into our characters. The drama and emotion that the face contains really makes us look inside ourselves and seek to understand and identify with a character. If animating the body makes us entertainers, then animating the face makes us actors.

Facial animation could fill many volumes on its own, but here we'll get into the bread-and-butter techniques that give us a great starting point. No two animators work through the face the same way, and you can build your own dramatic philosophies on the essential tools in this chapter.

Planning and Prep

W E ARE GOING TO WORK THROUGH some facial animation techniques using a simple example of a typical close-up shot. This keeps the staging simple and makes it easy to focus on just the face, while also being a very common shot style found in film, TV, and games. To make the exercises as straightforward as possible, the body has been blocked in for you, so you only need to worry about the face.

When doing any kind of dialog shot, it's important to thoroughly plan your animation. Don't just dive right in and start keyframing. Listen to the audio by itself, over and over, until all its accents and nuances are thoroughly engrained in your mind. Also think about the context of the line, along with the character's internal thought process and motivation for saying it. It's quite possible to animate a line in completely different ways, yet when played in context with the surrounding shots, only a specific approach will ring true.

In our case, we don't have a context, just a single line to use for practicing some animation technique. For the sake of consistency, we'll pretend that the ideas in this planning section are what a director has instructed us to do. In the real world, this planning and prep would have been done before the body was animated, as it would influence our decisions in that regard as well.

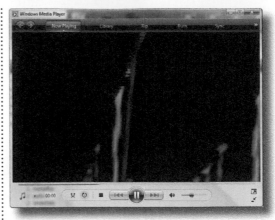

"I have nothing to say."

1 In the Sounds folder in this chapter's project directory is a .wav file with a short dialog clip (nothingtosay.wav). Open it in your favorite media player and listen to it on looped playback. Use headphones if possible. Write down the line and listen to its nuances.

"I have..."
-slow blink on head raise
-head tilts back
-eyebrows raise

"... nothing to..."
-eyes flare slightly
-upper lids still touch iris
-head tilts more
-make brow pose asymmetrical

"... say."
-head comes down
-tilt is opposite of up position
-brows lower some
-eyelids stay lowered

4 Reference is always a good idea. Act out the line and create some video reference for yourself. Make notes on the brow poses, eye darts, blinks, etc. You can also make thumbnails, have a friend act it out, whatever you find useful in determining what you will animate.

"I have nothing to say."

"I have nothing to say."

faceAnimation_
START.ma
faceAnimation_
END.ma

attitude: uncooperative, resistant, possibly hiding something, knows more than he is saying
subtext: "I have nothing to say to you, I don't want you to find out what you are asking me."

2 I hear two distinct accents in the line, on the "noth-" (first syllable) in "nothing," and on "say." The pitch goes up to "nothing" and down on "say." This is also reflected in the body animation. Mark the accents down in your notes.

3 Next I think about the tone of the line and the subtext it may be communicating. The way he says it sounds like he's being uncooperative. It feels like he means "I have nothing to say to you in particular," to whomever he's speaking to. This is more material for our notes.

HOT TIP

To import a sound file into your scene, go to File > Import and select the audio file. Then right click on the timeline and choose the file from the Sound menu.

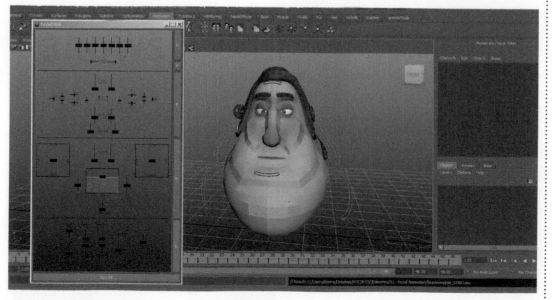

5 Once you've decided on the acting choices and know why you've made them, it's time to start working on the face. Some animators do the lip sync first, while others do it last. I find it helpful to first do a few full face poses to use as a structure. Open faceAnimation_START.ma. The main head control has animation, but the face is stuck in its default blank stare, which we'll fix soon enough!

11 Facial Animation

Core Poses

I T'S VERY FEASIBLE to animate the face in a layered fashion, but I've found I get better results when I first block in some initial expressions to use as a foundation. The accents we indicated in our planning stage create a perfect framework on which to base these poses. This also helps make the work stronger, since we can focus on just a few expressions and not worry about making fluid motion yet. We'll put in four poses total: the accents on "nothing" and "say," the anticipation pose on "to," and the starting pose. Things will get moved around a little when we refine them, but you'll likely find that these core poses really help keep you on track.

Cenk is a very powerful and versatile rig. We're going to try to make sure to take a very simple approach to the facial posing so that we don't get inundated with keyframes early on in the process. You will also notice we are referencing the Cenk rig into our scenes now—don't forget the great referencing cheats from last chapter!

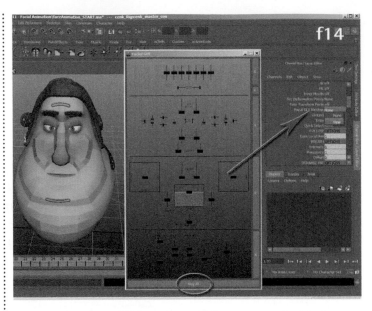

1 Open faceAnimation_START.ma. Select Cenk's master control and, in the Channel Box, select Facial GUI Window and select View. Now change the time slider to frame 14 and hit the Key All button on the Facial GUI.

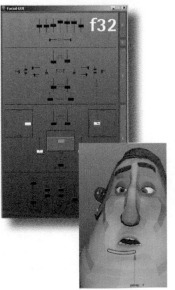

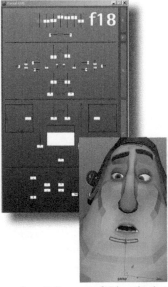

5 At f32, set a key on the face controls. Bring the brows down, lift the lids some, and expand and shape the mouth for "say."

6 Copy f14's pose to f18 by selecting all face controls and MM dragging in the timeline to f18 and setting a key. This will hold that pose for five frames.

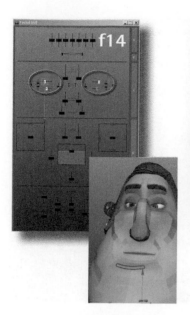

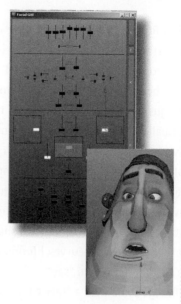

faceAnimation_
START.ma
faceAnimation_
END.ma

2 Cenk's pupils and irises are a llttle small—if we scale them up he will be more appealing. Make the Iris size 1, and the pupil size .5.

3 Start with the brows: raise them and make the shape slightly asymmetrical. Raise the lower lids a bit and make the L eye upper lid slightly higher to complement the higher L brow.

4 For the mouth, bring the corners down and inward. It's roughly the mouth shape for "ha-," but we don't need to be concerned with it too much right now. Curl the lips out a bit and shape the mouth.

HOT TIP

In the timeline's right click menu, go to the Sound options box. There you'll find an offset attribute if you need the sound file to start earlier or later a given number of frames.

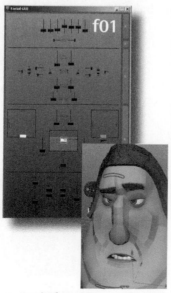

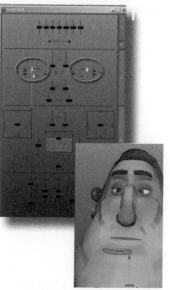

7 Key the face at 24. Raise the brows even more, lift the lids, and shape the mouth for the "to" sound.

8 Key the face at f01 and create the starting pose. We want to convey him being slightly defiant. Lower the brows, but not enough so he looks angry.

9 A slightly open frown helps show that he's displeased about the situation, but not gruff or stewing.

Facial Animation

Lip Sync 1–Jaw Motion

WITH THE CORE POSES COMPLETED, we're in a good spot to start on the lip sync. As we've seen time and time again, the approach of starting broadly and adding detail in phases will work beautifully here. We won't worry about mouth shapes yet, just the jaw movement. Once that is working, everything else usually falls into place pretty smoothly. It's easy to overlook the variety of timing in the jaw movement. In a given line of dialogue, there is usually a wide range of sharp and smooth movements. One trick that helps make them a bit more tangible is to say the line while holding your hand underneath your jaw. You'll be able to feel the words with sharper timings and then translate that into your curves. I found that the biggest accents were on "I," "nothing," and "say."

Normally rigs come with a "face cam" that is used for animating lip sync. This is especially useful in scenes where the character is moving all over the place, doing twists and turns, etc. Cenk does not come with a face cam, partly due to the fact he is basically one giant face to begin with. If you want to create one, simply create a camera and position it in front of his face. Then select his head_local_con and parent constraint the camera to it.

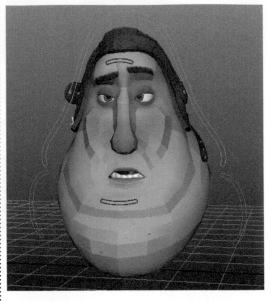

1 Start with the scene you just animated, or with my Lipsync1_Start.ma.

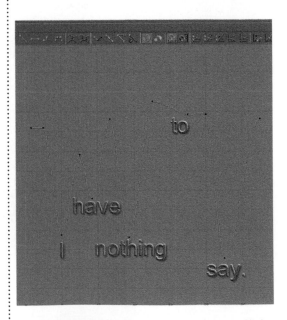

4 This is the curve I came up with for the first pass. Notice the accents on "I," "nothing," and "say," while "have" and "to" are much smaller.

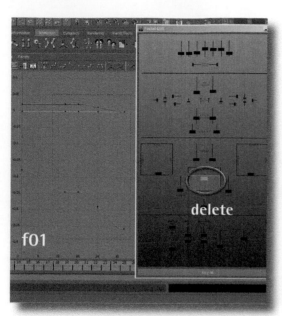

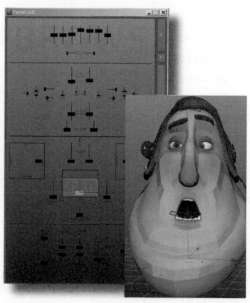

Lipsync1_Start..ma
Lipsync1_End.ma

2 It will help to start fresh with the jaw animation. Select the Jaw control in the facial GUI, and in the Graph Editor, delete all of the keys except the one on frame 1.

3 Do a first pass just to add the open/close movement. Just get the general timing for now. Do an open/close for each open mouth shape, or four total. Keep in mind that you want the open to be a few frames before the actual sound.

HOT TIP

Animate the physical movement of what's being said, rather than simply basing it on the words. If you open/close every syllable, the mouth will chatter pop. Analyze yourself saying the line and only put in what you actually see.

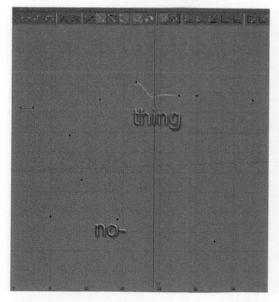

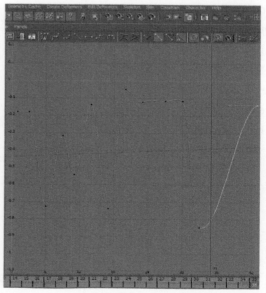

5 Tweak the timing and get the little bump that happens on "-thing." I like to save these secondary bumps for after the main accent so the mouth doesn't get too chattery.

6 Work on the timing of "say," which he draws out longer in the clip. I added a key to hold it open longer, and a longer ease in at the end.

253

Facial Animation

Lip Sync 2–Mouth Corners

THE JAW IS JABBERING AWAY, so it's time to work on the mouth corners. With this rig, the corners are accessible using the left_Mouth_Con and the right_Mouth_con in the facial GUI. The four directions are labeled Smile, Frown, Narrow, and Wide. The two directions we're focusing primarily on in this pass are Narrow and Wide. Other rigs might have more controls for the mouth shapes, but the idea at this point is the same: add another level of detail without going overboard. There's plenty of passes left, so we don't need to do everything at once. Because the mouth rig is so simple, we're basically only worrying about if the corners are in or out at a given time. As for up and down, they will stay in a downward frown position for the entire shot. This is the point where we can start thinking about basic mouth shapes and phonemes. If you're new to animating lip sync, there are plenty of charts online and in classic animation books to study extensively. For this exercise, we'll just walk through the ones we need for the dialogue. Remember, we're not doing the full mouth shapes yet, just the positioning of the corners to get us on the right track.

1 Open Lipsync2_Start..ma. At f07, move both corners out for the "I" sound.

2 Move to f13 and bring them in some for the "ah" sound in "have."

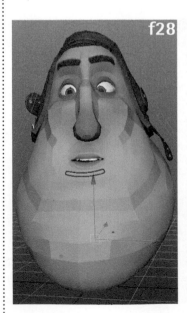

6 At f28 bring the corner back in for the "to" sound.

7 Hold that shape until f34, then at f40 the corners come out again for "say." Bring out his L corner more to give a nicer shape on this last word, so it has a slight drawl to it.

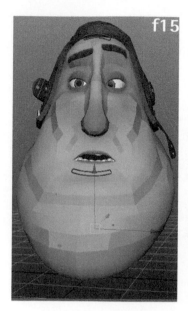

f15

f18

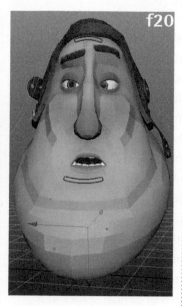

f20

Lipsync2_Start..ma
Lipsync2_End.ma

3 Key the mouth corners slightly wide on frame 15 to get a good read of the "N" of "nothing"

4 On frame 8, we need an "o" shape for "nothing."

5 Copy the key from frame 18 to frame 20, and on frame 24 give him a nice wide shape.

HOT TIP

Don't forget to animate to the camera primarily, rather than the face cam if your shot has one. Use the face cam as a helper, but ultimately the shapes need to look their best in the shotCam.

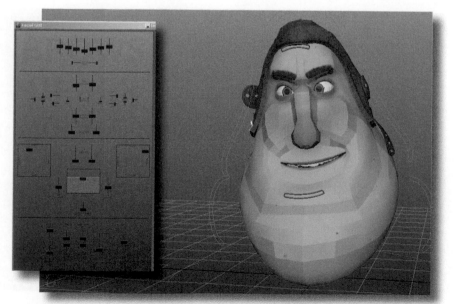

8 Finally, we want a nice ease in to the ending pose, as the mouth relaxes into his final expression.

Facial Animation

Lip Sync 3–Mouth Shapes

ET'S CONTINUE REFINING our lip sync by fleshing out the mouth shapes. This is one of the more organic parts of the process, where you need to experiment a little and do some back and forth to get things working.

The following cheat is a guideline, rather than a step-by-step process.

Remember that less is normally more. With the jaw open/close pass working with the lip corners narrow/wide pass, we are generally about 85 percent of the way done. These two passes need to be really close to perfect in order for the lipsync to read well to an audience. By adding this pass of custom shapes we're getting much closer to the final performance.

1 Open Lipsync3_Start.ma. I've removed the keyframe on the jaw on frame 3, and on frame 7, the corners of the mouth need to be wider to get the "I" shape.

2 On frame 14, create the "F" shape by using the bottom lip roll slider in the facial GUI.

6 Key the lip up/down controls, as well as the jaw and sneer controls on frame 28, then build a nice, toothy, snarly "S" shape on frame 30.

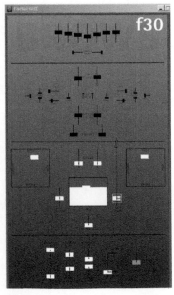

7 I keyed all of the mouth controls on frame 30, then slid all of the keys starting on frame 31 three frames forward. He needs to hold the S longer.

f15

3 On frame 15, we need to see his teeth a bit to get a read on the "N" of "nothing." I used the lip up/ down controls and a bit of sneer.

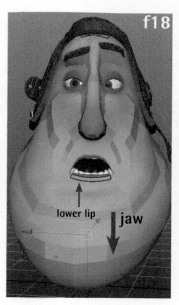

f18

lower lip

jaw

4 The "O" shape was a little too overdone on frame 18, I toned it down.

f20

5 Let's get another nice read on the teeth on frame 20.

Lipsync3_Start..ma
Lipsync3_End.ma

f32

8 Finish that hold on the "S" by middle mouse dragging the key on frame 30 to frame 32 on all mouth controls except the jaw.

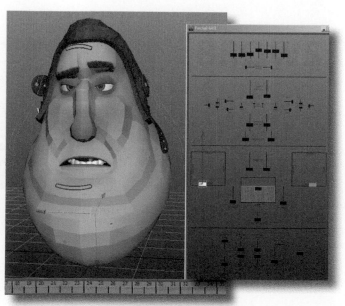

9 Watching the animation back a few times, it definitely feels like there is too much of a pose change in the corners of the mouth at the very beginning. I think this wider start pose feels better.

HOT TIP

Be sure to give any closed shapes at least two frames. Ms, Bs, Ps, Fs, Vs, etc all need to be held at least that long to not look like mistakes or hitches.

Lip Sync 4–Tongue

THE FINAL STEP to really sell the lip sync is to get the tongue moving on the right sounds, in particular "no-" and "-thing," the "T" sound on "to," and the "S" sound on "say." Unless it's an extreme close-up or something like that, the tongue mainly just needs to be seen when it's touching the top of the mouth, for example on "N" sounds, and when it moves back to the floor of the mouth. Otherwise it generally just needs to stay out of the way.

We can get away with a lot of cheating when keyframing the tongue. Again, since a viewer will normally only see the tongue peripherally when watching the animation, we can build a tongue "flick" and copy it to the correct frames later.

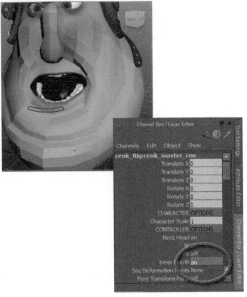

1 Open Lipsync4_Start.ma. On frame 37 (because the mouth is open), select the master controller and turn on the inner mouth controls either by typing in "1" or "on" and pressing enter.

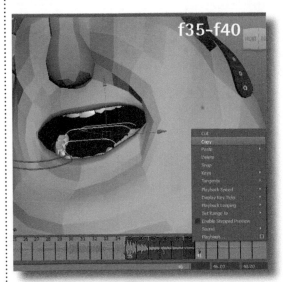

f35-f40

4 On the timeline, press *Shift*+LMB and draw a selection from frame 35 to frame 40. Right click on this range and choose Copy. Now anywhere we need this tongue "flick," we can paste it.

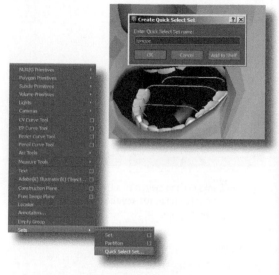

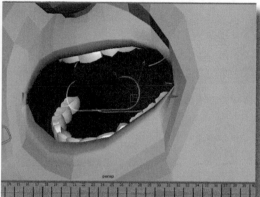

Lipsync4_Start..ma
Lipsync4_End.ma

2 Select all three tongue controls and make a quick select set by going to Create > Sets > Quick Select Set... . Type in the name "tongue" and choose Add to Shelf. This makes it really simple to select the tongue.

3 On frames 35 and 40, hit **S** to set a key with the tongue in default position. On frame 37, key the tongue in an upward pose like this. The tongue controls can be translated as well as rotated.

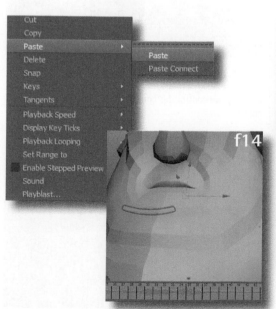

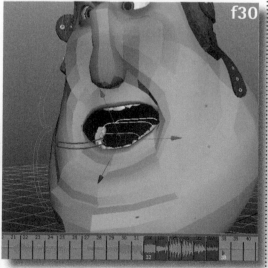

5 On frame 14 (two frames before we need the tongue in the up position), right click on the timeline and hit Paste > Paste. All three keys are pasted and are still in the clipboard for us to paste again.

6 Paste this animation again at frame 20, and frame 27. Delete the animation on frames 35–40 and paste your clipboard again on frame 32, or, if you feel comfortable, in the Graph Editor, delete the keys on frame 35 and slide the keys on frames 37 and 40 back 3 frames.

11 Facial Animation

Blinks

BLINKS ARE A VITAL PART of facial animation and acting, and a great way to add more life and interest to your character. Before we continue with the lip sync animation, let's take a look at doing a typical, standard blink. This is a common approach to doing them, but you want to make sure you don't do all your blinks this way. There are many different kinds of blinks – fast, slow, half blinks, fluttering eyes, takes, disbelief, etc. The approach you use will be dictated by the emotion and thought process of the character. Nevertheless, this is a tried and true way to get a nice, organic-looking blink and is a great starting point for building a "blink library" in your animation toolset.

Remember, we've learned some great ways to copy keys to the clipboard and export animation, so you can take a blink that you create in one file and use it throughout your animations, over and over. Just be sure to add some customization and "flavoring" to each blink to match the scene.

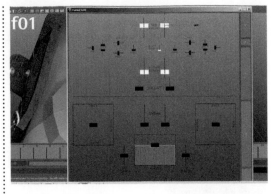

1 Open Blinks.ma and switch to a front view. Select the eyelid controls, and at f01 key the upper and lower lid controls where they are.

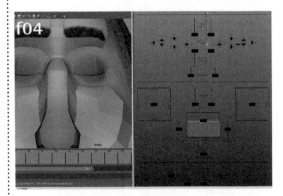

4 On f04 the lids are closed. Normally the upper lids come down about 75% and the lower lids 25%–on the Cenk rig, we control this contact point with the Eye Height control.

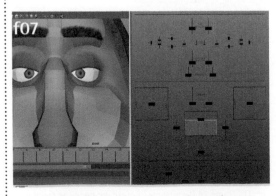

7 At f07 both lids are almost back to the starting pose. Unless the eyes are completely open or closed, I generally like to keep the lids touching the irises on the way up or down, as it makes the blink feel smoother.

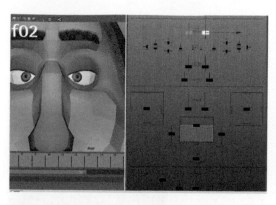

2 On f02 key the upper lids down slightly to create a slight ease out.

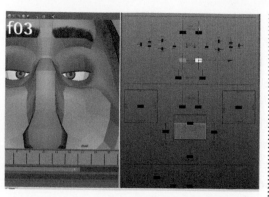

3 At f03 bring the upper lids down so they touch the top of the pupil, and start bringing the lower lids up slightly.

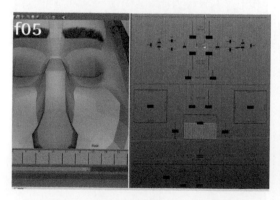

5 We'll hold the eyelids closed for two frames, but move the contact point down just a bit. Use the Eye Height control to key this.

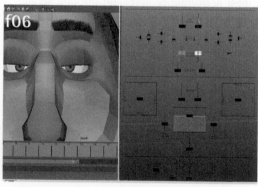

6 At f06, the eyes are opening back up. For a standard blink, I like to have the upper lids be around halfway past the irises on the way back up. The lower lids start to go back down as well.

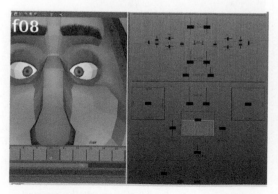

8 Instead of ending on f08, do a nice ease in from f07 to frame 10 to cushion into the pose and make it feel more organic.

9 For an extra bit of polish, do another four frames of very subtle ease-in cushioning on the upper lids. This is what the curves look like. Look at Blinks_End.ma for the final result.

Blinks.ma
Blinks_End.ma

HOT TIP

Another nice touch for blinks can be adding some very slight up and down in the brows. It depends on the situation, but sometimes adding a barely perceptible amount of motion here can help make things more organic.

Blink and Brows

L ET'S REFINE THE BROWS and add a blink to our face animation. We'll have Cenk blink when his head raises, since its speed fits well with the motion we have going. We'll keep it fairly close to a standard blink, except that the closing will be a bit slower since that fits his uncooperative, slightly indignant attitude. Then we'll tighten up the timing of the brows rising, and add an accent in the brows and eyes to bring out the the final word of the shot, "say."

You may find that you are doing a little bit of back and forth with the timing of lids and brows. Indeed, you need to have a workflow that allows for this process to happen so you can "discover" the best performance. We'll go through adding some blinks to the scene and brow movement, but experiment with some different values and timings in your own shot to get the best result.

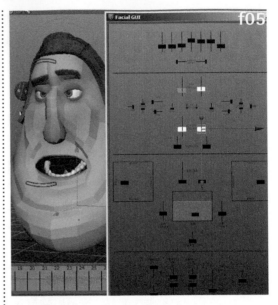

1 Open BlinkBrows.ma. Start the blink on f05. Key the upper and lower lids in their current position.

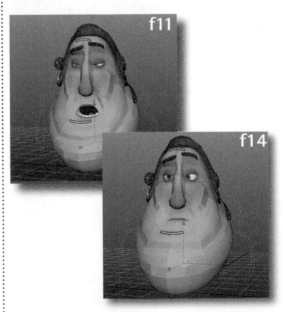

4 A slower opening fits this blink as well. The eyes start opening at f11, and at f14 the tops and bottoms of the irises are still touching the lids.

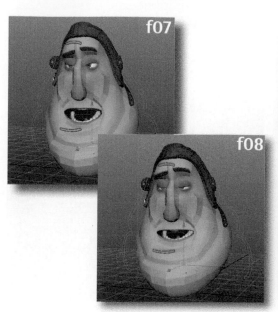

f07

f08

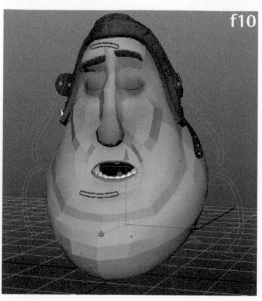

f10

BlinkBrows.ma
BlinkBrows_End.ma

2 Let's make the transition down into the closed pose a total of four frames. Here are f07 and f08. Notice that we always see part of the iris when the eyes are open any amount.

3 On f09 and f10 we have the closed pose.

HOT TIP

When doing any kind of blink, keep the irises partially visible in all of the opening and closing poses. This avoids flashes of only eye whites, which will pop in an unappealing way.

f18

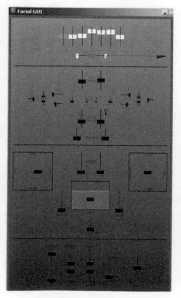

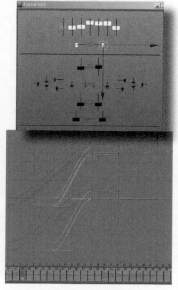

5 The eyes continue to ease into their pose at f18.

6 Now let's work on the brows during the blink. We want to have some overlap, with the brows going up leading the eyes opening slightly. Select all the brow controls.

7 Move the start of the brows' motion to f08, right before the eyes are closed at f09. At f14 they should hit their up pose.

Blink and Brows (cont'd)

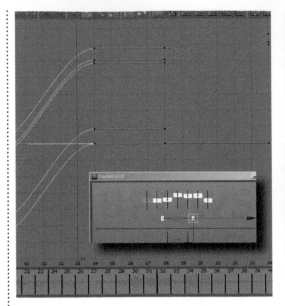

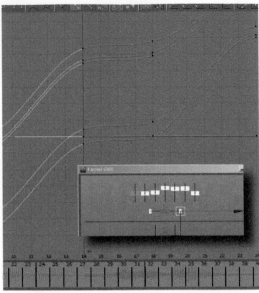

8 A quick trick for doing cushions for the flat curve sections is to move to the frame before they hit the pose, in this case f13.

9 MM drag in the timeline from f13 to f14 and set a key. Now f14 is almost the same value it was, but drifts through to f19. Fix the tangent handles and you instantly have a nice subtle drift to make things more organic, and not frozen for a stretch of frames.

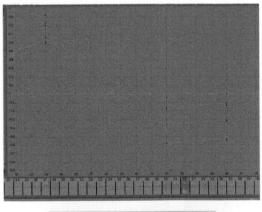

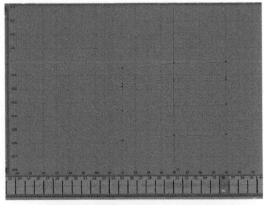

13 At f36, set a key on the brows so they have the same pose as f32. Then at f32, pull the brows down just a small amount to create a little overshoot.

14 Key the brows at f40 and add a little cushion starting at f36.

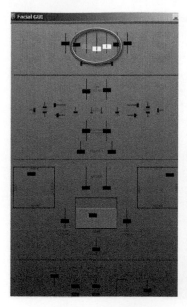

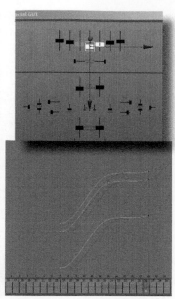

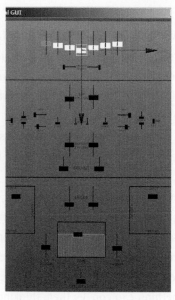

10 To add a bit more fleshiness to the brows, I often like to make the apex lead the rest by a frame. Select the three brow controls shown here.

11 These are the apex of the brow pose, so select their keys at f08 and f14 and slide them one frame earlier to lead the rest of the brows. It's subtle but a nice little touch.

12 Let's move to the end of the animation, on the word "say." Right now the brows and eyes just stop on that last pose at f32, so let's add a little accent. Select the brow controls.

HOT TIP

The brow sections that lead the rest depend on the pose you're hitting at a given time. Use the apex as a guide.

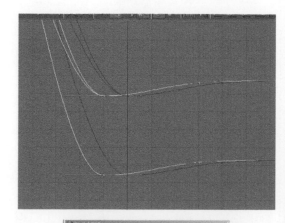

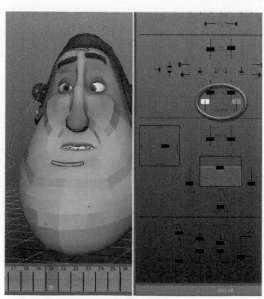

15 Select the three middle brow controls and from f32 onward move them one frame earlier so they lead the rest of the brows.

16 Make a very small complementary squint with the eyes that trails the brow by a frame. It will help give the feel that his face is working as an organic unit, rather than an assembly of moving parts. See BlinkBrows_End.ma for the end result.

Facial Animation

Eye Darts

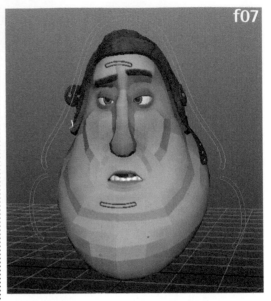

f07

ANOTHER IMPORTANT ELEMENT of organic facial animation is eye darts. They're often used for "keep alive" moments, where a character isn't really moving much but needs to look like they're still a living being. They show that a character is thinking about something and that they have an internal monologue happening. And just on a practical level, our eyes rarely stay focused on the exact same spot for more than a second or so, and usually less.

Eye darts can definitely go deeper than that, however, and should be thought about with as much attention as any other element in a character's performance. An eye dart at the right moment can communicate things that nothing else could. A character's eyes darting away as they're trying to convince someone of something can convey them thinking, "Are they buying this?" or show worry, realization, doubt, or any other internal emotion. This is something that we as animators need to be constantly thinking about.

We'll go through a simple eye dart workflow, but keep in mind it's a starting place. Your decisions about eye darts ultimately depend on what you need to communicate about the character's internal mental state.

Rather than bouncing them around randomly, it helps to create a subtle pattern with the darts. Shapes like triangles, rectangles, etc. can be good guides for plotting the path the darts make, provided you don't make them too obvious. Varied timing and amounts of movement can help with this. Shapes make sense because we often look back and forth between a person's eyes and mouth when we're conversing. For this exercise, we'll do three darts, and form a triangle shape with their path. They're traced in the example as they're very hard to see in still pictures. Be sure to follow along with the Maya file.

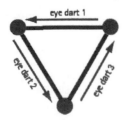

1 Open eyeDarts_Start.ma. If your eye control is not visible, select the master control and change the eyes attribute to "on" or "1". Then switch to the front panel to key this action. Hit **S** to set a key on f07.

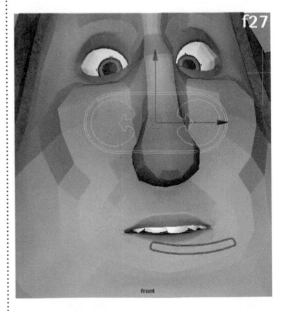

f27

front

4 Now we'll bring it back to the start position, starting on f25 and ending on f27. You can even middle mouse drag the key from f7 to f27 to be sure.

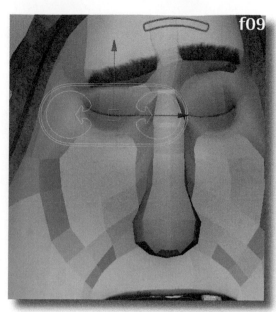

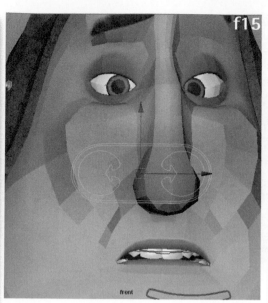

eyeDarts_Start.ma
eyeDarts_End.ma

2 Eye darts are generally 2 frames long at 24fps, so on f09 move the eye target slightly to the left in the front panel and hit **S**. It's okay that his eyes are closed – in fact eye darts work just as well hidden within blinks.

3 Now do another dart, this time downwards. Key the eyes where they are on f13, then move the eye target downwards and slightly back towards the middle on f15.

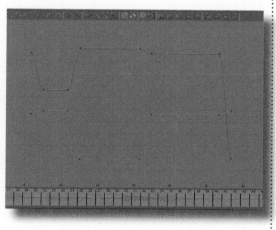

5 I did one more eye dart from f38 - f40, from right to left. Often our eyes dart between the eyes of the person we're speaking to, so this last dart reinforces the idea Cenk is talking to someone directly.

6 Here's what the curves look like for these darts. Our eyes move VERY quickly, so it's not necessary to spend too much time cleaning this up. Watch eyeDarts_End.ma for the final result.

Final Touches

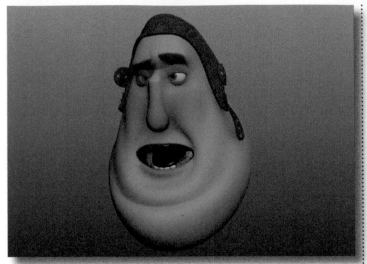

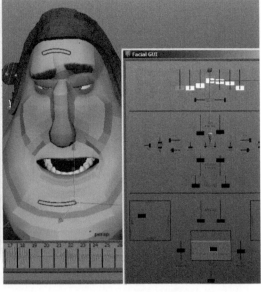

1 Open eyeDarts_End.ma. The first thing to do is give a slight anticipation down before the brows move up. It's another detail that will help things feel less mechanical and more organic. Select the brow controls.

W E'RE IN THE HOME STRETCH with this face animation! All that's left is some tweaks and polishing to make it look as good as possible, which we'll go over in this cheat. No matter what kind of facial rig you run into during your career, the principles remain the same. The face is working as an organic whole, yet some parts are influencing others (brows can influence the lids, mouth corners can push up the cheeks, etc.). From ears to nose flares to a dozen lip controllers, modern production rigs are capable of most any expression possible. Remember, the face has to support the body animation.

Most novices get very excited when they first encounter a sophisticated facial rig, like Cenk. The result is normally a very finely tuned face performance on a lackluster body. Do not do this! The great thing about Cenk is that he is a bouncing ball, so there is no reason that your "body" performance shouldn't be really solid before moving on to the face. And when you venture out into the animation world and use different characters, remember the basics you learned with Cenk. Happy animating!

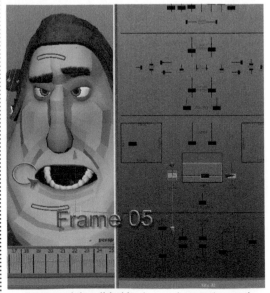

4 Another subtle polish thing is to make sure the mouth corners have nice little arcs in them when moving in and out. It's another one of those details that isn't obvious, but just helps everything feel a little nicer.

2 I added a key to f03, and on f08 brought the eyebrows all down slightly. Notice how nice and fleshy this makes the face feel.

3 On second look, it looks like the up pose at f14 is still hitting a bit too hard. Select the keys at f13 and f14 and pull them down to make the cushion a little bigger. Now they won't stop so quickly and will look more natural.

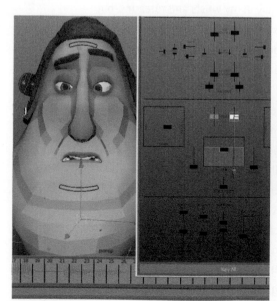

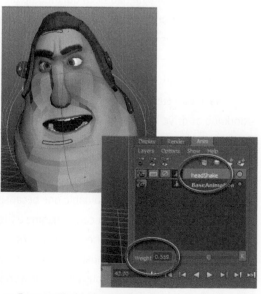

5 I added more sneer to the "N" of "nothing." The nose is easy to over-animate, so be careful when doing this.

6 For some final texture, I added the head control to an animation layer and animated a little shake on the word "nothing." I animated it just a little big, and then used the weight parameter to dial it down until it looks nice and subtle. Watch the final in faceAnimation_Final.ma.

Repetitive Stress Injury

by Eric Luhta

REPETITIVE STRESS INJURY, or RSI, is a very real hazard of working on a computer all day, as animation requires us to do. The stress you can put on your hands and wrists doing tiny movements day in and day out can add up to a very painful and debilitating condition that can jeopardize your ability to work. Taking precautions, being conscious of ergonomics, and working smart can keep you happily keyframing for many years.

I've been a victim of RSI, though it was before I became an animator. When I was in music school, I was practicing the piano eight hours a day, and also worked part-time as an IT supervisor for the university's music computer lab. If I was awake, chances are I was playing or typing and using a mouse. Everyday I was constantly using my hands without much of a break and it didn't take long before I pushed myself to the breaking point. The pain had been building up gradually in my wrists and forearms, but I shrugged it off until it became too much to ignore. This was before RSI was common knowledge, as it is now, and I went from doctor to doctor trying to figure out what was wrong. Eventually I found one who was experienced with this growing phenomenon of the computer age, and could treat me.

It wasn't an easy road to recovery though. At the worst point, I couldn't turn a doorknob or drive because of the pain. I didn't play music for about four months, and had to deal with the possibility of not playing ever again. I had to get lots of physical therapy, quit my job that helped support me through school, postpone classes, and put everything I loved to do on hold. It was an extremely difficult experience to get through, but ultimately an invaluable one because it taught me how important it was to take care of my body. If you can't imagine a life of not animating or at best being in pain whenever you do, you need to make working smart a priority.

Animation is extremely mouse intensive, and until we come up with a better interface, we need to be cautious about our working style. The standard computer mouse is actually one of the worst ergonomically designed devices in the history of civilization. Hold your forearm with the opposite hand and rotate your palm down as it is when using a mouse. You will feel your forearm bones twist over each other, tightly pulling your tendons and muscles above your wrist together. Tension equals friction, and over time your tendons will become inflamed and possibly develop scar tissue that exacerbates the problem.

So step number one: get a better mouse or mouse alternative. I use a Wacom tablet to animate, and since I started with it years ago (along with doing some of the other practices I'll mention), I've had no issues with RSI. It takes a week or so to get used to it, but once you do, you'll find it puts much less stress on your body. Many artists use tablets nowadays, and every place I've worked at had them available upon request.

If you really like using a mouse, research and find a quality ergonomic one. Evoluent (www.evoluent.com) makes a great vertical mouse that's very comfortable to use. It's oriented vertically to avoid the forearm twisting mentioned earlier. I've seen plenty of these in animation studios as well.

Take lots of breaks! Every hour or so you should take at least 5–10 minutes away from the computer to rest your eyes and hands. It may be hard during a crunch but in the long run it will make you more productive. Besides, it gives you a legitimate reason to make use of the studio's ping pong or pool tables!

Use good posture when working. If you work at home, the investment in a good chair and desk will pay for itself in keeping you healthy. Research ergonomics and find a combination that works for you.

Exercise and eating right is the last element of staying in the animation game. Exercise releases the tension that builds up in your body from sitting and working long hours. Doing some weight training will stretch your tendons and muscles and make them more resilient and flexible. Since I've stayed with a weight regimen and followed the above advice, I've been working happily with no issues and no pain my entire career.

RSI is very real and its effects can be devastating to your career. Do your homework, insist on working only in proper conditions, and your body will reward you by always being there for you.

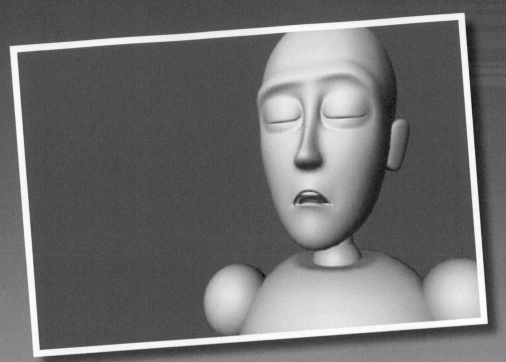

■ Undecided? Animation layers will let you organize and create unlimited variations in your work. Much like layers in Photoshop, you can control what curves are playing where and how much they influence the final result. Mix and match to your heart's content and come up with new ideas.

12

Animation Layers

SINCE THEIR INTRODUCTION, animation layers have been one of the most powerful tools yet introduced in computer animation. They exponentially increase the ease of creative tasks like trying different approaches and variations, and they make working with curves much simpler and more compartmentalized.

However, they're still a relatively new tool in Maya. I've met many professionals who don't even know they exist, yet their benefits can't be overstated. They allow a flexibility and simplicity in animation curves that is on completely another level compared to how many of us learned Maya. This chapter will show you how to employ this incredibly powerful feature in what will likely evolve into a new and vastly improved workflow for you.

How Animation Layers Work

IF YOU'VE USED GRAPHICS PROGRAMS like Photoshop, then understanding Maya's Animation Layers will be a short leap from there. Layers let us stack multiple versions of spline curves on top of each other, which Maya then mixes together the way we want. This default behavior is one of two available layer modes, and is called Additive mode. A simple example would be two layers for the Translate Y attribute:

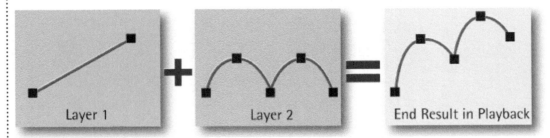

You can see how the two Y curves are mixed together for the end result. While this alone can make working with curves simpler, particularly with more complex examples, the real flexibility is in how we can adjust the weight of each layer, much like opacity in a graphics program.

Instead of editing the curve itself, simply turning the weight of Layer 2 down to 50 percent reduces its influence on the final result by half. It looks like this:

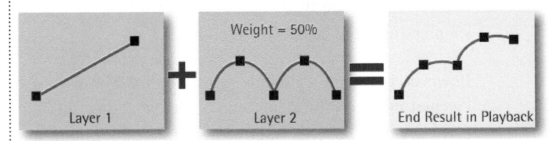

Likewise if we switched that concept, and reduced the weight of Layer 1 to 50 percent, we get this:

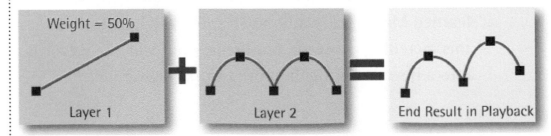

Since the weight is just a slider, we can instantly experiment with any ratio of weights, giving us exponentially more options with no extra spline editing.

Green = layer currently being keyed (possible for multiple layers to be keyed simultaneously)

When we use layers, any animation we've done before the first animation layer was created will be labeled as BaseAnimation in the editor. BaseAnimation is not actually an animation layer, so we can't adjust its weight or turn it off.

Creating animation layers stacks them on the base layer. As far as Additive mode layers (which is the default) go, the order doesn't really matter and the results should look the same. Override, the other mode, does take the order into account. When we set a layer to this mode, it essentially mutes any animation on layers below it that share the same controls or attributes. Animation above an Override layer will be added into the end result.

Override Layer (bold)

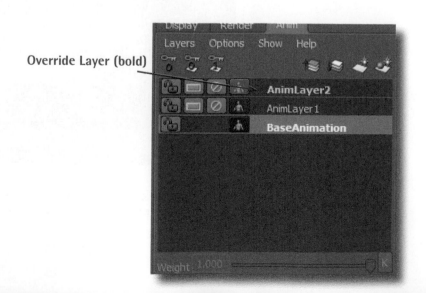

275

Animation Layer Basics

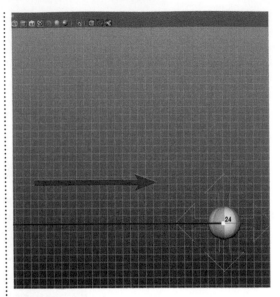

N OW THAT WE UNDERSTAND how animation layers work, let's see in Maya the example that was just illustrated. The Translate Y curves are exactly the same as the previous pages' example, to keep things consistent. You'll be able to experiment for yourself and see how the weighting of a layer affects the animation. Weighting can also be animated just like anything else, so curves can have different amounts of influence throughout an animation, continuing to expand the possibilities. Finally, layers offer some nice organizational colorizing, complete with different colored ticks in the timeline, which can be a lifesaver if you're using many layers.

After this cheat, we'll use layers to make some improvements to a completed facial animation scene and create some new variations.

1 Open layerExample.ma and switch to front view. Right now only the BaseAnimation is active, which is the ball translating in X from left to right.

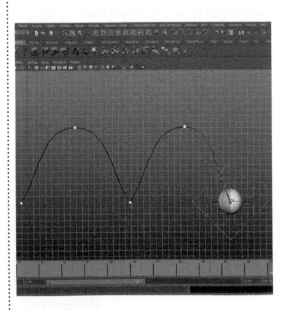

4 Re-mute Layer1 and unmute Layer2. You can see the Translate Y curve from Layer 2 in the illustration on page 274 at work.

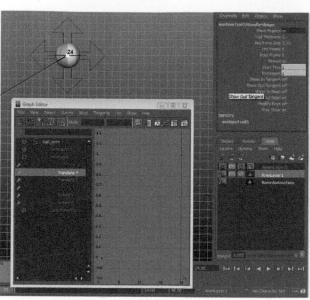

layerExample.ma

2 In the Layers panel, switch to Anim layers. There are the two layers above the base, with the same animation as in the example on pages 274–5 we just talked about. Currently both layers are muted.

3 Click the Mute button for Layer1 to unmute it. Our Translate Y curve from the illustration on page 274 is now active and the ball travels upward. Muting is a great feature for comparing how different curves affect the end result.

HOT TIP

If you have lots of layers and the Graph Editor is getting crowded, right click in the Graph Editor's left panel and select Animation Layers Filter > Active. Now only the active layers' curves will appear.

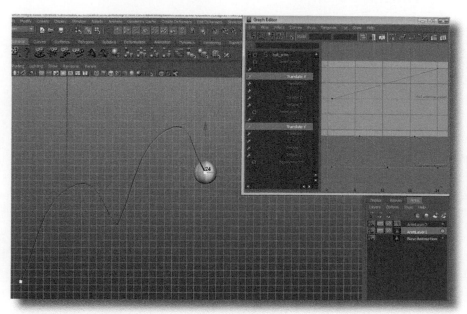

5 Unmute both and they are added together in the final result. You can see that there are two separate Translate Y curves in the Graph Editor, separated by their layers.

Anim Layer Basics (cont'd)

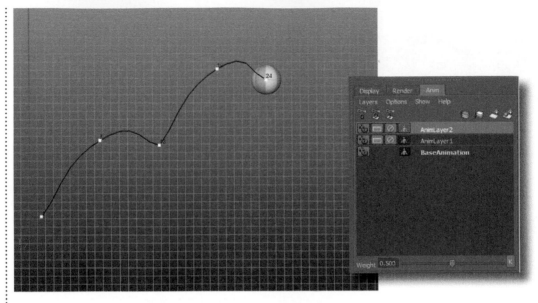

6 Select Layer2 and move the weight slider down to .5, or 50%. Now the peaks of the Layer2 Translate Y curve are half of what they were. Remember that we haven't changed the actual curve at all, only the amount of it that is combined into the final result.

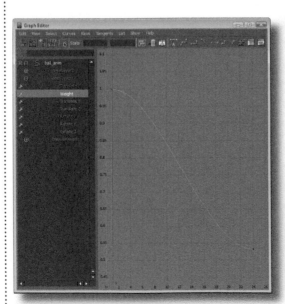

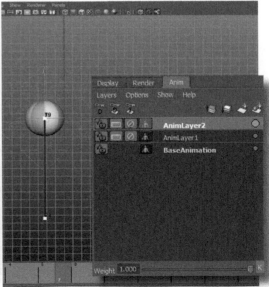

8 The K button next to the weight slider keys the weight attribute. You can set a layer's weight to different amounts throughout an animation. Once you set a key on it, a curve called "Weight" will appear under the layer's name in the Graph Editor, and you can edit it as normal.

9 Right click on Layer2 and select Layer Mode > Override. The name turns bold and the ball only moves up and down. Override causes a layer to not evaluate the layers below that have the same controllers. Since the ball's move control is animated in everything below, they are overridden.

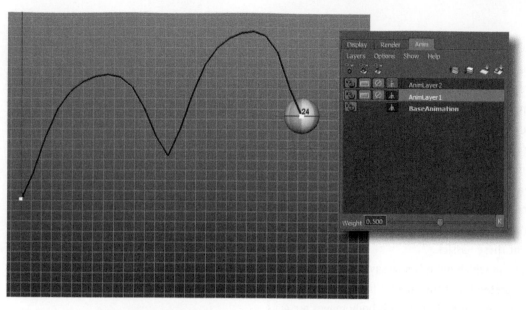

7 Set Layer2's weight back to 1 (100%) and slide Layer1 to .5. Now the ball only reaches half the height it used to at the end, but the bounces are back to their full sizes.

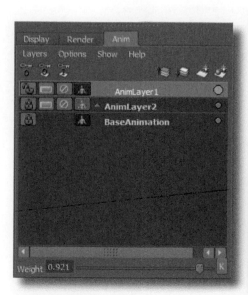

10 MM drag to reorder layers, and the lock button protects them from being keyed or changed.

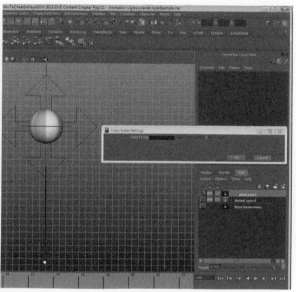

11 Right click on the colored Ghost button to set the layer's color. This will make all the key ticks for that layer in the timeline the color you choose. Clicking on the Ghost button will also enable ghosts for that layer in the color as well.

Creating Variations

ONE OF THE COOLEST THINGS about animation layers is they give you freedom to try new things without messing up what you've already done. This is especially useful if you're doing work for someone else, and they're undecided about which direction they want. Rather than having to save multiple versions of a scene and jump back and forth, you can keep everything in a single scene, yet separated the way you see fit. Better yet, I've been in plenty of situations where I've shown three or four versions, and they liked something from each. That can be a nightmare to put together sometimes! Animation layers eliminate all of these hassles.

We'll open a scene in which goon is now saying "I've got nothing to say", and pretend that the director likes what we've done, but wants to see what it looks like if his body moves are a little bigger and more exaggerated. We'll use layers to augment what we already have, and switch between the versions with a click of the mouse.

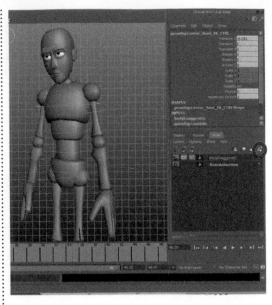

1 Open variations_start.ma. Select the body control and in the Anim layers panel click the Create Layer from Selected button. This automatically puts the control into the new layer. Name it "bodyExaggerate."

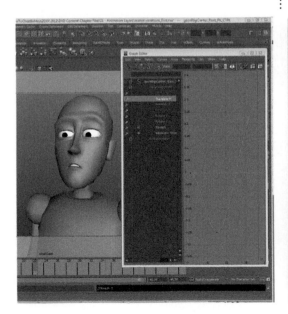

4 At f22, key the body up, pushing his peak higher.

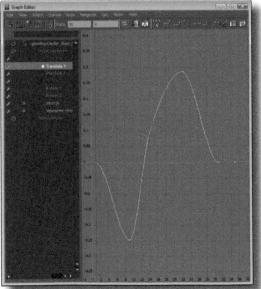

5 At f31, the new Y curve goes back to zero. Continue to tweak the curve until you're happy with his up/down motion.

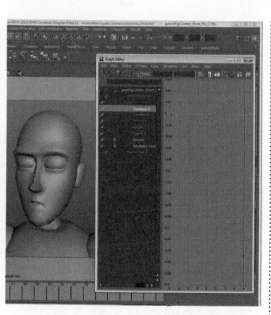

variations_start.ma
variations_end.ma

2 Click the lock button on the BaseAnimation so we don't accidentally alter our original. Then right click on the bodyExaggerate layer's Ghost button and change its color.

3 In the new bodyExaggerate layer, key the body at f01, then give Goon a bigger dip downward in Translate Y at f09 so his body arcs downward before it travels up.

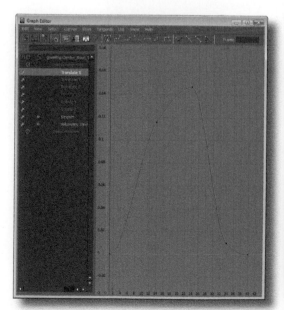

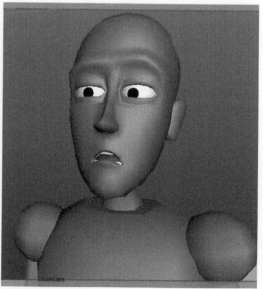

6 I also pushed him screen right more in X to go along with the bigger Y movement, again zeroing out at the end of the motion.

7 He now has a bigger body movement and we can switch between it and the original simply by muting the bodyExaggerate layer. If we wanted to see something between the two, adjusting the layer's weight will work beautifully.

Creating Variations 2

SIMPLE VARIATIONS, like we just did, are pretty straightforward. But sometimes it's useful to start with animation we've already done and alter it in a new layer. This lets us use the original curve and change it where we need to, while still keeping the original version to compare. Maya makes this a simple process, and it can be very powerful when we want to see subtle variations in an animation.

In this exercise we'll pretend that the director wants to see Goon close his eyes when he raises his head, to make him a little more arrogant. He'll keep his eyes closed until he comes back down on the words "to say". First we'll extract the original animation on the eyes and put it on a new layer, then copy that layer again for another version to make changes on. When you extract animation, you remove it from the original source, BaseAnimation, and place it into a new layer. Copying the extracted layer lets us keep the original, while having a duplicate to make any adjustments on. Then we'll use the Override mode so only one version is played back at a time.

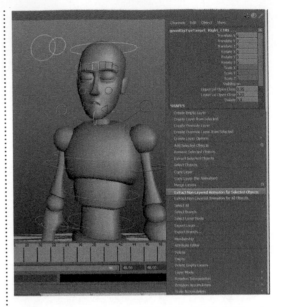

1 Open variations2_start.ma. Select the Goon's right and left eye controls and in the Layer panel menu bar select Layers > Extract Non-Layered Animation for Selected Objects. This takes the eye animation and places it onto a new layer.

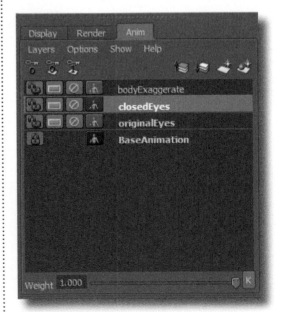

4 Name the new layer "closedEyes" and choose a new color for it. You can also lock the BaseAnimation and originalEyes layers to keep them from being accidentally changed.

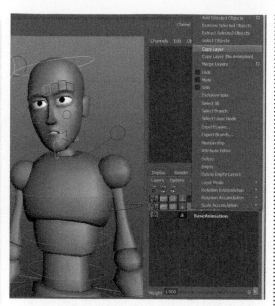

variations2_start.
ma
variations2_end.ma

2 Rename the new layer (double click the name) "originalEyes" and choose a distinctive color for it. This is where we'll keep the original version of the animation. Note that extracted layers are Override mode (name in bold) by default.

3 Right click on the originalEyes layer and choose Copy Layer to make a new layer (in Override mode) with the same eye animation.

HOT TIP

Instead of extracting, you could have just copied the curves from one layer to another in the Graph Editor. This keeps the curves on the BaseAnimation. It's just personal preference to separate the variations into layers for organization.

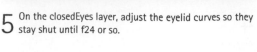

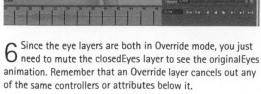

5 On the closedEyes layer, adjust the eyelid curves so they stay shut until f24 or so.

6 Since the eye layers are both in Override mode, you just need to mute the closedEyes layer to see the originalEyes animation. Remember that an Override layer cancels out any of the same controllers or attributes below it.

Layers for Texture

THE ANIMATION IS LOOKING quite a bit better with our recent additions, and we can instantly go back to the original version at any time. Such is the power of layers. Yet it still needs a little something. A little shake when he raises his head and closes his eyes will add a nice bit of texture.

Creating layers to add in texture is a technique that can save you tons of work, especially if working for a picky or indecisive director. It's easy enough to add in the headshake as normal, but if you're then asked to tone it down or take it out, you have to go back in and edit the original curve quite a bit. Using a layer for the shake, you can simply turn the weight down until they're happy. And best of all, it makes your curves simpler to work with. If you were asked to start with the head rotated further in Y, you can simply adjust the original curve while the head shake stays the same in its own layer, rather than having to tweak where Rotate Y starts and all the shaking keys after it.

In short, layers have lots of uses and you'll figure out plenty more as you continue to use them and tailor them to your workflow. Happy (easier) animating!

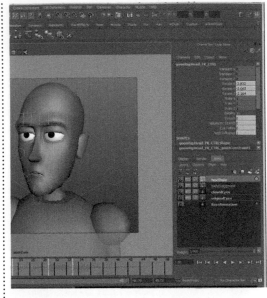

1 Open texture_start.ma and select the head control. In the Anim layers click the Create Layer from Selected button. Name it "headShake" and give it a unique color.

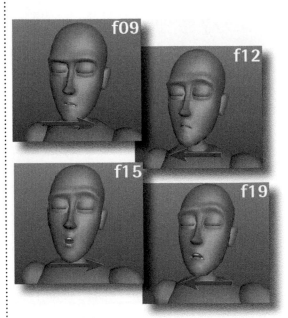

4 The subtle shake.

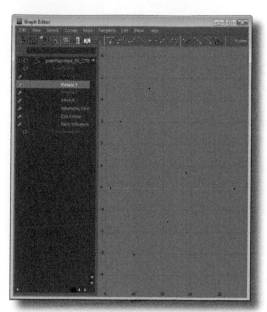

2 In the headShake layer, starting at around f07, rough in a back and forth "no" movement in Rotate Y as he raises his head.

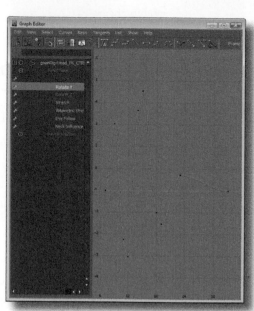

3 Work with the curves until the shake looks good to you. I added some more ease in on some of the shakes.

texture_start.ma
texture_end.ma

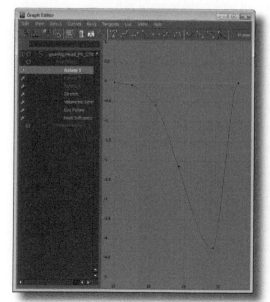

5 With the bigger movement in the body, I noticed his head needs to drag more in Rotate X. Add that in on the headShake layer, or put it on a new layer if you like.

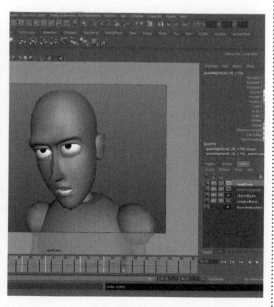

6 Now you can really tweak things to your heart's content. Using the layers and their weights, experiment with different amounts of head shake, body exaggeration, eye versions, and anything else that you want to try!

Your Demo Reel:

New Guidelines for a Changing Industry
by Kenny Roy

THERE HAVE BEEN MANY demo reel guides written over the years. However, the industry is changing so fast these days that an updated guide to creating the ultimate demo reel is in order. Use this guide if you are sprucing up your current reel or if you are creating your first reel. The advice given here I've written in part as an animator who's worked at the largest studios on major films, but also in part as an employer myself. Having made the transition, I have some advice I think you'll find handy.

The first rule that is changing rapidly is the rule about how often to apply to a studio. Back when I started in this industry, it was common that a studio would keep your reel on hand for a year or longer, and that if you fit a particular project, you would be contacted by the studio. With a huge influx of students from schools entering the market, the sheer number of applicants has made it so the major studios are too inundated with reels that arrived that week to really take the time to hunt down candidates that might have shown promise a year ago. If you are one of these students, it makes sense that you will want to send your current reel as soon as it is ready. On the other hand, if you have a reel that garnered no responses the first round of sending it out, it's really time to consider how the industry has changed. This means you should spend very little time polishing old work on your reel in lieu of creating new work. A good rule of thumb is, you can send a new demo reel into a studio as long as it has been over two months since you sent the last one, and you have at least two major new pieces of work to go on it. A ten-plus-second multi-character dialog shot would be considered major, as would a character modeled, textured, rigged, and animated in a few short physical tests. A flying logo animation, a particle simulation created from default settings, or mocap editing would not qualify. Studios want to know that applicants are constantly bettering themselves. They want to know that, on the job, you are concerned at all times with creating the greatest result you can. Constantly updating your demo reel is a great way to demonstrate that you are familiar with the rigors of the job and are ready for production. So remember, wait to resubmit your reel for at least two months and until you have at least 20 seconds of new, polished animation on your reel.

The second change that is happening in the industry is again due to the large influx of students graduating from school. Playblasts will no longer suffice, unfortunately. The reason is that many animation curriculums start with a general CG education in Maya, then move on to the finer points of performance and character animation. While it is debatable how well this prepares students for the larger studios where specialization is essential to competing, this situation does change the rules for an animator's demo reel somewhat. Since only a small percentage of the available jobs in this industry are in major 1000+ employee visual effects and feature animation powerhouses, the small-to-midsized studios are enjoying the benefits of having animators who are generalists, and more well-rounded. Again, while most high-end projects need the kind of expertise that typically only an animation specialist can deliver, you need to cope with the fact that your competition may know how to model, UV, texture, rig, light, and write MEL script. If your demo reel is a series of grey-shaded playblasts, it will take a serious amount of disparity in the animation quality for a potential employer to overlook the fact that you have no generalist skills. I know from owning a boutique studio that I can relax just a little bit if I know that a generalist that I can hire based on their animation quality alone will come through in a pinch when I need help on other areas of the pipeline. So, to compete in the largest employment pool of the animation industry (small-to-midsized studios), at the very least light and render your animations for your demo reel. Spend a little time finding rigs to animate with that have nice textures and shaders, and experiment with lighting setups and render settings just a little bit. Spend the most time polishing your performances, but don't be left behind because of your boring playblasts.

Since the animation industry only gets more competitive, your reel should be even more specific. This is an old demo reel tip, but it is even more important now. Professionals used to say, "Your demo reel should match the work you are applying for. Don't send animations of gory insect robots to a company that makes fluffy animations for children's games." This is still applicable, but you should realize that you are probably competing for a job against people that have some VERY specific animation on their reel. Case in point: one of the animators on *King Kong* was a lighter before that film who turned in a reel comprised of a dozen or so gorilla tests. Naturally, with so many examples of gorilla animation on his reel, he was a shoo- in for a spot on the animation team. One of the lead animators on that film who worked on the sequence of the brontosaurus stampede had just finished a film in which he worked on a stampede of elephants. Employers truly do cast their animation. So what can you do to be more specific? Follow the trade and visual effects blogs for news as to which films are ramping up their animation and create a short piece of animation tailored specifically for that project. It is not too hard to find news on major studios' websites about what projects they have coming up. Best- case scenario, tailoring your animation tests will put you in the lead position for a job on a specific show; worst-case scenario, your reel just got updated with more fresh work!

Another guideline has to do with demo reel length. Most advice out there right now says to put all of your best animation on your reel, and to keep it under two minutes. This could be a problem if you just graduated. If you graduated from a popular school whose rigs are very well known, employers are already getting a little tired of seeing the same characters over and over. Even at the expense of demo reel length, it is a good idea to get original-looking animation on your reel. Many deformable rigs are available online, which is a good start for getting a unique look to your reel. This also means that your bouncing ball and flour sack tests should be the first thing to go. I've heard of animators being hired from a reel that is only 30 seconds long. Speaking as an employer myself, I can say that it is much better to have a very short reel of consistent quality than even a marginally longer one with different qualities on display. Why? Because I know that the animator can do at least what I've seen. If older work is on the reel, I start to think what I'm seeing might be what the artist can achieve at most. I will ask an animator whose reel is too short but has great work on it for some more material, or if they would be willing to do a test for the work. Definitely keep the reel under 2 minutes though; that rule still applies!

To DVD or not to DVD? Ten years ago, a DVD was a must for an animation applicant. Today, however, normally a digital file will suffice. You have to call or email the recruiter at the company you are applying to and ask them what they prefer. You will find that most studios prefer digital files these days; we work with digital recruiting databases, and the ability to link your demo reel file to a clickable link on your recruiting file saves everyone that is part of the hiring process valuable time. DVDs also take up space, can deteriorate or stop working, may have region or format issues, and they cost money to produce and ship. It's no wonder they are falling out of style. What this means for you, however, is that you should learn to compress your demo into a file that is high quality but small. H.264 compression is a standard that nearly 100 percent of PCs and Macs will have no trouble playing. Play with bit rate, compression quality, image size, and sound codec to keep your reel under 50MB for a "high quality" version, and under 10MB for a "low quality" version. In your email to a recruiter, give them links to a fast URL they can download either file from, and remember to specify each version's filesize.

Finally, never put anything on your reel that you don't have permission to show. This is another one of the old tips that still pertains. Ten years ago, I remember it was commonplace to sneak out a couple of shots to show recruiters. The thinking was "I'm only going to show it to the recruiter, what's the harm?" Well, now that the industry is so full, and the world is getting smaller and smaller with communication between studios, you are going to be in a lot of trouble if you sneak even your playblasts out of the studio. People will talk, and you will be avoided. In the time of DVDs it was a little different because you could be sure to take the DVD with you when you left the interview. I even had a couple interviews like that early in my career. But now that we are sending digital files, you must remember the internet is forever; sending a digital file that you do not have permission to send is inviting a world of trouble.

The old guidelines have been repeated over and over, and they are still very good. Only put your best work out there. Don't copy a well-known character. Don't use offensive imagery or themes. Don't blast heavy metal music; use music that is very low-key, if any at all. Clearly label your reel with your name, phone number, and email at the head and the tail. Don't bother recruiters every day with phone calls or emails; they WILL contact you if they are interested.

As the animation industry changes at a rapid pace, however, you must adapt and learn to work within some new guidelines in order to be competitive. Remember just one thing: no amount of demo reel magic will improve the animation quality, and the quality alone will get you the job. Focus on improving your craft of performance, polish your workflow, and then do what the rest of us do: send in your demo reel and cross your fingers!

Mike Gasaway

MIKE GASAWAY HAS BEEN AN ANIMATOR, supervisor, director, producer and writer on various projects such as *The Adventures of Jimmy Neutron: Boy Genius*, *Back at the Barnyard* and *Planet Sheen*.

WHAT WAS YOUR FAVORITE MOVIE GROWING UP AND WHY?

As everyone in this business, *Friday the 13th*. Wait, it's not? Yeah, I'm weird. I loved *Star Wars* but that's not the reason I got into this business. It was Bugs Bunny's fault.

TELL US A LITTLE BIT ABOUT YOUR DECISION TO CHANGE CAREERS FROM ARCHITECTURE TO COMPUTER ANIMATION.

First, it was a very difficult decision. I wanted to be an architect since I could put two Legos together. Luckily, I took architecture classes in High School and then got accepted into one of the top schools in the nation. After going there for four years, I realized that architecture just wasn't where my heart was. I "found" animation, ironically, while working at an animation firm. The University of Cincinnati had a co-op program where you went to school for a quarter and then worked basically as an intern for a quarter. One of these co-ops, I worked in the Computer Aided Drafting department of a firm and found I was very efficient on the computer. I came back for the school quarter and saw a short by PDI called "Gas Planet." That pushed me over the edge. I wanted to do whatever it took to do a film like that. I was bitten.

     The hard part, though, was moving and leaving everyone to finish my schooling. Everyone said I was crazy but I did it anyway.

WHAT DO YOU THINK IS THE MOST NOTABLE DIFFERENCE BETWEEN ANIMATING FOR FILM VERSUS TELEVISION?

The biggest is by far the time. We had to do SO much footage each week to keep the television machine rolling. We couldn't noodle the shots and make them super awesome. We had to also develop a methodology to make the process faster/more efficient.

WHAT IS IT LIKE TO PRODUCE YOUR OWN FILMS?

A LOT of work. The problem I'm finding is that not only do you have to be the creative force, but also the producing force. That side of my brain doesn't work fully. Honestly, I'm not sure if I have that part of my brain. I guess that would explain why I lean to one side all the time. The nice part, however, is that I do have full creative control. You don't have that any other way.

DO YOU HAVE ANY HOBBIES OUTSIDE OF ANIMATION?

Watching animation, critiquing animation... I LOVE writing. That's my passion. Guitar playing is something I miss—I used to play quite a bit but never enough. My kids take up the rest of my free time.

YOU WORKED ON SOME MEDICAL ANIMATIONS EARLY ON IN YOUR CAREER. DID YOU FIND THIS HELPFUL TO YOUR CAREER NOW?

Immensely. Because I NEVER WANT TO DO IT AGAIN. It did give me a sense of respect for the industry. I had to work through a lot of work that I didn't want to do to get to where I wanted. I'm not sure I would respect the work as much as I do if I didn't go through it. Plus I learned a lot about cellular mitosis.

ARE THE "TOOLS" INVOLVED IN ANIMATION (FAST COMPUTER, LATEST SOFTWARE) REALLY IMPORTANT TO A GOOD END RESULT?

I don't think they are necessary but they sure help. When I first started, I had to wait overnight for a simple render. That taught me to be very certain with my acting choices and do a lot of fixes before hitting that render button. I'm also not one that uses a lot of the bells and whistles. I'm not sure if that helps or hurts me but it still gets me the desired result. I will also say that the most important thing is a good animator. I have always said that a good animator can animate with match sticks. That being said, a fast computer helps.

AS AN ANIMATOR AND DIRECTOR, HAVE YOU TAKEN ACTING OR IMPROVISATION CLASSES AND IS THAT IMPORTANT?

Most definitely. I have taken them and highly recommend them. Improv is great because it teaches that acting is reacting. Having that skill helps the animator develop choices — something key in acting — especially from a director's point of view. Acting classes are great because they force you to look into the character and find some reasons why a character will/might react. I have done everything from taking classes, doing improv to even reading books on... how to pick up women...The last part was by accident because I found this book that was on body language. I perused it and thought it was great because it gave reasons for how people reacted. I bought it and didn't realize until I got it home that the book was actually on how to pick up women. It's still a great book.

DO YOU THINK IT'S IMPORTANT THAT ANIMATORS OF ALL LEVELS TAKE ADVANTAGE OF AN OPPORTUNITY TO CRITIQUE OTHERS' WORK?

The only way to get better is to learn and to get different opinions. You should always try to get better each day. Once you're done learning, you're dead. Critiquing is also great for the critique-er. When you look at someone else's work, you can always glean something from it, thus making your animation better.

DO YOU HAVE ANY ADVICE FOR SOMEONE LOOKING TO GET INTO ANIMATION?

Prepare to work your tail off but don't be in a hurry. Learning this skill takes a long time and can't be rushed. You will need a lot of patience in your work too. I think it's best to learn animation through baby steps and thoroughly understand the rules of animation and the workflow. This takes quite some time. Also realize, there is a lot of competition and you need to set yourself apart. Great animation will help that quite a bit.

WHAT DO YOU THINK ARE THE MOST COMMON MISTAKES YOU SEE IN YOUNG ANIMATORS?

Failure to plan. I see a ton of animators that just want to hurry up and get on the computer to start animating. What they don't realize is that planning the shot, doing vid ref and thumbnails is actually animating. The more you pore over your shot before getting into the computer, the better off you'll be. I've seen plenty of animators short change this step and then make changes way too late in the process. This makes their animation even weaker. Get in the habit of planning from the get go so it's a part of your workflow.

BRIEFLY DESCRIBE WHERE YOU SEE ANIMATION GOING IN THE NEXT TEN YEARS.

I'm not 100 percent sure where it is going but I can tell you where I hope it isn't. I hope that live action directors don't think that they can "easily" direct animation by shooting the movie in film and simply giving it over to animators to put it in the computer. I'm not a fan at all of motion capture at all either. I would be very happy if that went away.

YOU HAVE STARTED ON THE PATH TO CREATING A FEATURE FILM, CAN YOU TELL US HOW YOU DECIDED TO MAKE THAT LEAP?

I had a great agent who sent me to a bunch of producers and production companies to pitch my stories. I had a ton of great responses and even had second and third meetings. What I kept running into was everyone was looking for something "proven" or something with an audience. It was almost like no one wanted to take a chance on something they thought was good. They needed someone else to tell them what was good. I then decided to create my own "following." I've been doing a website called "The Path to a Movie" at www.gasmangroup.com/blog. It's a site where I chronicle what I go through each day from writing the idea/novel and then script and follow the whole process from producer meetings to pre-production. The site is slowly growing daily and I haven't missed a post just yet and don't plan on stopping until the movie comes out.

Joe Ksander

JOE KSANDER IS AN ANIMATION DIRECTOR AND SCREENWRITER. He has worked at several studios including Rhythm & Hues and Industrial Light & Magic. His credits include *The Chronicles of Narnia: The Lion, the Witch, and the Wardrobe, Yogi Bear*, the animated feature *9* and the upcoming *Pacific Rim*. He is currently developing his first feature film.

WHAT IS YOUR FAVORITE FILM YOU'VE WORKED ON AND WHY?

This sounds like a cop-out, but the most recent one, whatever that happens to be. I feel like I'm still learning how to do this stuff, and the more I do it, the more I like it. Sure, sometimes it can be totally frustrating, but I keep coming back for more.

CAN YOU GIVE US SOME INSIGHT INTO THE DIFFERENCES BETWEEN DIRECTING ANIMATION FOR LIVE ACTION VERSUS FULL CG?

The biggest difference is that in live action, when you are on set, you have to be able to communicate to the crew what the animated characters will be doing when they are completed six to nine months after the shoot is finished. You need to give the actors a clear idea of what is going on in the shot and who they are acting against, even though their scene partner is a CG character that they can't see. Once the shoot is finished and the film cut together, the process is very similar to an animated feature. Another difference is that in live action, many of the people involved don't have a lot of experience with animation, so it's important to be patient and willing to collaborate to find creative solutions to complex problems. But the goal is the same: performance in service of story.

WHAT IS YOUR FAVORITE PART ABOUT BEING ANIMATION DIRECTOR?

I love working with talented artists — including (but not limited to) designers, animators, actors and cinematographers. I am always amazed when a team comes together and is able to produce work that is so much more impressive than any individual could have achieved on their own.

WHAT ARE SOME MEDIA SOURCES OR EVENTS IN REAL LIFE THAT HAVE INFLUENCED YOUR ANIMATION?

I grew up watching Ray Harryhausen monster movies, which really inspired me to get into this field. Science fiction of all kinds has also been a huge influence on me, but especially writers like Ray Bradbury and Isaac Asimov. More recently I have fallen in love with theatre, and my current obsession is stand-up and improv comedy.

DO YOU HAVE A SECRET TOOL OR TECHNIQUE YOU LIKE TO USE WHEN ANIMATING?

The only real trick I have is what I call "fine-tuning my bullshit detector." Which is a punchy way of saying be your own worst critic. I never felt like I was a "natural," but I kind of think that there is no such thing. The way I make my stuff work is to take a look at it and ask myself if it is any good. If not, I keep going until it is.

SHARE WITH US YOUR THOUGHTS ON THE IMPORTANCE OF DIVERSITY IN LIFE OUTSIDE OF THE WORK PLACE.

Are you talking about having a life outside of work? If so, I'd say it's really important that you take care of yourself and your life because the studios aren't going to. Even the nicest corporation in the world is a still a corporation — it has its own goals. When those goals align with yours, then things are awesome. But when they don't, you are on your own. That being said, the only way to get good at this stuff — animation and making movies — is to spend all your time doing it. And if you do, you will be making sacrifices. You just have to be okay with that.

DID YOU ALWAYS KNOW YOU WERE GOING TO BE IN ANIMATION?

No, I didn't. After I saw *2001*, I was going to be an astronaut. After *Raiders of the Lost Ark*, I was going to be an archaeologist. When I saw *Jurassic Park*, it was palaeontology. Being an animator is how I get to be all of those things.

HOW DID THE FILM *9* DIFFER FROM OTHER FILMS YOU HAVE WORKED ON?

9 was a smaller budget but bigger scope than a lot of the films I had worked on, so it was a challenge to achieve the things that we were aiming for. But it was also a lot of fun and almost like being in film school again, because we would find ourselves huddling around editorial at ten o'clock on a Friday night trying to solve problems. On Monday you'd hand out your direction to the team, and they'd bring it back at the end of the week and blow us away. Then we'd get up and do it again.

DO YOU HAVE ANY ADVICE FOR YOUNG ANIMATORS THAT ARE JUST STARTING THEIR CAREERS?

Aim high — it can actually be easier to get a job in the industry than you might think, but if you really want to be good, then you should have higher standards than just "good enough for the job." Don't limit yourself to looking to your heroes — look to their influences and then find out what those influences were influenced by. There is so much information available out there nowadays about animation and making movies that your only real limit is your level of commitment.

CAN YOU LIST SOME BOOKS OR RESOURCES THAT HELPED YOU BECOME THE PERSON YOU ARE TODAY?

There are great books on technique, *The Illusion of Life* or Richard Williams' book for example, that were really helpful for me in the beginning. But I had some great teachers who pushed me in other directions and showed me that animation is more than just technique. So I got exposed to books like Robert McKee's *Story*, and Bruce Block's *The Visual Story*. Getting inspired is not easy, but I try to cast a wide net. I do a lot of science reading. Online lectures like the TED talks are a great resource. From a pure entertainment perspective, there is no better teacher than comedy so I look to artists like Louis C.K., Patton Oswalt, George Carlin or Sarah Silverman. It's almost embarrassing how much information is out there nowadays. But it's great for me because I'm such a nerd about this stuff.

WHAT ARE SOME QUALITIES YOU LIKE TO SEE IN COLLEAGUES THAT WORK BESIDE YOU?

There is nothing better than somebody who is passionate about the project. Of course there are going to be times when you are not but have to go to work anyway. But the best artists I've seen and worked with find ways to get excited even in the most difficult circumstances, and usually that makes the whole enterprise get better.

IF ANIMATION DIDN'T EXIST, WHAT DO YOU THINK YOU'D BE DOING TODAY?

In a time-travel counter-factual kind of a way? I'd like to have been a cosmologist. The math was too tough for me but I bet I could have gotten through that. In a more realistic way, these days I'm finding a great deal of creative satisfaction writing, and would have been happy to have started doing it professionally a lot sooner. But I know that all my animation experience has made me a better storyteller, so I probably couldn't have been a writer without having gone though all of that anyway.

Dan Barker

DAN BARKER IS THE CHARACTER DEVELOPMENT SUPERVISOR at Blue Sky Studios. He has worked on *Horton Hears a Who, Ice Age: Dawn of The Dinosaurs, Rio, Ice Age Continental Drift*, and is currently working on *Leafmen*.

WHAT IS THE MOST REWARDING ASPECT FOR YOU OF WORKING ON IN-HOUSE FEATURE ANIMATIONS?

For me one of the most rewarding aspects is the collaborative creative environment. Early on I was really reluctant to show people my work, honestly because I thought they would think it was bad, and I didn't want to hear any negative criticism. But what I found is that by working with other people, not only do they help you when you are struggling with something, they help you be the best artist you can be!

Obviously the other aspect for me in particular is helping define how new characters are gonna act, and behave. Helping define the personality traits of the characters is an incredibly rewarding process. I love being able to speak to the director, the story team, the art director about how a character should look and behave. Then you finally get to animate them, you understand them and can hopefully make them sincere, and believable for the film.

And then simply animating them. Animation is a lot of fun! Working on an IN-HOUSE feature you get to have fun for work! That in itself is pretty rewarding!

WHAT IS YOUR AVERAGE QUOTA FOR SHOTS PER WEEK?

Our average depending on complexity is about 75 frames per week.

PLEASE DESCRIBE YOUR WORKFLOW FOR DECIDING ON PERFORMANCE CHOICES.

Depending on the character I would speak to the character leads. They generally will have a lot of reference and info on how the character should act, and perform, and more importantly on how he shouldn't act or perform. I will look at the reference and the character pages first. Then I will look at the boards and the full sequence to get a good idea as to where my shot fits into the overall sequence. I try to identify what the character's arc is in the sequence and where my shot fits into that. Once that is complete I would shoot reference. If I can't get what I am looking for in my acting I would get someone else to act it out. Jeff Gabor is always a good guy to go to for that! Then once I have something I like I generally will do one or two drawings based on the reference, trying to push my character more. Once I have this I would show the other supervisors or the director to get a buy off on it. And then I start blocking it out.

DO YOU HAVE ANY CHEATS FOR COMPLETING A SHOT THAT HAS THE DIRECTOR'S SPECIAL ATTENTION?

Yes, listen to what the director wants. Get to know how your director works, what he/she generally responds to, and what they don't respond to. Depending on the director this may be taking his notes word for word, or sometimes it's trying to decipher the underlying meaning of what he wants. Sometimes if your shot is not working a director will give you notes like "Maybe have him come in slower from the left." And when you try to actually have the character come in slower from the left, the acting is thrown off, or the energy isn't right, or it simply doesn't work. In moments like this I try to get understanding of what "feels" wrong, rather than identify frame by frame what's wrong. More than likely my whole shot is not working and I need to redo it with the right "feeling." And other times I just need to have the character come in slower from the left. It really is getting to understand your director. That's the secret! SO I would go to sweatbox a lot, read the notes other guys are getting. That helps you understand the director's sensibility.

DO YOU SHOW THE DIRECTOR YOUR THUMBNAILS AND PLANNING PHASE, OR IS IT JUST FOR YOUR OWN PERSONAL WORKFLOW?

Yeah, I always try to show the director as early as possible. Things inevitably change from your reference/thumbnails to what you actually have in your shot, but if your idea is strong and clear, that remains constant, and if the director has bought off on that earlier you are in a better place. Try to show other animators as well. They will let you know if your acting is bad, or cliched. Try show them before you show the director.

WHAT SORT OF BREAKS DO YOU TAKE WHEN YOU'VE BEEN WORKING ON A SHOT TOO LONG? WHAT HELPS YOU CLEAR YOUR MIND?

Sometimes just going home and not thinking about it. Watching films, playing a sport or an instrument. Something to get your mind off your work really helps. Going to the pub and having a shot, to stop thinking of my shot! Sometime you just need to remove yourself from the shot, and more importantly stress associated with it. I sometimes would talk with the production supervisor about getting an extension if things really are not working. Reducing the pressure to perform, on something that is taking a long time helps.

After a little break, like an afternoon off, my mind is cleared and when I get back in there I generally nail it! Another thing that helps is going onto another shot if you can. Sometimes the creative juices that flow on the other shot give me the impetus to go back into the shot I am struggling with and bring it to the finish line.

WHAT IS YOUR FAVORITE STYLE OF ANIMATION TO WORK ON? CARTOONY? PUSHED REALISM? OTHER?

I am a fan of all animation, but if I had to choose I would say I prefer cartoony. It's a lot of fun to really exaggerate your poses and acting choices, which cartoony lends itself to. And then there is the contrast in a cartoony film where the character has to be played more straight, and sincere. I feel we get to get a good range. For me pushed realism is actually a lot harder to do. So I respect those guys a lot!

HOW DO YOU ADDRESS CONTINUITY ISSUES BETWEEN SCENES OR CHARACTERS?

It's important to communicate with the animators on either side of your shots. If you know someone is going to be starting a shot later than you, and say the end pose of his shot will dictate all of your shot, I try brainstorm with him/her on what they would be thinking for their shot. That way continuity is generally not that much of an issue. And sometimes if I see a problem, I will go back into my shot and correct a pose to make it feel the same. Communication is the key!

WHEN YOU RECEIVED YOUR FIRST JOB AS AN ANIMATOR, WHAT ONE PIECE OF INFORMATION DID YOU WISH YOU WOULD HAVE KNOWN?

Not to be afraid to ask for help, out of fear of people finding out I was a hack! I think all artists go through periods where they are confident with their work, and then they think that they are completely useless. To this day I would love to go into all of my shots and redo them with what I have learned. But the big thing I found is getting feedback from other animators in the know. You don't have to take it all, but it's good to get them to look at stuff and give you feedback. I think I would have grown a lot quicker had I realised that early on.

ANY ADVICE FOR STUDENTS AND YOUNG ANIMATORS WHO WANT TO WORK FOR STUDIOS THAT PRODUCE FEATURE FILM ANIMATIONS?

Be open to criticism. One of the key aspects of working at a major studio is having a well-trained eye. And if you can't see that there are problems with your work, then your eye isn't trained well enough to pick up some of your mistakes. Try to get feedback from people in the know. And if you feel the feedback is harsh, it probably is because your work isn't strong enough. Don't take it personally, just try hit the notes the best you can as you slowly develop your eye. The other advice is that there are a lot of people trying really hard to get into the studios, and they are putting a lot of hours in, days and nights. You are probably gonna have to work as hard if you wanna get considered. Lastly if you get rejected, don't take it personally, just try get feedback as to what was not right, and then improve that, and resend your reels out.

The other BIG BIG thing is not to put everything you have ever done on your reel. Keep it short and only put your best work on. Only was I started taking part in reel reviews did I realise how brutal the review process is. As soon as there is something that is not strong, or has bad polish, or the acting choices are cliched, the reel comes out DVD Player and goes into the rejection pile. So make sure your strongest stuff is right at the beginning.

Printed and bound by CPI Group (UK) Ltd, Croydon, CR0 4YY

22/10/2024

01777531-0001